D1196492

The music of
PRAISE

✣ GORDON GILES ✣

The music of

PRAISE

MEDITATIONS ON GREAT HYMNS OF THE CHURCH

HENDRICKSON
PUBLISHERS

ACKNOWLEDGMENTS

I have been helped and supported in the writing of this book by a number of people, but in particular I would like to thank my wife Jessica, and also Paul Grimwood for making comments on the text. Any writing about hymns has to be rooted in the singing of hymns, and so I am also indebted to the Organists, Vicars Choral and Choristers of St Paul's Cathedral, London, who have inspired me musically on a daily basis over the last few years, and whose leading of hymn-singing is always exemplary.

Almost all of the hymns used in this book are in the public domain, but three are not and have been reproduced with permission gratefully acknowledged:

'God in whose image we are made'. This text by Michael Saward is reproduced with the permission of the author, and is © Michael Saward/Jubilate Hymns.

'O Christ the Same' by Timothy Dudley-Smith is reproduced by the permission of the author.

'For the Love of Jesus' (first line 'All for Jesus') from 'The Crucifixion.' Music by John Stainer, words by the Rev. W.J. Sparrow-Simpson. Copyright © Novello & Company Limited. International Copyright Secured. All rights reserved. Reprinted by permission.

For Jessica

They shall awake as Jacob did, and say as Jacob said, Surely
the Lord is in this place, and this is no other but the house of
God, and the gate of heaven, And into that gate they shall
enter, and in that house they shall dwell, where there shall be
no Cloud nor Sun, no darkness nor dazzling, but one equal
light, no noise nor silence, but one equal music, no fears nor
hopes, but one equal possession, no foes nor friends, but one
equal communion and identity, no ends nor beginnings, but
one equal eternity.

JOHN DONNE, *XXVI SERMONS*, 1627/8, PUBLISHED 1660

O may we soon again renew that song,
And keep in tune with Heav'n, till God ere long
To His celestial concert us unite.
To live with Him, and sing in endless morn of light.

JOHN MILTON, 'AT A SOLEMN MUSICK'

CONTENTS

INTRODUCTION

Henry Venn Elliott, the brother of Charlotte Elliott, who wrote 'Just as I am, without one plea', wrote of his sister's talent as a hymn writer, 'In the course of a long ministry, I hope I have been permitted to see some of the fruit of my labour, but I feel that far more has been done by a single hymn of my sister's.'

We *are* our hymns; they inform our faith, and are invariably written from a standpoint of faith. It is sometimes said in liturgical circles, '*Lex credendi, lex orandi*', which means 'What they pray, they believe', implying that whatever we say in formal prayers, we end up believing. This is why it is so important to get our 'official' worship publications, if we have them, just right. It's also why there is so much discussion about what those prayers should be, sometimes leading to debates about individual words. In recent debates before the publication of the Church of England's *Common Worship* material, which was a major revision of all of the Anglican liturgy, a great deal of time and energy was spent discussing the meaning of the Greek word *ek*, which is found in the Creed. Jesus the Son is born *ek* the Holy Spirit and the Virgin Mary, and it became a matter of doctrine to clarify whether *ek* means 'of' or 'from'. Eventually the Liturgical Commission and the General Synod of the Church of England agreed the phrase 'was incarnate from the Holy Spirit and the Virgin Mary' for use in the Nicene Creed.

Some would say that this is all technical stuff and need not concern most of us, while others see it as being of profound importance, but much of this debate pales into insignificance when we consider some of what we regularly *sing* in church. Hymns are not generally subject to such scrutiny, not least because there are no 'official' hymns in most churches, and none that *must* be sung. The only exception might be the *Veni Creator Spiritus*, sung at ordinations and coronations (see the chapter on that hymn, p. 158).

Nevertheless, we are equally if not more influenced by what we sing than by what we say. Our understanding of Psalm 23 is probably more affected by the hymn 'The Lord's my shepherd' than by any translation found in a Bible, and if someone were to whistle the tune of CRIMOND we would find the words of at least the first line leaping to our lips. The same may be true of the tune 'DOMINUS REGIT ME', the tune used for 'The king of love my shepherd is', which was used at the funeral of Diana, Princess of Wales in September 1997. The tune or words, or both, bring the hymn into focus, and so do the circumstances under which it was sung.

This is important, for there is something about human nature that leads us to keep mementos of special events and places. Words or music or both can evoke occasions or memories, such that any substitution of words or music can have a negative effect. Try singing 'I vow to thee, my country' to any other tune or, indeed, setting other words to Thaxted. The result will probably be unsatisfactory, and will be unlikely to succeed as an alternative version of the hymn. People can usually tell you what hymns they sang at their wedding or at the funeral of a loved one. We associate pieces of music with holidays or friends or periods of our lives. I personally believe that modern popular music is partly created with the intention that this should happen: we are intended to relate what is happening in our lives now to what we hear. Pop music, by its very nature, is more transitory than Mozart or Beethoven, and much of it speaks to a particular and short-lived age at a particular moment in time. This is both an advantage and a disadvantage, but it significantly distinguishes it from older music which retains its popularity over hundreds of years. It may well become the case that some Beatles or Abba songs stay with us for a very long time as they are rediscovered and reclaimed by succeeding generations who feel that they transcend their original context. As such, though, they are 'exceptions that prove the rule'!

In a way, the same is true of modern Christian music and some of our more established hymnody. In this book I have confined discussion to the latter, not because I believe it is better (or worse!), but because it is not quite the same thing. There are hymns that take us back to early Christian culture in Greek and Roman times, and we still sing them today. It is fascinating to peer into the past and try both to understand it a little and also to appreciate that it is the same Jesus Christ, yesterday and today, whom we have worshipped, followed and adored for two thousand years.

Nevertheless, hymns, even the older ones, are not so far removed from popular music. Some hymns are far more well-known than the current 'number one', not only because they have been around for longer, but also because they are sung by so many people. Hymns are meant to be sung and, as well as our regular worship in church, the BBC's *Songs of Praise* broadcasts on Sunday evenings ensure that millions of people are drawing on the spiritual heritage of praise that is stored in the hymn treasury.

Some of those hymns still gleam golden when we sing them, and are polished with use. 'Thine be the glory', that great Easter hymn with its splendid tune by Handel, never loses its popularity. Ironically, it is hymns like this that can surreptitiously instil faith and nurture it, even if the hymn is being sung by non-believers. Christmas carols are a supreme example of this phenomenon.

Other hymns have become a bit tarnished over the years, either because they have become associated with unfortunate circumstances or because we have realized that some of the sentiments expressed in them do not appeal any more. 'Onward Christian soldiers' and 'And did those feet in ancient time' are rarely heard in Sunday worship these days. They are rare and extreme cases of hymns which appear to advocate positions or theologies that many people do not want to sing about any more. Ironically, to the unchurched they are two of the best-known hymns. But like everything else in heaven and earth, they can be redeemed, and redemption is better than boycott.

Alexander Pope (1688–1744) was speaking of our age as well as his own when he wrote, in *An Essay on Criticism*, in 1711:

> *As some to church repair,*
> *Not for the doctrine, but the music there.*

From time to time the English press will discover a vicar, or perhaps an organist, who has strong feelings about not allowing 'Jerusalem' or 'I vow to thee, my country' to be sung at a wedding or funeral, and the nation's attention will suddenly, and briefly, be turned to asking whether this is indeed a hymn and whether it is appropriate for Christian worship. The Church will be accused of being out of touch, and someone will allege that the reason that no one goes to church any more is because 'I vow to thee, my country' and 'Jerusalem' are banned, when really they are fine hymns with rousing tunes, evoking green English fields and a bit of acceptable national pride.

In reply, others will write to the newspapers defending a ban and saying that 'unquestioning sacrifice' in warlike contexts is not to be applauded or encouraged, and pointing out that the hymn in question is hardly appropriate for a wedding anyway. Given the distinctive lack of specifically 'wedding' hymns, this is a brave thing to say. Others will make fun of it all, suggesting that the words should be changed to something like 'I vow to thee, my husband', although this would make the phrase 'and there's another country' rather suspicious.

Then, after a day or two, some real news will occur and the question will be forgotten, left to smoulder in the hearts of those who feel that the Church of England has rejected them by 'banning' the hymn that Princess Diana had at her wedding (and her funeral). 'Why can't we have a jolly good sing?' they will ask, and no one will dare to answer. Denying the British non-churchgoing public the opportunity to have a jolly good rendition of 'I vow to thee, my country' or 'Jerusalem' every few years is not something that anyone in the Church wants to do publicly. Hence these hymns remain in the 'National' section of many hymn books, and will likely stay there for many years to come.

In one sense, it is all a fuss about nothing. But this perennial debate raises questions about what hymn-singing is for, what worship is all about and what the people's involvement in it is or should be. The issue also raises questions about how the active Church is to minister to and include those who attend rarely, if at all. The ministry of crematorium funerals, for example, involves, for most ministers, a twenty-minute service which includes a reading, a brief sermon and one or two hymns, combined with the two-minute liturgy in which the deceased is actually commended to God. The majority of the congregation on such occasions are not regular churchgoers, and yet they often expect and want to sing a couple of hymns. Inevitably, the choice for them is limited, and is in some sense divorced from what happens on Sunday mornings.

'I vow to thee, my country', for example, while popular at funerals and weddings, is hardly ever sung in Sunday church worship. Many clergy and organists are either a bit frightened of it, because they think that a proportion of their regular congregation will object that it is 'unChristian', or they are sick of singing it on weekdays at funerals. (This is also why 'The Lord's my shepherd' does not find its way into many Sunday services these days.) Or, in some cases, the clergy (and people) of a congregation do actually believe that the hymn is a little unsatisfactory, if not downright dodgy.

In this day and age, some hymns have suffered and may fall into disuse because they are littered with non-inclusive language. There is a move to 'inclusivize' such hymns, such that now 'Be thou my vision' may not speak of 'man's empty praise', but of 'all the world's praise'. Personally I do not have a problem with changes to a translated text such as this, any more than I would object to the New Revised Standard Version of the Bible translating the writings of Paul in a gender-inclusive way. Some people object to any change in a hymn because it affects them when they sing it (it means that they can no longer sing it without thinking about the words)—but part of me would therefore want to change a word or two every time a hymn is sung in order to enable everyone to think about, take in, and *believe* what they are singing!

On the other hand, there are great hymns written in English, the poetry of which we should preserve. Here the analogy is with the 1662 Prayer Book, which cannot be changed, only replaced. 'The Lord will come and not be slow' by John Milton (1608–74) is a fine text, beautifully carved out of Psalms 85, 82 and 86, and is usually sung to the tune ST STEPHEN. The second verse, which is beautifully constructed, bears through it a floral image:

> *Truth from the earth, like to a flower,*
> *Shall bud and blossom then;*
> *And justice from her heavenly bower,*
> *Look down on mortal men.*

Milton did not know about inclusive language (if he had, he would probably have used it), and it is clear that in order to change the verse we might have to unpick the whole image as well as becoming as fine a poet as Milton himself. *Paradise Lost* has not been inclusivized; nor should this hymn be. Sadly, it has not found its way into one of the most recent of hymn books because some editors would rather lose the hymn than include these lines or attempt to change them. The second part of such a decision is correct, at least. It also has to be acknowledged that for a significant number of churchgoers in the UK (and especially for many who do not come to church often), inclusive language is simply not an issue. Change takes a while to take effect, and many people have never seen the phrase 'fellow men' or 'mankind' as referring to anything more or less than the whole human race. At this time hymnody is in a no-win situation over this issue, because if the words are changed someone will complain, and if they are not changed someone else will complain! The sad consequence of this will be that the repertoire is diminished as hymns fall into disuse. Readers of this book will notice that it has been my intention to use inclusive language myself, and to quote from the NRSV, but also to print the hymns as they appear in their original form.

Printing hymns in their original form in some cases means printing more verses than we are familiar with. In the case of other hymns, there are sometimes lots of extra verses, some of which I have quoted from within the text, in order to avoid printing out extensive long-forgotten verses. In general, I have taken the *New English Hymnal* as my baseline for hymn texts, as most of the hymns discussed appear in that volume, and are out of copyright. Those few hymns which do not are taken from other reputable sources.

The selection of hymns, prayers and meditations that make up this book are offered as both a reference and a weekly reading tool. During Lent, and sometimes in the other penitential season of Advent, many people find a tradition of daily reading helpful. The value of daily Bible reading hardly needs defending, and in Lent many people read another book besides, while both the Archbishops of Canterbury and Wales recommend a book each year. This book is not really intended as a Lent book, but rather as a book for the whole year, to be read perhaps once a week. For that reason the hymns are grouped seasonally. Readers who are familiar with the *Common Worship* Calendar will notice that I have generally stuck to that classification and ordering of Sundays. With Easter being a movable feast, complications arise when suggesting a hymn for each week of the year. Depending on where Easter falls in any given year, readers may find themselves 'running out of hymns' towards the end of the Trinity season, and may also find that unless Easter is very late, the 'pre-Lent' weeks are not all needed. If and when that happens, the first few pre-Lent hymns may be read at the end of the Trinity season. There are 53 hymns covered in this book, so I hope that most years can be accommodated, albeit with a bit of juggling!

On the other hand, it is not my intention to be prescriptive at all, and so I offer these thoughts on some of our greatest and most interesting hymns in the hope that they may delight, inspire and comfort us, especially when we sing them together as we make the music of praise.

WAKE, O WAKE!

✣

Wake, O wake! with tidings thrilling
The watchmen all the air are filling,
Arise, Jerusalem, arise!
Midnight strikes! no more delaying,
'The hour has come!' we hear them saying.
Where are ye all, ye virgins wise?
The Bridegroom comes in sight,
Raise high your torches bright!
Alleluya!
The wedding song
Swells loud and strong:
Go forth and join the festal throng.

Sion hears the watchmen shouting,
Her heart leaps up with joy undoubting,
She stands and waits with eager eyes;
See her Friend from heaven descending,
Adorned with truth and grace unending!
Her light burns clear, her star doth rise.
Now come, thou precious Crown,
Lord Jesu, God's own Son!
Hosanna!
Let us prepare
To follow there,
Where in thy supper we may share.

Every soul in thee rejoices;
From men and from angelic voices
Be glory given to thee alone!
Now the gates of pearl receive us,
Thy presence never more shall leave us,
We stand with Angels round thy throne.
Earth cannot give below
The bliss thou dost bestow.
Alleluya!
Grant us to raise,
To length of days,
The triumph-chorus of thy praise.

WORDS: PHILIPP NICOLAI (1556–1608), TRANS. F.C. BURKITT (1864–1935)

TUNE: WACHET AUF, MELODY BY PHILIPP NICOLAI, HARMONY BY JOHANN SEBASTIAN BACH (1685–1750)

✛

This great Advent hymn owes its words and music to one man, Philipp Nicolai, although for most English-speakers his thrilling handiwork is hidden behind the pens of others. Johann Sebastian Bach has harmonized the tune that Nicolai wrote, and several translators have turned the text into English. The text given here is the one written for the *English Hymnal*, and there are other translations, among them those by Catherine Winkworth (1829–78) and Frances Cox (1812–97).

The original German words (*'Wachet auf, ruft uns die Stimme'*) were probably inspired by a poem by Hans Sachs (1494–1576), who was a Meistersinger from Nurenburg. 'Meistersingers', or 'mastersingers', were state-employed court musicians. Sachs is almost a legendary figure, and appears in the music drama *Die Meistersinger von Nürnberg* (1867) by Richard Wagner (1813–83). He was a Lutheran poet whom Nicolai evidently admired.

Like his father, Nicolai was a Lutheran pastor, who studied theology at Erfurt and Wittenburg universities. He suffered persecution at the hands of Spanish counter-reformation troops in Herdecke an der Ruhr, and then in Cologne, where Lutheran congregations were not welcome. He then worked as pastor in Unna, Westphalia, but there was unhappiness there too, as nearly 1400 people succumbed to plague in

1597–98. Very much affected by the deaths of his parishioners, Nicolai read *City of God* by Augustine of Hippo (354–430), and in 1599 he published *Freudenspiegel des ewigen Lebens* ('Joyous Mirror of Eternal Life'), in which are found his two most famous hymns, 'Wake, O wake' and 'How brightly shines the morning star' (*Wie schön leuchtet der Morgenstern*). Two years later he moved to the parish of St Katherine's, Hamburg, where he served until his death seven years later.

Nicolai's experience of plague was by no means unique. In England in the following century, another pastor, the Reverend William Mompesson (1639–1709), found himself serving a rural community in Eyam, Derbyshire, which, due to a quirk of bad luck, found itself exposed to the plague of 1665–66. It was the only village infected in that part of the country (by a bolt of cloth brought from plague-infested London), and Mompesson sealed off the village in order to prevent the disease from spreading. Tragically, it took hold, killing 259 people from a total of only 76 families, Mompesson's own wife among them. It was under circumstances such as these that Philipp Nicolai laboured, burying his parishoners daily, and at constant risk of infection.

His hymn is not about plague, of course, but it points us to the end time when Christ will come again in glory, as Bridegroom to the faithful. The original title of the hymn made specific reference to the brides-maids who await the bridegroom's return with their lamps lit (Matthew 25:1–13). They have to wait a long time, and their lamps go out. Half of them have spare oil, but do not share it with the others because there is not enough. The unwise ones go to fetch more oil, but the bride-groom arrives, and the party begins. When the others return, they are too late, the door is closed and they miss the party.

In telling this parable, Jesus is saying, 'Be prepared.' We know neither the time nor the place of his return. He will come like a 'thief in the night', as the apostle Paul puts it (1 Thessalonians 5:2). Paul continues, 'You, beloved, are not in darkness, for that day to surprise you like a thief; for you are all children of light and children of the day; we are not of the night or of darkness. So then let us not fall asleep as others do, but let us keep awake and be sober; for those who sleep sleep at night' (1 Thessalonians 5:4–7).

Nicolai's hymn wakes us up. 'Wake, O wake! with tidings thrilling' is a clarion call to be ready, and also a dramatization of the moment when the wise bridesmaids see their Lord approaching. The expansive melody, so majestically harmonized by Bach, makes the image of the bridesmaids rising to greet him all the more vivid. Yet it is not just them, it is all Jerusalem, all of the city of God, who must arise and take their place in the welcoming party. As the text continues into the second verse, we realize that this is not just a dramatization of the parable, it is also a future vision of the second coming, also encompassing the watchmen of Jerusalem (see Isaiah 52:8). The bridesmaids are representative of all of us, and we all rejoice to see Christ descending from heaven in glory. Just as the crowds sang 'Hosanna' as Jesus entered into Jerusalem on Palm Sunday (Mark 11:9–10), here again the triumphal shout of welcome goes up. This time, though, we *will* follow and not abandon our Lord as we follow him to the eucharistic feast that he has given us: 'Then I saw an angel standing in the sun, and with a loud voice he called to all the birds that fly in midheaven, "Come, gather for the great supper of God"' (Revelation 19:17). The second half of the hymn addresses Jesus as we pass into eternal life through the pearly gates of Revelation 21:21, and it ends with Nicolai's expression of the desire to be able to sing God's praise throughout our lives, and into eternal life.

Both the text and music have had an interesting and varied career. Bach harmonized Nicolai's melody, which had already been harmonized by Michael Praetorius (1571–1621), but he also used it in one of his cantatas. For each week of the ecclesiastical year, Bach wrote a musical meditation for use in church, and *Cantata BWV140* was written for the 27th Sunday after Trinity, 1731 (a rare date, found only in years when Easter falls in March). It takes its name and musical theme from Nicolai's hymn, which was well-known, although a contemporary of Bach, Christian Gerber, complained that Bach's version of the chorale was unsingable by the congregation. Sometimes there is no pleasing people with church music!

In the cantata, Bach interleaves the verse of the chorale with arias and duets commenting upon and illustrating them. Thus, between the first and second stanzas there is sung a bass and soprano duet which is a dialogue between one of the bridesmaids and Christ. She tells him she is waiting with her lamp lit, and he replies that he is on his way. The setting is like a love duet between bride and groom, and in it we can sense the idea of Christ as bridegroom to the Church, a popular and traditional view of marriage. Thus the bass soloist sings, 'Then come within to me, my chosen bride! I have been betrothed to you from all eternity. I will set you on my heart and on my arm like a seal.' The last phrase is a direct quotation from Song of Songs 8:6 and shows how Bach, like Nicolai before him, has explained and illustrated the parable of the wise and foolish bridesmaids by reference to related texts, in order to inspire and uplift our faith as we wait for the return of Christ.

O Lord, enlighten our waking hours, and guard us when asleep, that awake we may be found ready and waiting for Christ, and asleep may rest in the peace of his love, until that great day when he returns in clouds of glory to lift us to your heavenly throne. Amen.

GOD, IN WHOSE IMAGE WE ARE MADE

✣

God, in whose image we are made,
strengthened to face life unafraid,
we adore you,
stand before you;
filled with delight at all you give
morning and night that we may live,
to your praises
our heart raises
joyful praises
gladsome praises
to your honour.

God, who in marriage has begun
through male and female, bound as one,
culmination
of creation;
give to your children love and peace,
patience and trust that will not cease,
to your praises
our heart raises
joyful praises
ceaseless praises
for your mercy.

God, in whose family we are heirs,
give sons and daughters to be theirs,
bringing pleasure
in good measure;
that in the home that is to be
all may find fruitful unity
to your praises
our heart raises
joyful praises
heartfelt praises
as our duty.

So, Holy Trinity above,
we, who rejoice to feel your love,
knowing gladness
tinged with sadness;
then, as we face the gates of death,
drawing at length our final breath,
to your praises
our heart raises
joyful praises
heaven's praises,
in your presence.

WORDS: © MICHAEL SAWARD (B. 1932) / JUBILATE HYMNS. USED BY PERMISSION
TUNE: LASST UNS ERFREUEN, RALPH VAUGHAN WILLIAMS (1872–1958)

✤

I have to confess that the inclusion of this brand new hymn is little short of self-indulgence on my part, although I do want to commend it to wider usage, as very few people have come across it.

Canon Michael Saward, who is a well-known contemporary hymn writer, wrote it for my wife Jessica and me, for our wedding in St Paul's Cathedral in September 2000. We requested the tune, Vaughan Williams' great LASST UNS ERFREUEN, not only because we like it and it is well-known, but because it is not sung so often. It is also used for 'All creatures of our God and King' and 'Ye watchers and ye holy ones'. The tune was first used for the latter of these two in 1906, but can be traced back to Cologne in 1623, where it first appeared in the hymn book *Geistliche Kirchengesang*.

The hymn, we hope, may become a hymn for weddings, as there are so few hymns that are distinctively appropriate for Christian marriage. The words speak very clearly of the expectations and elements of marriage that the Church advocates and teaches. Friendship, sex, children, trust and a dimension of eternity are all expressed.

In the history of the Anglican Church there have been various Prayer Books, each with their own slant on the Marriage Service, but the theological thinking has hardly changed. These days, brides do not promise to be 'bonny and buxom in bed', as they did in Thomas Cranmer's time, although many couples do still opt for the 1662 Book of Common Prayer service, in which they 'give and pledge their troth' to one another. Many phrases from this version, which was the only legally authorized one for hundreds of years, have found their way into the English psyche. Phrases such as 'til death us do part', and 'let him now speak, or else hereafter for ever hold his peace' are instantly recognizable. Even in 1928, when the Church of England tried unsuccessfully to persuade Parliament to accept a new Prayer Book, the service was hardly altered, although the Preface at the beginning was made more palatable (references to 'carnal lusts and appetites', 'brute beasts' and 'the gift of continency' were removed). This 1928 revision is still very much in use, although many prefer a modern language version, such as the recent revision found in the *Common Worship* services. Whichever service is used, though, the reasons for marriage have not changed, even if their order of significance has.

In the older Prayer Book services of 1549 and 1662 there are three 'causes' for matrimony given: first, procreation of children; second, to encourage only appropriate sexual activity; and third, as a source of enduring friendship. In the more modern services, these purposes are still mentioned, but in a different order: first comes friendship, then sex, then children. This change says more about our modern attitude to human relationships than it does about theology. The attempt is not being made so much to prescribe the purposes of marriage, as to reflect what brings couples to the altar. The theological thinking comes as an application of the gospel to modern life, rather than the often preferred model of ordering our lives according to gospel teachings.

Where human marriage and relationships are concerned, this may not be such a bad thing, and it may even reflect what God himself has done. The marriage service in the Church of England says that a couple 'shall be united in love as Christ is united with his church'. The phrase originates with St Paul: 'anyone united to the Lord becomes one spirit with him' (1 Corinthians 6:17), and although he is speaking of individuals, the same has been said of the whole Church.

During Advent we are particularly reminded that Christ is the 'bridegroom' for whom we wait. Jesus says of himself, 'The wedding guests cannot mourn as long as the bridegroom is with them, can they? The days will come when the bridegroom is taken away from them' (Matthew 9:15).

In saying this Jesus places himself in a tradition by which the people of Israel have seen themselves as like a bride waiting for the bridegroom, the Messiah. Now as we await the second coming of Christ, the *parousia*, the imagery is still helpful and relevant.

In Isaiah we find the idea of marriage being presented as a model to which the relationship between God and his people will match up: 'For as a young man marries a young woman, so shall your sons marry you, and as the bridegroom rejoices over the bride, so shall your God rejoice over you' (Isaiah 62:5).

Israel is to understand how the Lord will treat and love them by thinking of their weddings, and how brides and grooms rejoice over each other. On the last day, when all shall be revealed, God and they shall be united like a married couple. The union between Christ and the Church is seen in terms of the temporal and worldly union of husband and wife. Other texts, most notably the Song of Songs, supposedly written by King Solomon, are also taken to support this view.

It is often supposed that what is being said is that the union between human beings reflects the union of Christ and his Church, the relationship between God and his people. For Isaiah, it is the other way around: we are invited to see the relationship between God and his people as in some way based upon the relationship between man and woman. In the narratives of creation, God gives Adam a partner, not because doing so will reflect an ideal relationship between himself and Adam, but because 'it is not good that the man should be alone' (Genesis 2:18). Here is the basis for human marriage in creation, and the origin of 'the two shall become one flesh' (Matthew 19:5).

Human marriage comes first. In what may appear to be a kind of spiritual version of the chicken and egg dilemma—which comes first?—it seems that marriage does, for it leads to an understanding, offered by God himself, of how we are to relate to him. Through Isaiah and St Paul, God is saying, 'Take the fundamental form of human relationship, one of the most rewarding forms of relationship' (and, we might add, the most difficult, most complex and most time-consuming form of human relationship), 'and think of my relationship with you in that way.'

Our relationship with God and our marriages are not always easy, and can be stretched to absolute limits sometimes. But both are rewarding, almost *because* they are not so simple or easy to get right. And we can be helped to understand each by reference to the other. Communication, trust, intimacy and a balanced perspective don't come easily in either faith or marriage. This is perhaps why the idea of marriage is something on which God has drawn over the ages as a way of explaining in scripture how we can, should or may relate to him, as the Bride of Christ.

O God, our partner in life and love, our rock in times of trouble and the enabler of our joy, give us your grace to follow your way of faith to our lives' end, that we may share with you in all our joys and pains, until that last day when we will be united with you through the saving grace of Jesus Christ our Lord, Amen.

I HEARD THE VOICE
OF JESUS SAY

✣

I heard the voice of Jesus say,
'Come unto me and rest;
Lay down, thou weary one, lay down
Thy head upon my breast':
I came to Jesus as I was,
Weary, and worn, and sad;
I found in him a resting-place,
And he has made me glad.

I heard the voice of Jesus say,
'Behold, I freely give
The living water, thirsty one;
Stoop down, and drink, and live':
I came to Jesus, and I drank
Of that life-giving stream;
My thirst was quenched, my soul revived,
And now I live in him.

I heard the voice of Jesus say,
'I am this dark world's Light;
Look unto me, thy morn shall rise,
And all thy day be bright':

I looked to Jesus, and I found
In him my Star, my Sun;
And in that light of life I'll walk
Till travelling days are done.

WORDS: HORATIUS BONAR (1808–89)

TUNE: KINGSFOLD, ENGLISH FOLK SONG, ARR. RALPH VAUGHAN WILLIAMS (1872–1958)

✧

The tune KINGSFOLD is one of the most lyrical melodies in the modern hymn repertoire. Like many of our best tunes, the composer's identity has been lost in the mists of time, even though the music still rings clear today. It was originally a folk tune discovered by Ralph Vaughan Williams sometime between 1902 and 1906 while visiting small towns and villages, notating the local music. The melody was known as 'Dives and Lazarus', and after fitting it to Bonar's words for the *English Hymnal* of 1906, Vaughan Williams was to use it again in a 13-minute work for harp and string orchestra entitled *Five variants on 'Dives and Lazarus'*.

The title evidently refers to Jesus' parable about the rich man and Lazarus (Luke 16:19–31). 'Dives' (pronounced 'Dyvees') is Latin for 'rich man', whereas Lazarus is a variant on Eleazer, which means 'God has helped'. This Lazarus is not to be confused with Jesus' friend Lazarus whom he raised from the dead (John 11:1–44).

Not only is the tune based on a folk tune, but the story may have been a folk tale. The parable of Dives and Lazarus is all about a rich man (Dives) who, having died, finds himself in hell. Gazing up to heaven, he sees Lazarus, whom he recognizes as a beggar. He calls on him for help, but there is a great gulf fixed between heaven and hell. Dives is told that Lazarus is now being helped by God, while he is getting his richly deserved reward for having lived a selfish life. Dives then asks that his family be warned of their future torment, so that they may act to prevent it (he cares about his family, at least!). But again, this is impossible, and the gospel parable concludes with the chilling prophecy: 'If they do not listen to Moses and the prophets, neither will they be convinced even if someone rises from the dead' (Luke 16:31). In using this story, which may already have been well-known as a Middle Eastern folk tale, Jesus adds a distinctive prophetic slant, making the tale refer to himself as the one 'sent from the dead'.

It is hard to know whether Horatius Bonar or Vaughan Williams intended the hymn to make any connection with this story. When we read the opening lines of the hymn, however, we can imagine Lazarus resting in peace on Christ's breast. We might also be reminded of the apostle John, reclining next to Jesus at the last supper (John 13:23–26). Lazarus is weary, and worn, and sad, but found in Jesus his resting-place, and Christ has made him glad. The key text for this verse, though, is surely 'Come to me, all you that are weary and are carrying heavy burdens, and I will give you rest. Take my yoke upon you, and learn from me; for I am gentle and humble in heart, and you will find rest for your souls. For my yoke is easy, and my burden is light' (Matthew 11:28–30).

In the second verse the perspective moves away from the weary disciple to the Samaritan woman at Jacob's well, near the city of Sychar (John 4:5–30). This time it is Jesus who is weary, and he rests in the heat of the day. She comes to draw water, and he asks for a drink, but she is surprised because he is Jewish, and Jews did not associate with Samaritans. Jesus says that if she had known who he was she would have asked for 'living water', which, if drunk, quenches all thirst. He says: 'Everyone who drinks of this water will be thirsty again, but those who drink of the water that I will give them will never be thirsty. The water that I will give will become in them a spring of water gushing up to eternal life' (John 4:13–14).

The third verse reminds us of Jesus saying, 'I am the light of the world' (John 8:12). We may be reminded of that famous picture by the pre-Raphaelite painter William Holman Hunt (1827–1910) in which Christ stands at a closed door with a lantern. The door has no handle on the outside, and is overgrown with weeds, indicating that the entrance to the heart is disused. Christ knocks, but the door can only be opened from inside. Only we can open our hearts to Jesus, who will not force his way in. Versions of the painting hang in Keble College, Oxford, and St Paul's Cathedral in London. In the picture, and in this third verse of the hymn, we are reminded of Christ as a light shining in the darkness, the light of redemption conquering the darkness of sin, and the light of love illuminating the darkness of fear and despair. It is the great theme of the Advent season, but it is an important aspect of all Christian spirituality. At any time of year we can look to Jesus, and find in him 'my Star, my Sun'.

The hymn offers three kinds of personal reflection, three 'persons' to whom the 'I' might refer. Firstly, there is the 'I' of the character in the stories alluded to. There is the 'I' of Lazarus, and of the Samaritan woman, and of the fearful sinner, to whom Christ offers light. In John's Gospel the saying 'I am the light of the world' follows the story of the woman caught in adultery, which may seem appropriate, but there is no real suggestion that the two are linked. Yet all three of these people represent us in some way: we are all sinners, we all seek the living water, and we are all weary travellers walking the path of life. Thus secondly there is the 'I' that is you or me, empathizing with these people who meet Jesus.

Thirdly, there is the 'I' of the author, Horatius Bonar, who, when he wrote the hymn in 1846, was Pastor of North Kelso in Scotland. He wrote more than 600 hymns, but this is the one by which he is most often represented today. His hymns were usually inspired by the circumstances in which he lived—a babbling brook, waves on the Edinburgh coast, or even a railway train. We can easily imagine him on a Scottish hillside being inspired to write of the 'life-giving stream'.

The tune that Vaughan Williams so aptly arranged for Bonar's words also has a flow to it like a running stream. The first, second and fourth melodic phrases are almost identical, and there is very little harmonic movement. The tune is very much in E minor, and would seem repetitive if it weren't for its innate beauty, and the fact that at the end of the first and third lines the composer employs musical 'suspensions', which leave the final chord lingering, unresolved. When the resolution does come, it leads us straight into the next line, thereby keeping us moving along, like that stream of living water that carries us until our travelling days are done.

In the *New English Hymnal*, KINGSFOLD is also a second tune for 'How shall I sing that majesty'. Fortunately Ken Naylor's (1931–91) COE FEN has gained a good foothold, and KINGSFOLD has been largely displaced from there. More recently it has been twinned with 'If Christ had not been raised from death, our hope would be in vain' by Christopher Idle (b. 1938), and also 'Two thousand years since Galilee' by Brian Hoare (b. 1935), but in both cases the placidity of the tune does not really suit the strength of the words. Understandably those who put words and tunes together want to use KINGSFOLD more, but there has not been a pairing more apt than 'I heard the voice of Jesus say'.

Lord Jesus, spring of living water, grant us the comfort of your love and your light, that in you we may find our resting-place, and that, our hearts gladdened by your voice, we may walk in the light of life until our travelling days are done, for your dear name's sake we pray, Amen.

WHEN CAME IN FLESH
THE INCARNATE WORD

✣

When came in flesh the incarnate Word,
The heedless world slept on,
And only simple shepherds heard
That God had sent his Son.

When comes the Saviour at the last,
From east to west shall shine
The judgment light, and earth aghast
Shall tremble at the sign.

Then shall the pure in heart be blest,
As mild he comes to them,
As when upon the Virgin's breast
He lay at Bethlehem:

As mild to meek-eyed love and faith,
Only more strong to save;
Strengthened by having bowed to death,
By having burst the grave.

Lord, who could dare see thee descend
In state, unless he knew
Thou art the sorrowing sinner's friend,
The gracious and the true?

Dwell in our hearts, O Saviour blest;
So shall thine advent's dawn
'Twixt us and thee, our bosom-guest,
Be but the veil withdrawn.

WORDS: JOSEPH ANSTICE (1808–36)

TUNE: WALSALL FROM W. ANCHORS' *A CHOICE COLLECTION OF PSALM TUNES*, 1721

✣

A 21st-century British Christmas involves various ingredients. We consume a great deal, eating, drinking, and spending; we sing Christmas carols, and we send Christmas cards. Some people go to church, others reunite themselves with their families—and family reunions at Christmas can cause as much sadness as joy, according to the various welfare charities that report on our national life.

Another aspect of Christmas these days is that it lasts for far too long. Liturgically speaking, Christmas begins at midnight on Christmas Eve, but for many it begins sometime in late November, and so when the Church is beginning to get excited about the birth of Jesus—the incarnation of our Lord—many people are fed up with Christmas, sometimes literally! The same is true of Easter, to a certain extent. A shopping culture is a culture of anticipation, where all the trade and energy is put in before the event, rather than after it. Many people think that Easter Week is the week before Easter Day, when it is in fact the week afterwards; and Easter Saturday is really the Saturday after Easter, not the Saturday before it, which is called Holy Saturday or Easter Eve, just as the week before Easter is properly called Holy Week.

While the focus of Christmas may be different depending on whether you are in the shopping mall or in church, the sense of anticipation is common to both. The December period is, of course, Advent, and during Advent we wait. Many wait for Christmas, for the presents and food it may bring, while others wait for the second coming of Christ.

As well as waiting during Advent, we also prepare. All the shops extol the virtues of preparing for Christmas, and the Church does also. Advent used to be a time of fasting, not unlike Lent, and it is still observed in many churches as a penitential season. It can be quite hard to maintain this flavour of Advent while there is a demand for carol services in the first half of December. In schools, charities and many other organizations that have an annual carol service, necessity forces the celebration of Christmas well back in December. For some, then, Advent can be a confusing time, as we are already singing the praises of the newborn king, while at the same time apparently waiting for him. He is both here and not here. The salvation, promise and hope of the incarnation are both now and not yet.

This juxtaposition of future hope and present joy is coincidentally very important for Christians. We know, as it says in this Advent hymn, that the 'incarnate Word' has come, and yet we are waiting for his return. This hymn, which has a lovely tune and is not as well-known as it should be, is one of only a few that capture the blend of past, present and future with which Advent and Christmas force us to juggle in December.

Little is known about the music, except that it has at various times been attributed to the great English composer Henry Purcell (1659–95). Whether he wrote it or not, it found its way into William Anchors' collection of Psalm tunes published in 1721. The words we have here were not written until 1836, and were dictated by Joseph Anstice as he lay dying in Torquay, aged only 28. After his death, his wife published *Hymns by the late Joseph Anstice, M.A., formerly Student of Christ Church, Oxford, and Professor of Classical Literature, Oxford, and Professor of Classical Literature, King's College, London*. The book contained 52 hymns and was published in Bridgwater, only four months after his death in February 1836.

Anstice was evidently something of a theologian as well as a classical scholar. This hymn begins with a doleful verse, suggesting that no one other than the shepherds noticed when Jesus was born. The reference to 'the incarnate Word' comes from John 1:14, and the shepherds are found in Luke 2:8–20. A great event such as the birth of Christ was only recognized by humble shepherds, and some people might equally lament the fact that the true meaning of Christmas is often overlooked today.

The second verse moves straight from the lowly and unnoticed incarnation to the opposite extreme—a bright second coming, seen from east to west, and all 'earth aghast' to witness it. Jesus may have crept in quietly last time, Anstice wants to say, but next time we will all see it clearly. Verse three combines the two, as we do today, in as much as the author talks of the pure of heart being blessed at the second coming, just as Jesus was mildly cradled at Bethlehem. For those of faith, he says, the second coming will be peaceful, and yet also frightening to any that are not prepared to welcome him, who returns this time after having already defeated the power of the grave:

> *Lord, who could dare see thee descend*
> *In state, unless he knew*
> *Thou art the sorrowing sinner's friend,*
> *The gracious and the true?*

The final verse, which, like this one, is addressed directly to Jesus, combines the post-incarnational Christ with the one who is yet to come. Both, who are one and the same, are invited into the singers' hearts, so that when we keep Christmas *and* Advent we may be able to see Jesus clearly, and not as through a veil.

In this hymn, then, we have a blend of Advent and Christmas which speaks to the sometimes confusing mix that is experienced in contemporary life. When we sing it, it may well help us to disentangle Advent and Christmas, and also, at the same time, to appreciate the advantages of handling them together.

Lord our God, as we turn our eyes and prayers towards your incarnation among us, gladden our hearts with the news of your coming; hold our friends and families in your love, and turn any sorrow to deeper joy, in the light of the eternal promises made secure in our Lord's birth, death and resurrection, through the same, Jesus Christ our Lord, Amen.

O COME, ALL YE FAITHFUL

✣

O come, all ye faithful,
Joyful and triumphant,
O come ye, O come ye to Bethlehem;
Come and behold him
Born the King of Angels:

O come, let us adore him,
O come, let us adore him,
O come, let us adore him, Christ the Lord!

God of God,
Light of Light,
Lo! he abhors not the Virgin's womb;
Very God,
Begotten, not created:

See how the Shepherds,
Summoned to his cradle,
Leaving their flocks, draw nigh with lowly fear;
We too will thither
Bend our joyful footsteps:

Lo! star-led chieftains,
Magi, Christ adoring,
Offer him incense, gold, and myrrh;
We to the Christ Child
Bring our heart's oblations:

Child, for us sinners
Poor and in the manger,
Fain we embrace thee, with awe and love;
Who would not love thee,
Loving us so dearly?

Sing, choirs of Angels,
Sing in exultation,
Sing, all ye citizens of heaven above;
Glory to God
In the Highest:

Yea, Lord, we greet thee,
Born this happy morning,
Jesu, to thee be glory given;
Word of the Father,
Now in flesh appearing:

WORDS: LATIN, 18TH CENTURY, TRANS. FREDERICK OAKELEY (1802–80),

WILLIAM MERCER (1811–73) AND OTHERS

TUNE: ADESTE FIDELES, JOHN FRANCIS WADE (1711–86)

✛

Carols have become almost exclusively associated with Christmas. This was not always the case, and occasionally we hear of 'Easter Carols' (such as 'This joyful Eastertide' or 'Ye choirs of new Jerusalem' which can be found as the last entry in *100 Carols for Choirs*, edited by John Rutter and David Willcocks), but the use of the word in that context has almost completely died out. Benjamin Britten (1913–76), one of the 20th century's greatest English composers, wrote 'A New Year Carol', using words by an unknown writer, but almost all the other carols we might come across today are Christmas carols.

The word 'carol' comes from two Latin words: *cantare*, 'to sing', and *rola*, which is an exclamation of joy. Thus in Italian we find the verb *carolare*, which means 'to sing songs of joy'. There is no mention of Christmas here, although we can see why Christmas, the feast of the nativity of our Lord, or of the incarnation of the Word made flesh, should be associated with exclamations of joy! The first exclamations of joy, the first Christmas carol perhaps, is the *Gloria in Excelsis*, the song of the angels proclaiming the good news of Jesus' birth to the shepherds (Luke 2:14). In medieval times, carol singing was often accompanied by dancing, and both had a place in worship, as they had since the time of the Psalmist: 'Let them praise his name with dancing, making melody to him with tambourine and lyre' (Psalm 149:3).

Carols are still very popular, at least at Christmas, and some of the old traditions associated with them still survive. We still see groups of people wandering the streets singing carols, exchanging gifts, being offered refreshment and generally enjoying themselves in the 'spirit of Christmas' even in our high-tech postmodern world, even if there is not so much dancing these days. Christmas itself has survived the process that has demoted Christian festivals in the social consciousness, and one of the reasons that Christmas is still 'celebrated' must be that Christmas music is as popular as it ever was.

The traditions of Christmas live long, and it should be remembered that when Rome was Christianized in the fourth century, Christian festivals displaced pagan ones. Christmas replaced the festival associated with the birth of the Roman god Mithras (a temple in whose honour can still be seen in the heart of the City of London). Just as St Valentine's day replaced *Lupercalia* (a Roman love-lottery festival), we have to admit that some of the original flavour of these festivals has survived Christianization, and is still present today. The feast of Mithras' birthday and other festivals associated with the winter solstice and the shortening of days, such as the Santa Lucia festival celebrated in Scandinavia around St Lucy's day (13 December), have left their mark on Christmas, even today.

In one sense, all carols are hymns, and many hymns are carols. If a carol is a song of joyful exclamation, then many of our hymns qualify, and rightly so. Yet many of our carols can be considered as hymns, for they are surely poems designed to be sung in praise to, or of, God. 'O come all ye faithful' is one of the most famous, popular and well-known carols. Many people can sing several verses without checking the words, and of all hymns this is one where even those who do not sing in choirs often have a crack at the wonderful fifth-verse descant by Sir David Willcocks (b. 1919). That soaring descant, with its trumpet like 'O come' in the refrain has established itself as part of the carol, even though it was composed recently.

The tune itself is quite old, and it is now thought to have been written by John Francis Wade, who also wrote the original Latin words. He was an English Roman Catholic who became involved in the Jacobite rebellion in Scotland. Charles Stuart (1720–88), also known as 'Bonnie Prince Charlie', was defeated at the Battle of Cullodden in 1746 and, with many followers, fled to France. Many of the exiles settled in Douai, then in Flanders. Wade was a supplier of music to these expatriate Roman Catholics, and this may explain why his relatively modern hymn was written originally in Latin, which in the mid-18th century was still very much the language of the Roman Catholic Church. It was published in Wade's *Cantus Diversi*, in 1743. Manuscripts of the carol from Ireland dated 1746 suggest that Wade composed the tune between 1740 and 1743, and it has been suggested that he lifted it from *Ottone*, an opera written in 1723 by George Frideric Handel (1685–1759).

A carol in Latin was never going to become popular in reformed Anglican Britain, until Frederick Oakeley translated it in 1841. The fourth and fifth stanzas were not translated by Oakeley but by William Mercer (1811–73), who, like Oakeley, was an Anglican priest. Ordained in 1828, Oakeley worked from 1839 at the church now known as All Saints', Margaret Street, in London. In 1845 he became a Roman Catholic priest and in 1852 a Canon of Westminster Cathedral, the most significant Roman Catholic church in England.

The carol tells the story of Christmas in a very clear way, although there is a confusion among the verses about to whom the hymn is being sung. The difference of sources no doubt explains this, but we notice that the first verse summons us to worship, as a gathering-call, and the refrain 'O come let us adore him, Christ the Lord' repeats this invitation after each verse. The second verse expresses the theology of incarnation and quotes the Nicene Creed, reminding us of the deep significance of this Christ-child whom we are to come and adore. The next two verses describe the nativity, joining us to the adoration of shepherds and magi, for 'we too' will worship. The fifth verse is slightly different, as it addresses the child Jesus directly, suggesting that Jesus is poor and in the manger because of us. Here we notice some atonement theology creeping into the manger. Christ died for us, and Christ was born for us, but we don't often hear the view that Christ had a lowly birth *because* of us. Is it human sin that causes there to be no room at the inn?

'Sing, choirs of angels' is often the final verse, and ends the hymn with shouts of praise in true 'carol' style. The angels' *Gloria* is repeated and we end with great praise—except on Christmas Day, that is, when we have to go one better. Musically this is handled with a stupendous organ part (again by Sir David Willcocks), crowning the hymn with appropriate panache, while the words turn to a restatement of St John's theology of Christmas (John 1:14), here addressed to Jesus the incarnate Son. The phrase 'now in flesh appearing' can send a tingle down the spine, because it is reserved only for one day of the year, and its use gives a special significance to *this* day, the day when God became human, when the salvation of humanity was launched from on high. And on this day we greet the Lord and welcome him into our hearts, adoring him alone, for he is Christ the Lord.

Lord Jesus, as we follow the light of your star to Bethlehem, to greet your appearing and hail your presence among us, grant us, your faithful people, so to adore and follow you, not only on this day, but all the days of our lives until we come to dwell with you, and sing your praise with choirs of angels and all the citizens of heaven, Amen.

STEPHEN, FIRST OF CHRISTIAN MARTYRS

✛

Stephen, first of Christian martyrs,
Let the Church in hymns proclaim;
Following close the Saviour's passion,
Thus he won immortal fame:
For his foes he prayed forgiveness
while they stoned him unto death,
To the Lord his soul commending
As he yielded up his breath.

Holy Spirit, gift of Jesus,
Shed thy light upon our eyes,
That we may behold with Stephen
That fair realm beyond the skies,
Where the Son of Man in glory
Waits for us at God's right hand,
King of saints and hope of martyrs,
Lord of all the pilgrim band.

See him who went on before us
Heavenly mansions to prepare,
Who for us is ever pleading
By his wounds of glory there;
In that blessèd home of splendour
Christ our Saviour reigns above,
Calling us to share his rapture
In the Father's boundless love.

Glory be to God the Father,
Glory to his only Son,
Dying, risen, ascending for us,
Who the heavenly realm has won;
Glory to the Holy Spirit,
To One God in Persons Three,
From the saints in earth and heaven,
Glory, endless glory, be. Amen.

WORDS: CHRISTOPHER WORDSWORTH (1807–85)

TUNE: EVERTON, HENRY SMART (1813–79)

✛

It may seem a little strange that in the Church's calendar we com-memorate a very unpleasant event the day after Christmas. For many, 26 December is merely 'Boxing Day', the day on which there was a tradition of giving a 'box' of money or treats to servants as a kind of belated Christmas present. For many today, Boxing Day is simply the slightly deflated holiday after Christmas, when the leftovers are eaten and the family gathering begins to disperse. For many clergy, Boxing Day is the day when, at last, the busyness of the previous day is over and, feeling less fatigued, the vicarage family can have *their* Christmas.

All of this is very ironic, because 26 December is not merely the second day of Christmas. It is also the feast day of St Stephen, the first Christian martyr, whose witness of word and death we encounter in Acts 6—7.

There is a stunning depiction of the stoning of St Stephen by Sir Anthony Van Dyck (1599–1641), painted between 1622 and 1624, and kept at Tatton Park in Cheshire. Charles I described Van Dyck as a 'Genius of Painting', and in *The Stoning of St Stephen* he portrays Stephen dressed in martyr's red, wearing a deacon's dalmatic robe, and gazing upwards to 'that fair realm beyond the skies' as five men raise stones against him. In the picture they have yet to strike—we are spared the bloodstained reality. Above the saint hover two cherubs, ready to receive him as he forgives those who are about to kill him, saying, 'Lord, do not hold this sin against them' (Acts 7:60). In the middle ground of the painting, we see St Paul (then 'Saul'), standing on

Stephen's clothes, explaining to another onlooker what is happening.

And yet, glorious and beautifully depicted as the painting is, there is something unsatisfactory that makes us forget what is actually happening as these five boulder-wielding thugs set upon a man who has done little more than deliver a sermon. The art helps us to see through what is going on, to a greater glory as Stephen goes to his maker with a serene expression on his face. So too, to a certain extent, does the hymn, with its major-key melody and virtuous words. The story of St Stephen is so often portrayed as a vaguely pleasant one, indicating how sweet and decorous it is to die for one's faith. In the painting particularly, the reality of death is withheld—we are protected from it—as the moment is frozen in an almost idyllic scene.

In another of Van Dyck's paintings, of the adoration of the shepherds at the birth of Christ, completed in 1632 for a church in Dendermonde, Belgium, we see the same style, the same heavenward gazing, the same cherubs in the sky watching over as the coarse shepherds pay homage to a splendidly dressed Madonna displaying her clean white baby. Paintings such as this find their way on to our Christmas cards and Christmas pudding labels! They are indeed masterpieces: there is no question as to their value as works of art, nor of their status as objects of devotion, nor of the authenticity of the artist's intentions.

And yet, paintings that depict the mother and child in pastoral elegance with rich robes and a clean stable floor are in some sense unrealistic, just as pictures or hymns suggesting that someone is enjoying their martyrdom are unrealistic. Conventions of hymnody or painting can disguise the truth with their sweet words and honeyed melody. They can affect our vision, helping us to forget the reality of the events portrayed. Cake-tin depictions of martyrdom or incarnation veil us from the realities of thuggery, intolerance and bigotry; or from the pain, fear and danger of natural birth in a first-century Middle Eastern cow-shed, with all the lack of hygiene and risk of disease that that brings.

In the world of art, which mirrors the imaginations of our own hearts, we are more than content to witness a cosy martyrdom, or believe in a gentle and pale-skinned Madonna cradling a clean and sleeping baby. But of course, it wasn't like that. There was a lot of blood, dirt and pain on those occasions, and likely more besides.

And yet, we must have our art, we must have our painters, composers and poets who show us the heavens and depict a greater significance. We need interpretations and descriptions that point us beyond the surface facts to deeper truths. We need artists who can *show* us that the Christ-child is the Saviour of the world, artists who can show us and hymn writers who can help us believe that Stephen was not a victim of just another street-lynching. We need these people to tell us the stories and point us beyond the facts, to the Truth.

St Luke, that great storyteller who gives us the most extended account of Jesus' birth, is also the one who writes, in Acts, of Stephen's death. Both stories capture our imaginations and our hearts. But we must not let go too easily. There are realities of birth, of life and of death that we must face—realities not only of who we are and how we act, but also of how we relate to these over-familiar events.

It's so easy, in that carol by Christina Rosetti (1830–94), 'In the bleak midwinter', to sing, 'If I were a wise man, I would do my part'. But would you? Could you? Dare you?

It takes some conviction to follow a call to a dingy animal-shed to greet a divine child, and more still to speak out against those who would harm you for it. Sadly, Stephen was the first in a very long line, and it is quite deliberate that we commemorate him on the first day after Christmas.

Most of us are never asked to submit to martyrdom, so the question of whether we would be prepared to do so is not often asked. When it does get asked, as it might do on St Stephen's day, it is too easy to hide behind a pretty picture of red robes and angels singing as a worthy soul is carried to heaven. It can be so easy to romanticize martyrdom, just as it can be so easy to romanticize Christmas. Such fantasy feeds on reality. Fantasy cloaks a bloodstained, dirty baby in pure white linen, and a martyr in red silk. Fantasy talks of peace and goodwill on earth, but at no cost. That amounts to cheap grace, salvation bought cheap, suffering ignored. Fantasy covers reality in candy, and peddles it for pennies like a cheap Christmas present.

At Christmastide, we are meant to encounter birth and death in quick succession. Both of them involve us, they are *for* us. If we really buy into Christmas, we become involved in the birth at Bethlehem, and we watch in real horror as a man whose job is to help the poor is slaughtered by persecuting fanatics. It is not hard to become involved, and easy to want not to become involved, because these events happen around us all the time. We enjoy sharing with families who have had a new baby, and we cannot help but be moved by stories of violence in our news media. These are not fantasies, but realities of real pain and real joy.

Dear God, who gave us the supreme gift of your Son at Christmas, help us not to lose our ability to celebrate new birth, and prevent us from becoming spiritually immune to the horror of killing, so that our lives may be real and whole, and our hearts filled with wonder and compassion, today and always, Amen.

O GOD, OUR HELP
IN AGES PAST

✠

O God, our help in ages past,
our hope for years to come,
our shelter from the stormy blast,
and our eternal home.

Beneath the shadow of thy throne
thy saints have dwelt secure;
sufficient is thine arm alone,
and our defence is sure.

Before the hills in order stood,
or earth received her frame,
from everlasting thou art God,
to endless years the same.

A thousand ages in thy sight
are like an evening gone,
short as the watch that ends the night
before the rising sun.

Time, like an ever rolling stream,
bears all its sons away;
they fly forgotten, as a dream
dies at the opening day.

O God, our help in ages past,
our hope for years to come,
be thou our guard while troubles last,
and our eternal home.

Words: Isaac Watts (1674–1748) (Psalm 90)

Tune: St Anne, William Croft (1678–1727)

❖

On 1 January 1901 there was a service in St Paul's Cathedral to celebrate the start of the 20th century. Ninety-nine years later, on 2 January 2000, the Cathedral was again full of people celebrating the start of the 21st century. The 20th century, it seems, lasted for only 99 years. It was short-changed, deprived of a year. And to a certain extent, so was the last millennium, which seems to have lasted only 999 years.

No matter, I hear you say, we had a good year—in London we built a great big covered space in Greenwich, a sightseeing wheel and a bridge across the Thames. No matter indeed—no matter to us really that we got our measurements wrong, and that, to us, a thousand years in our sight are the same as 999. No matter, of course, then, to God, to whom, as the hymn puts it, 'a thousand ages in thy sight are like an evening gone'.

It doesn't matter to God *when* we celebrate the birth of Christ—*when* we reflect on the incarnation, the Word made flesh—what is important is that we do remember and celebrate it. Human beings have a great interest in celebrating anniversaries and in marking the passing of time: our lives are very time-ful, it might be said. We want to make every step we take, in that ever-rolling stream of life, matter. We want to make a difference—we want our achievements to be measured, just as we seek to measure time accurately and constantly.

But to our millennium-measuring, time-consumed culture, Psalm 90, of which Isaac Watts' words are a rewriting, has a very different message. This hymn has always been associated with William Croft's hymn tune St Anne, and here we have a 17th-century reworking of a hymn used in the second Jewish temple, half a millennium before the birth of Christ. And it speaks now, as it has done throughout all those years. The author of Psalm 90 (thought by some to have been Moses) and Isaac Watts after him want to say to us, 'Wait—hold it—God is eternal, God lasts, for ever.'

Whatever day of the week it is, whatever year it is, whatever millennium it is or whatever planet we are on, God is above all, in all, throughout all. And the honest fact in the face of this is that we are frail and short-lived. Very short-lived. Short-lived, that is, on this timeful, fast-spinning, modern planet.

The hymn speaks of God as our 'eternal home', but also of *our* God: God is *our* home, he always has been and always will be. Stormy blasts can last for a thousand years, and yet nothing changes. Watts subtitled his rendering of the psalm 'Man frail and God eternal', and he makes sure that the positive nature of God as 'our eternal home' is emphasized. The last line of the first verse brings us 'home' to that eternal promise, which we, in our immense frailty, very much need. The rhythm of the hymn, so perfectly set by Croft, is established immediately as steady and sure, steady and sure as God under whose shadow we walk our unsteady path through life.

The permanence of God is referred to in the third verse, and there is that image of the mountains and hills standing to attention, like troops on parade, in honour of, and in awesome response to, their creator. Indeed there is good reason for awe, as presented in a verse that is seldom if ever sung:

> *Thy word commands our flesh to dust,*
> *'Return, ye sons of men'*
> *All nations rose from earth at first,*
> *And turn to earth again.*

Psalm 90 found its way into the burial service in the 1662 Prayer Book and, in an age that was readier to reflect on mortality than ours is today, these words took deep root in the spirituality of the English-speaking world. The hymn was originally written by Watts in 1714, just before the death of Queen Anne, at a time when there was some question as to who would succeed her. The hymn is often sung on Armistice Day, as well as at funerals. We can here see humanity as part of that ever-rolling stream which, although it bears our loved ones away, bears them to their, and our, eternal home, in timeless peace with God, *our* God.

Again, a lesser-known verse emphasizes this point:

The busy tribes of flesh and blood,
With all their lives and cares,
Are carry'd downward by thy flood,
And lost in following years.

This is not a bleak way of saying, 'The dead are swept away, forgotten', but a reminder that all are swept up in the love of God, in all times and places. The ever-rolling stream is seen not as unstable, but as bearing us back to where we started, with God as our home. And we reach that home at the end of Watts' setting, with a new and fuller understanding of the one upon whom we can rely in this transient, dangerous and weak world, in which we are so vulnerable. Thus, at the end of the psalm, we come to rest at 'home':

Be thou our guard while troubles last,
And our eternal home.

Our frailty in the face of God can be a frightening prospect, or it can be a comforting prospect—frightening, if we fear oblivion and being forgotten, and count our immortality as consisting in the remembrances of those who travel the road behind us; or comforting if we envisage a cosy eternity with God, freed from time and space.

But for most of us, there is a blend of the two. The life we have is held dear by us, and by those whom we love and who love us. We do fear the future, at least a little, and we value the past and try to learn from it; and we do count our years, centuries and millennia. These, on one level, may not matter to God, because he is timeless and a thousand ages are like an evening gone to him, but they do matter to us, and therefore they matter to God.

In those timeless words of Psalm 90, we hear not only of God who transcends all time and space, but of God who shelters us—our help in ages past and our hope for years to come—that is, *our* God, who cares. Thus, what matters to us matters to God. Our attempts to live, to love and to grow are of incalculable value to God, even if we cannot adequately do the sums by which we measure our lives. Our lives, however small, or however short, are of infinite value to *our eternal* God.

O God, helper of all your people, support and encourage us in this life, that at our lives' end, we may be borne away in the eternal tide of your love to dwell with you in glory, for ever and ever, Amen.

BETHLEHEM,
OF NOBLEST CITIES

✛

Bethlehem, of noblest cities
None can once with thee compare;
Thou alone the Lord from heaven
Didst for us incarnate bear.

Fairer than the sun at morning
Was the star that told his birth;
To the lands their God announcing,
Seen in fleshly form on earth.

By its lambent beauty guided
See the eastern kings appear;
See them bend, their gifts to offer,
Gifts of incense, gold and myrrh.

Solemn things of mystic meaning:
Incense doth the God disclose,
Gold a royal child proclaimeth,
Myrrh a future tomb foreshows.

Holy Jesu, in thy brightness
To the Gentile world displayed,
With the Father and the Spirit
Endless praise to thee be paid. Amen.

WORDS: LATIN, AURELIUS CLEMENS PRUDENTIUS (348–C.410) TRANS. EDWARD CASWALL (1814–78)

TUNE: STUTTGART, CHRISTIAN FRIEDRICH WITT (C.1660–1716), *HARMONIA SACRA*, 1715

❖

Epiphany, 6 January, is also known as 'Twelfth Night', and is thought of by many as the last day of Christmas. In 'The Twelve Days of Christmas', it is the final day on which 'my true love' gives to me no less than 78 presents, among them five gold rings, a dozen lords, and another partridge to go with the eleven that I already have.

In many parts of the world, 6 January is celebrated as Christmas Day. As Western Christians pack up their Christmas trees and decorations, the Greek Orthodox world and Catholic Spain are giving presents and celebrating with the wise men, or magi. Epiphany is Christmas Day for them, although in Spain there is also a tendency to celebrate Christmas on 25 December as well, which means that Spanish children get two sets of presents! But what better time to exchange presents than on the day when the magi brought Jesus their famous gifts? For the gifts they brought emphasize Jesus' immense significance for the world.

There is gold to remind us that this baby, born in a humble stable, is the Prince of Peace and King of Kings. As another carol puts it:

Born a king on Bethlehem plain
Gold I bring, to crown him again—
King for ever, ceasing never,
Over us all to reign.

Gold is for kingship, proclaiming the royal child. There are prophetic echoes of this in Psalm 72:10–11, 15: 'May the kings of Tarshish and of the isles render him tribute, may the kings of Sheba and Seba bring gifts. May all kings fall down before him, all nations give him service… Long may he live! May gold of Sheba be given to him.'

In this text lies the origin of the mistaken idea that the wise men, or magi, were kings of some sort, but St Matthew's unique account of their visit does not support this. The popular 'We three Kings of Orient are', while it helps to explain the significance of the gifts, is not biblically accurate on this point. A sixth-century tradition gives the 'kings' the names of Caspar, Balthasar and Melchior. Origen (c.185–c.254) first suggested that there were three gift-bearers, largely because three gifts are mentioned and it was assumed from an early date that they brought one each!

Frankincense, modern equivalents of which are often used in worship today, reminds us of the astonishing fact that in Jesus, God became a human being. Resonances of Isaiah 60:6 are to be found here: 'All those from Sheba shall come. They shall bring gold and frankincense, and shall proclaim the praise of the Lord.'

Kingship is suggested here too, but with incense there is a more specific reference to worship. In the temple, prayer and incense were closely linked: 'Let my prayer be counted as incense before you, and the lifting up of my hands as an evening sacrifice' (Psalm 141:2). Incense indicates access to the presence of God, and emphasizes not only Jesus' worthiness to be praised but also his becoming a living human presence among us. Thus frankincense is for worship and incarnation:

> *Frankincense to offer have I;*
> *Incense owns a deity nigh;*
> *Prayer and praising, all are raising,*
> *Worship him, God most high.*

The third gift, myrrh, finds its significance at Calvary. After the crucifixion, Nicodemus and Joseph of Arimathea prepared Jesus' body for burial, using myrrh as an embalming fluid (John 19:38–39). Thus the shadow of the cross falls over the crib. We see the power of God revealed in symbols of weakness, in a borrowed manger and on a wooden cross. Here we see power handed over; power utterly controlled by love.

> *Myrrh is mine: its bitter perfume*
> *Breathes a life of gathering gloom;*
> *Sorrowing, sighing, bleeding, dying,*
> *Sealed in the stone-cold tomb.*

This idea that myrrh foreshows the future tomb is a popular and helpful one, but we should also remember that myrrh also denotes joy. Thus in Proverbs 7:16–18 we find: 'I have decked my couch with coverings, coloured spreads of Egyptian linen; I have perfumed my bed with myrrh, aloes, and cinnamon. Come, let us take our fill of love until morning; let us delight ourselves with love.'

Myrrh is symbolic of love (a similar idea can be found in Song of Songs 5:5), and so we might want to say that the third gift is about adoration as well as death. Christ's death on the cross is for love of the

Church, his bride, and thus love and death come together in the gift of myrrh.

'Bethlehem of noblest cities' is one of the oldest hymns in the book. It was originally written by (Marcus) Prudentius who, although Spanish, wrote in Latin. A lawyer until the age of 57, he retired and began to write poetry and hymns. Two of his collections, the *Cathermerinon* and the *Peristephenon*, have had most influence, and some of these early hymns are still in use today, among them 'Of the Father's heart begotten'. 'Bethlehem of noblest cities', which is sometimes known as 'Earth has many a noble city', was translated from the Latin *O sola magnarum urbium* by the Reverend Edward Caswall and first published in a hymn collection, *Lyra Catholica*, in 1849. Caswall was curate of Stratford Castle, near Salisbury, but on becoming a Roman Catholic in 1847 moved to Edgbaston in Birmingham, where he wrote 'See amid the winter's snow' and translated many hymns, among them 'Glory be to Jesus' and 'Hark a herald voice is calling'.

The German composer of the tune, Christian Witt, was organist at Gotha from 1686, and became court musician (*Kapellmeister*) in 1713. The collection from which STUTTGART is taken, *Psalmodia Sacra*, dates from 1715.

'Bethlehem of noblest cities' is an ancient Epiphany hymn, and makes reference not only to the significance of the gifts brought to Jesus but also to the importance of the city of Bethlehem. The town of Jesus' birth, the city of David has had a high-profile history, and still does today amid the sad circumstances of modern-day Palestine. Rachel, the wife of Jacob, is buried there (Genesis 48:7), and the story of Ruth is set in and around Bethlehem. Jesse, King David's father, was from Bethlehem and St Matthew makes use of this connection in his genealogy before describing the visit of the magi (Matthew 1:1–17). Matthew also quotes the prophecy of Micah, which locates Bethlehem as the birthplace of the Messiah: 'But you, O Bethlehem of Ephrathah, who are one of the little clans of Judah, from you shall come forth for me one who is to rule in Israel, whose origin is from of old, from ancient days' (Micah 5:2; Matthew 2:6).

In the hymn, Prudentius praises Bethlehem not only as the birthplace of our Lord but also because it had already been marked out as an important place. Jesus is descended from David, through the family of Joseph, and so the scene is set when Joseph has to return to Bethlehem for the census called by the emperor Augustus (Luke

2:1–5). While St Matthew places Jesus very much in a line of descent from great Jewish leaders, he also describes the visit of the magi, who were foreign Gentiles. Thus, at the very beginning of the story, St Matthew emphasizes that Jesus is not just the Messiah for the Jews, but the Saviour of the whole world.

O God who guided the magi by the light of a star, that they might bring gifts to the humble throne of your Son, guide us by your brightness, that through the ministry of your people, the lambent beauty of your love may be displayed to the whole world, to whom you sent the same, Jesus Christ our Lord, Amen.

ON JORDAN'S BANK

✛

On Jordan's bank the Baptist's cry
Announces that the Lord is nigh;
Come then and hearken, for he brings
Glad tidings from the King of kings.

Then cleansed be every Christian breast,
And furnished for so great a guest!
Yea, let us each our hearts prepare
For Christ to come and enter there.

For thou art our salvation, Lord,
Our refuge and our great reward;
Without thy grace our souls must fade,
And wither like a flower decayed.

Stretch forth thine hand to heal our sore,
And make us rise, to fall no more;
Once more upon thy people shine,
And fill the world with love divine.

All praise, eternal Son, to thee
Whose advent sets thy people free,
Whom, with the Father, we adore,
And Spirit blest, for evermore.

WORDS: CHARLES COFFIN (1676–1749), TRANS. JOHN CHANDLER (1808–76)

MUSIC: WINCHESTER NEW, ADAPTED FROM A CHORALE IN *MUSICALISCHES HAND-BUCH*, HAMBURG 1690

This hymn naturally reminds us of John the Baptist, although it is not really about him. We know very little about John, although he knew himself to be the forerunner of the Messiah and spoke in those terms. He witnessed to Jesus as the one whose shoes he was not worthy to untie, and he died for it. He is the only prophet of whom we have a record of martyrdom. St Stephen is usually honoured as the first martyr, but John was killed for his faith in Christ too. That John died before Jesus does not make his death any the less significant, and emphasizes his role as the messenger who clears a path before Jesus. It is in that role that we see John in this hymn.

He is there at the beginning of the hymn (the first verse is about him and his call in the wilderness to repent and be baptized, Mark 1:4–8), but just as St Mark uses him to start the Gospel, soon moving on to the greater figure of Jesus, so too does Charles Coffin in his 17th-century Latin hymn. John diminishes almost as soon as he appears, so that the imminent arrival of Jesus can be emphasized. The hymn is often sung during Advent, not only because it mentions Advent but because it expresses a mixture of penitence and hope that is so characteristic of that season. But the hymn is equally appropriate as we celebrate John's baptism of Christ at the river Jordan.

In the hymn we hear the good news of the coming of the Messiah, tinged with fear, but there is also the great hope and expectation which is so often expressed in terms of waiting before a feast. The Christian heart is 'furnished', like a banqueting house, ready to welcome Christ, who is sometimes (but not in this hymn) characterized as the Bridegroom. Whether he is or not, he is here seen as the healer, the saviour, even the one to nourish our souls with living water, without whom we would wither like a dead plant. The imagery is creative in that we often think of the Christ of Advent and Epiphany as being 'light', reminding us that all life needs light. Plants need light to grow and thrive, but they also need water, as we do.

Baptism, of course, of which John is a famous advocate, is conducted in and with water, and water is the substance of both plant and human life. We are about 75 per cent made of water; without it we could not exist, and while we can go for days without food, we cannot go for very long without water. In the hymn, we are reminded that just as water is the key to human and plant life, in the spiritual realm the waters of baptism signify the grace of God watering and nourishing our souls. We also use water to wash, as well as to drink, and it is no coincidence that the waters of baptism washing over us symbolize the washing away of sin.

To some extent we must give John the Baptist credit for a practice that Jesus instructed his disciples to adopt. John's baptisms have caused all kinds of controversy over the years. For not only is John overmodest about his baptism, suggesting that it is not good enough for Jesus himself when they meet, we also have no record of Jesus baptizing anyone. Baptism is regarded as a sacrament, not because Jesus did it but because he endorsed it by accepting John's baptism, and by instructing the apostles to go out and make disciples and baptize them in the name of the Father, the Son and the Holy Spirit (Matthew 28:19).

But when Jesus is baptized, he does not repent of his sins in the way John invited people to do, for he had no sin. Any repentance implied is on our behalf, and so there is here a premonition of Christ's death on the cross. Baptism is all about new life, and by it we first die to our old self. Thus, in baptism, we are baptized into our own death, and into the death of Christ which itself saves us from the death that would otherwise come to us at the end of our lives.

But while the Christian Church has adopted and adapted John's manner of baptism, it is important that Jesus affirms John's ministry. In being baptized himself, Jesus is placing himself very firmly in the prophetic tradition of which John is the captain—the one at the head of the line. Thus there is a continuity, an unbroken succession from Abraham to Jesus.

But also, with the arrival of Jesus, that prophetic tradition must decrease, and Christ must increase. In a similar way, in the hymn, John's presence fades as we progress through the verses. John has that rare gift of knowing when and how to let go. He has done his work, fulfilled the promise, and knows when to hang up his sandals at the end of the day. John has the gift of knowing his own identity, his role and his purpose. He lays down the reins, and none other than the Son of God picks them up. If he is not to smudge the good work he has done, he must recede, with dignity, honour and the blessing of later history.

John never competed with Jesus, never challenged his authority, but rightly and properly verified it (Luke 7:18–23). In this much he is a model to us all when it comes to standing in a tradition. For all traditions involve succession and handing on, from one generation to another. In that handing on lies a core of truth, enshrined in continuity.

We find a metaphor for this in the tune that is invariably used for this hymn. WINCHESTER NEW is an old German tune, in use in Hamburg in 1690, and it was introduced into England by John Wesley (1703–91) in his *Foundery Tune Book* of 1742. This book was partly the product of extensive research into the German hymn tradition, which led to many translations of German texts and the purloining of tunes such as this. Here is tradition handing on substance of value 'down the line', as it were, with the tune FRANKFURT giving up its name to become WINCHESTER NEW. The Reverend John Chandler translated John Coffin's words, and other editors of hymn books have tweaked them in places, but the words basically survive. The music survives too—the 'swift German tune', as Wesley called it, still bears words expressing the hope and truth of the second coming. As John the Baptist ministers, witnesses to and hands on truth, so too do many of our hymn writers and musicians.

Of John the Baptist himself we can say that he had a unique and special calling, combined with the gift of self-awareness. He was the captain of prophets, the last in a great line, pointing to Jesus and bringing forward a great tradition of truth that culminates in Jesus. This gives him an odd position perhaps, summed up best by Jesus himself: 'No one has arisen greater than John the Baptist; yet the least in the kingdom of heaven is greater than he' (Matthew 11:11).

Almighty God, whose servant and prophet John the Baptist was a witness to the truth as the forerunner of the salvation wrought in your Son: lead us to bear witness to the same Jesus Christ, who is the eternal light and truth, and lives and reigns with you and the Holy Spirit, now and for ever, Amen.

SONGS OF THANKFULNESS AND PRAISE

✣

Songs of thankfulness and praise,
Jesu, Lord, to thee we raise,
Manifested by the star
To the sages from afar;
Branch of royal David's stem
In thy birth at Bethlehem;
Anthems be to thee addrest,
God in Man made manifest.

Manifest at Jordan's stream,
Prophet, Priest, and King supreme;
And at Cana wedding-guest
In thy Godhead manifest;
Manifest in power divine,
Changing water into wine;
Anthems be to thee addrest,
God in Man made manifest.

Manifest in making whole
Palsied limbs and fainting soul;
Manifest in valiant fight,
Quelling all the devil's might;
Manifest in gracious will,
Ever bringing good from ill;
Anthems be to thee addrest,
God in Man made manifest.

Sun and moon shall darkened be,
Stars shall fall, the heavens shall flee;
Christ will then like lightning shine,
All will see his glorious sign;
All will then the trumpet hear,
All will see the judge appear;
Thou by all wilt be confest,
God in Man made manifest.

Grant us grace to see thee, Lord,
Mirrored in thy holy word;
May we imitate thee now,
And be pure, as pure art thou;
That we like to thee may be
At thy great Epiphany,
And may praise thee, ever blest,
God in Man made manifest.

Words: Christopher Wordsworth (1807–85)

Tune: St Edmund, Charles Steggall (1826–1905)

✣

Bishop Christopher Wordsworth was the nephew of the great English poet William Wordsworth (1770–1850). In this hymn he sought to explain the meaning of the Epiphany, telling the story of the season. Epiphany is not just 6 January, for it is a season of the Church's year, and it involves far more than the revealing of Christ to the magi at Bethlehem.

The word 'Epiphany' comes from the Greek *epiphaneia*, which means 'manifestation'. Wordsworth wants us to remember this, which is why he uses the same last line in every verse: 'God in Man made manifest'. In this single word and phrase we have the core of Epiphany, which is all about the manifestation of God, the appearing in real form of the human Christ. In the earliest Eastern Church calendars, Epiphany was associated more with the feast of the Baptism of Christ than with the Nativity, and it is in Jesus' baptism by John that he is first associated with the Holy Spirit of God, as the dove descends when he emerges from the water (Mark 1:10; Luke 3:22; John 1:32). By the third century, the story of the magi had been incorporated into celebrations of Epiphany, and it soon became the third principal feast-day of the Church, after Easter and Pentecost. The feast of the Nativity (Christmas) was considered to be far less significant in those days. The feast of Epiphany was adopted by the Western Church in the fourth century, but lost the emphasis on baptism. Mention of the first miracle at Cana also began to creep in. Nowadays a wider perspective is being regained, not least thanks to the efforts in past centuries of church leaders like Wordsworth. Thus, today, we have in many churches an Epiphany season during which we focus on the journey of the magi, the baptism by John *and* the wedding at Cana.

These three events are covered by Wordsworth in the first half of his hymn. In the first verse we see the star of Bethlehem (Matthew 2:2), which associates Christ with King David, revealing him to be the Messiah (Isaiah 11:1–10). In the second verse, Wordsworth moves us to the River Jordan, and thence to the wedding at Cana (John 2:1–11). At Cana, Jesus performs his first recorded miracle, manifesting himself in a new ministry, even though at the time he tells his mother Mary that his 'hour has not yet come' (John 2:4). The story is all about change, and it indicates that there is to be change in the world, for this Jesus, the Son of God, is going to change ordinary people into the best vintage in the kingdom of heaven. The symbolism of wine and blood, pointing to the cross and the eucharistic offering of himself, is also present.

The third verse takes us to Jesus' ministry of healing, which itself is a fulfilling of prophecy: 'The Spirit of the Lord is upon me, because he has anointed me to bring good news to the poor. He has sent me to proclaim release to the captives and recovery of sight to the blind, to let the oppressed go free, to proclaim the year of the Lord's favour' (Luke 4:18–19; Isaiah 61:1–2). The manifestation of God among us is also in compassionate ministry, which not only shows God's love for those who are healed, but indicates his power and authority and freedom to act where humanity fails. Wordsworth then mentions the temptations, the 'valiant fight' against the devil that takes place in the wilderness immediately after Jesus' baptism (Mark 1:12–13; Matthew 4:1–11). God is also made manifest in Jesus' ability to turn bad situations to good, such as in the raising of Lazarus (John 11) or almost any other miracle that we can think of.

The fourth verse, which is sometimes omitted, speaks of the

apocalyptic future when Christ shall return. All the events so far mentioned are the beginnings of an earthly ministry, and yet the story does not end with birth, death or even resurrection. The return of Christ in glory is not something we confine to Advent, nor even to Epiphany, but it is a key part of God's plan for the world. The fact that we have seen many events in history that were once supposed to be the beginnings of the end does not mean that such an end time, when Christ returns, is a fantasy: 'When you hear of wars and insurrections, do not be terrified; for these things must take place first, but the end will not follow immediately' (Luke 21:9). The Gospel writers describe a time when 'the heavens shall flee' (Luke 21:5–36) and the book of Revelation is full of such prophecies. Wordsworth was probably thinking of the words 'The fourth angel blew his trumpet, and a third of the sun was struck, and a third of the moon, and a third of the stars, so that a third of their light was darkened; a third of the day was kept from shining, and likewise the night' (Revelation 8:12). Such events are to be the final 'God in Son of Man made manifest'.

The last verse is less of a narrative, more of a prayer, offered in response to the awesome events which are associated with the appearing of Christ on earth first, and second time around.

Wordsworth was a theologian and a teacher, having been headmaster of Harrow School, Vicar of Stanford-in-the-Vale, Berkshire, Archdeacon of Westminster and finally Bishop of Lincoln from 1868. He was a scholar of Greek and Latin literature, and as well as writing a collection of hymns entitled *The Holy Year; or Hymns for Sundays and Holydays throughout the Year, And for other Occasions*, in 1863, he published the *Memoirs of William Wordsworth* in 1851.

Charles Steggall, who wrote the tune St Edmund, was a near contemporary of Wordsworth. He was a student, then professor, at the Royal Academy of Music in London, and was organist at Lincoln's Inn from 1864 to 1905. (Lincoln's Inn is one of the Inns of Court, home to barristers in the City of London.) Steggall spent all his life in London, and edited *Church Psalmody* (1849) and *Hymns for the Church of England* (1865).

Both writer and composer, therefore, were teachers at the top of their professions. The hymn 'Songs of thankfulness and joy' is clearly a teaching hymn, and speaking of his hymns, Wordsworth said, 'It is the first duty of a hymn to teach sound doctrine and thence to save souls', and in this hymn we can see him doing just that. In this day and age, when teaching the meaning and significance of the Christian faith seems to be more necessary than ever, we can do far worse than turn to some of these older hymns to learn from teachers of the past. For all their teaching points us both backwards and forwards to Jesus, our great teacher and Lord.

O Christ our teacher, who was made manifest to your people on earth, inspire us with the vision of your light and the sound of your clarion call, so that on that day when the sun shall be darkened and you return in glory, we may be made ready and whole to meet you, and to sing with the angels songs of thankfulness and praise, Amen.

O CHRIST THE SAME

✧

O Christ the same through all our story's pages,
Our loves and hopes, our failures and our fears;
Eternal Lord, the King of all the ages,
Unchanging still, amid the passing years:
O living Word, the source of all creation,
Who spread the skies, and set the stars ablaze,
O Christ the same, who wrought man's whole salvation,
We bring our thanks for all our yesterdays.

O Christ the same, the friend of sinners, sharing
Our inmost thoughts, the secrets none can hide,
Still as of old upon your body bearing
The marks of love, in triumph glorified:
O Son of Man, who stooped for us from heaven,
O Prince of life, in all your saving power,
O Christ the same, to whom our hearts are given,
We bring our thanks for this the present hour.

O Christ the same, secure within whose keeping
Our lives and loves, our days and years remain,
Our work and rest, our waking and our sleeping,
Our calm and storm, our pleasure and our pain:

O Lord of love, for all our joys and sorrows,
For all our hopes, when earth shall fade and flee,
O Christ the same, for all our brief tomorrows,
We bring our thanks for all that is to be.

WORDS: TIMOTHY DUDLEY-SMITH (B. 1926)

TUNE: LONDONDERRY, 'AIR FROM COUNTY DERRY' IN THE PETRIE *COLLECTION OF IRISH MELODY*

❖

'Danny Boy' is one of the best-loved and most well-known of Irish folk songs, and the tune alone can bring a tear to even the most smiling of Irish, British or North American eyes. The words of 'Danny Boy', now famous, were at once only one among about a hundred different songs that were sung to the tune. Today there are at least three sets of hymn words that are used, so popular is the tune. Bishop Dudley-Smith has also written 'Lord of the Church', a hymn for Christian unity, which is lent an ecumenical poignancy by the use of the Irish tune. Another hymn, 'I cannot tell', by William Young Fullerton (1857–1932) which is about the Passion of Christ, is less successful because the tune, while beautiful, can lend a certain syrupiness to words that need a more frank statement of their message.

'Danny Boy' itself is a real tear-jerker:

Oh Danny boy, the pipes, the pipes are calling
From glen to glen, and down the mountain side.
The summer's gone, and all the flowers are dying
'Tis you, 'tis you must go and I must bide.

And then we realize that the song is about separation of lovers by death:

You'll come and find the place where I am lying
And kneel and say an 'Ave' there for me.
And I shall hear, tho' soft you tread above me
And all my dreams will warm and sweeter be.
If you'll not fail to tell me that you love me
I'll simply sleep in peace until you come to me.

These words were composed by an English lawyer, Frederic Edward Weatherly (1848–1929), who was also a radio entertainer. In 1910 he wrote these words and a tune, but the song never took off. In 1912 his sister-in-law in America sent him the LONDONDERRY AIR and he realized that it fitted his 'Danny Boy' lyrics, and so he published a new version in 1913.

The tune that Weatherly thereby made famous was perhaps composed by Rory Dall O'Cahan in the 1600s, and was first published in 1855, in *Ancient Music of Ireland* by George Petrie (1789–1866). The untitled melody was supplied by Miss Jane Ross of Limavady, County Londonderry, who claimed to have notated it from the playing of a piper. Thus it became known as the LONDONDERRY AIR, although to Irish nationalists it is known as the AIR FROM COUNTY DERRY, and it was under that title that the Australian-born composer Percy Grainger (1882–1961) orchestrated it. The hymn tune version of the melody is known as LONDONDERRY, a name which emphasizes the English legacy to the part of Ireland from which it takes its name.

The melody itself is so well-known that it hardly needs description, and it is no doubt for this reason that some hymn writers seek to set words to it. The metre is virtually unique, and the verses make up some of the longest in the repertoire, which means that an enthusiastic congregation must also be an energetic one with plenty of breath.

Timothy Dudley-Smith's words are a fine accompaniment for such a lyrical tune, and the slight hint of nostalgia that he conjures up in the first verse is emphasized by the tune. Yet this is not a hymn to wallow in, for as well as speaking of wide human experience, it has powerful words to say about Jesus. Christ is the same, unchanging, in spite of the 'chances and changes of this fleeting world': whatever happens to us, wherever our loves, hopes, failures, fears lead us, Christ goes with us. Each verse emphasizes and expresses gratitude for the passing of time. The past, the present and the future are all prayed for and offered back to God in a hymn of thanksgiving and hope, and the final line is a statement of hopeful faith, an exclamation of commitment to the future that says 'Yes' to Christ, whatever may befall. The reason is given in the preceding verses: we can say 'Yes' to the unknown future because we know one thing, which is that Christ the same will continue to inhabit our lives and hopes, and that our remaining years will be spent under the banner of love that is Christ crucified and glorified for us.

The hymn was sung at the Service of Thanksgiving for the Golden

Jubilee of the Queen in St Paul's Cathedral on 4 June 2002. It is a good one for any event that marks change, whether that be a New Year service or a leaving service at a school or church, and it can also be sung very effectively at weddings. Congregations who do not know many hymns often know 'Danny Boy' better than they think they do, and the words are eminently suited to a wedding. Weddings mark change, just as Jesus' first miracle at the wedding at Cana (John 2:1–11) is all about change, and so it is good to be reminded of the past, and to give thanks for the joy and beauty of the 'present hour', the wedding service itself. Most importantly of all, it is a delight for the couple, with their families and friends, to be able to offer thanks in advance for all that is yet to be. The real poignancy of this hymn at weddings is realized when we remember that its basic message is that Christ doesn't change, even when everyone and everything else does change—he is the solid, unchanging friend who is the same through thick and thin, for better for worse, in sickness and in health. That said, this hymn should not be reserved exclusively for bride and groom, or even just for turning points in our lives or Golden Jubilees, for it reminds us of the continuing flux of our lives, of our smallness in time and space, and of the continual debt of gratitude that we owe to our God who created us, redeemed us in Christ and continues to sustain us in all events.

O unchanging God, we bring you our thanks for your sustaining and unchanging love that you show us each and every day. Inhabit our thoughts, our prayers and our hopes, dispel the fears and worries of our hearts and soothe the sorrows of our souls. This we ask for the sake of your Son our Lord Jesus Christ, the same yesterday and today, Amen.

HAIL TO THE LORD WHO COMES

✣

Hail to the Lord who comes,
Comes to his temple gate!
Not with his angel host,
Not in his kingly state;
No shouts proclaim him nigh,
No crowds his coming wait;

But borne upon the throne
Of Mary's gentle breast,
Watched by her duteous love,
In her fond arms at rest;
Thus to his Father's house
He comes, the heavenly guest.

There Joseph at her side
In reverent wonder stands;
And, filled with holy joy,
Old Simeon in his hands
Takes up the promised Child,
The glory of all lands.

Hail to the great First-born
Whose ransom-price they pay!
The Son before all worlds,

The Child of man today,
That he might ransom us
Who still in bondage lay.

O Light of all the earth,
Thy children wait for thee!
Come to thy temples here,
That we, from sin set free,
Before thy Father's face
May all presented be!

WORDS: JOHN ELLERTON (1826–93)

TUNE: OLD 120TH, 'WHOLE BOOK OF PSALMES'. MELODY BY THOMAS ESTE (1592),

HARMONY BY THOMAS RAVENSCROFT (C.1590–C.1623)

❖

2 February, the feast of Candlemas or 'The Presentation of Christ in the Temple', has often been forgotten or ignored, yet it provides a wonderful opportunity to celebrate the holy family's encounter with Simeon and Anna (Luke 2:22–38). John Ellerton's hymn, which was written especially for this time of the year, is a meditation on that most touchingly human of events.

Ellerton wrote it in 1880, by which time he was Rector of Barnes in West London, and already had quite a name as a hymn writer. It was perhaps his reputation that he had in mind when he wrote in a letter to Godfrey Thring, the editor of *The Church of England Hymn Book*, that 'you were quite right to abuse my Purification Hymn. I know it is very bad.'

Whether it is bad or not remains to be seen, but it does help us to reflect on its subject. Jesus is brought by Mary and Joseph to the temple, fulfilling the Jewish law that after a forty-day period, both mother and child should be presented in the temple. The event is rich in meaning, for when Jesus is brought, Simeon and Anna both recognize Jesus for the saviour that he is. It is almost as if they have always been there, waiting, like the whole world, for the coming of the Messiah. That this is a 'presentation' also reminds us that by incarnation, at Christmas, God presents us with the ultimate of presents, the gift of his saviour who will be 'the light of all the earth'. We are also reminded that if even Christ is presented to God, then we can and must present ourselves, our souls and bodies, to be a 'reasonable, holy and living sacrifice', as a prayer used after the eucharist puts it. Even at only forty days old, Christ's offering of himself has begun. By that offering, we also:

> *...from sin set free,*
> *Before thy Father's face*
> *May all presented be!*

Christ's presentation in the temple was done according to the Law of Moses. When the Israelites were allowed to leave Egypt after the final plague, in which the angel of death struck down the firstborn of the Egyptians, the Law decreed that in memory of their deliverance every Jew was to present, or consecrate, their firstborn male to the Lord. The child was offered in sacrifice, but then a pigeon would be offered as a substitute. This was known as 'redemption', a word which, for the Christian, has overtones of the redeeming work of Christ. Jesus' presentation in the temple is a symbolic precursor of what he is destined to do many years later. A pigeon takes his place, but later he will take our place.

The feast of Candlemas is all about meeting. Mary and Joseph introduce Jesus to the world: 'Here he is,' they say. There is always something very exciting about meeting a newborn baby, and in this story and hymn we are reliving the first time that Jesus met anyone in public. Jesus meets his people for the first time, and the first people whom he is recorded as meeting recognize who and what he is. It is a quietly promising start.

The idea of meeting has overtones for us today, for one day we hope and expect to meet Christ too. As St John puts it, 'we will see him as he is' (1 John 3:2). This puts us in mind of heaven, so as we commemorate the beginning of Christ's life we contemplate the end of our own lives, when we shall not only meet him in the flesh but be united with all the saints in light.

The most important theme of Candlemas, from which it takes its name, is that of light. In Advent we waited for Christ's light to come. At Christmas we celebrated the incarnation and arrival of Christ's light, and now, after Christmas, before we move towards Lent, we remember and celebrate Christ's light ever with us, for as Ellerton puts it, Jesus is 'Light of all the earth' and, quoting Simeon's *Nunc Dimittis* almost verbatim, 'the glory of all lands'.

The revelation of the child Jesus in the temple calls for rejoicing, but the prophetic words of Simeon, who speaks of the falling and rising of many and the sword that will pierce Mary's heart (Luke 2:34–35), point us to suffering and death. This season follows the Christmas and Epiphany periods and, with Lent close at hand, it is pivotal in the Christian year. It is as if we say, 'One last look back to Christmas, and now, turn towards the cross!'

John Ellerton's not-so-bad words have been set in many hymn books to the old tune used for Psalm 120, found in the *Whole Book of Psalmes* by Thomas Este, published in 1592. The tune was later harmonized by Thomas Ravenscroft for inclusion in his wonderfully titled *The Whole Booke of Psalmes: With the Hymnes Evangelical and Songs Spirituall. Composed into 4 Parts by Sundry Authors, to Such Severall Tunes, as Have Beene, and Are Usually Sung in England, Scotland, Wales, Germany, Italy, France and the Nether-lands*, published in London in 1621. Ravenscroft is not very famous today, but he holds the rare distinction of being the original composer of the round 'Three blind mice'. He began his career as a chorister of St Paul's Cathedral around 1600, which meant that he probably also spent time singing in Covent Garden and drinking copious amounts of ale (how things have changed!). When his voice broke, he taught at Christ's Hospital, a school which began life in the City of London but which subsequently moved to Sussex, where it thrives still. Ravenscroft published three books of rounds and 'catches', and one of his books, entitled *Melismata*, includes a song that some have identified as being the tune on which the British National Anthem is based. Such simplicity survives, and the OLD 120TH owes its survival to a straightforward tune, which hardly ever moves more than one step at a time, and which Ravenscroft harmonized simply and effectively. It is a shame that it has been allied almost exclusively to Ellerton's seasonally specific words, which means that this delightful tune is not sung as often as it might be.

Ellerton's text dwells on the theme of light and on the joy of those who were present as Christ was brought to the temple. He begins by stating his theme in two lines that carry us from Advent to Candlemas. The coming of the Lord is the great expectation of Advent, but here Ellerton reminds us of a different coming. He uses negatives to keep us in suspense, and yet also to remind us of other 'comings' that are to follow this presentation of Christ. The presentation is not kingly, nor noisy, nor triumphant, nor even very public. Instead it is intimate, with only a few onlookers, and Christ's throne, as Ellerton vividly paints it, is the mother's breast, the place of nourishment and security where Mary both presents and protects him. The young Christ, the baby Saviour, is portrayed as the centre of attention, not in a public speech, trial or execution but in a little family gathering with proud parents and friendly strangers. In the hymn, Simeon is mentioned, almost as we might include a modern-day godparent in the wider family of a child.

We too are welcomed into this family gathering as we welcome Christ. Christ's quiet presentation to the world at Candlemas reminds us that as he is presented to God, he is also presented by God, and it is the duty and service of the world to welcome him and to present ourselves in return.

O Christ our King and saviour, who was humbly presented in your Father's house to a waiting world, keep alive in us a welcoming heart and a burning love, so that we may live in the light of the glory of your redeeming power, revealed to all the nations in your birth, presentation, and resurrection, Amen.

O GOD OF BETHEL

✛

O God of Bethel, by whose hand
Thy people still are fed,
Who through this weary pilgrimage
Hast all our fathers led:

Our vows, our prayers, we now present
Before thy throne of grace;
God of our fathers, be the God
Of their succeeding race.

Through each perplexing path of life
Our wandering footsteps guide;
Give us each day our daily bread,
And raiment fit provide.

O spread thy covering wings around,
Till all our wanderings cease,
And at our Father's loved abode
Our souls arrive in peace.

WORDS: PHILIP DODDRIDGE (1702–51)

TUNE: MARTYRDOM, HUGH WILSON (1766–1824), ADAPTED BY R.A. SMITH (1780–1829)

BURFORD, CHETHAM'S PSALMODY 1718

STRACATHRO, C. HUTCHESON (1792–1860)

SALZBURG (HAYDN), MICHAEL HAYDN (1737–1806)

✛

The story of Jacob, on which this hymn is a reflection, takes up half of the book of Genesis—chapters 25 to 50. In my Bible that amounts to some thirty pages. Jacob's parents were Isaac and Rebekah, and Jacob was one of twins. He and his brother Esau fought even in the womb, and when they were born, Esau came out first with Jacob clutching his heel. Jacob's name means 'May he be at your heel'. From the beginning they were opposites: Esau was hairy and red while Jacob had smooth skin.

Esau became a hunter, Jacob a farmer; Isaac preferred Esau, while Rebekah, the mother, loved Jacob best (Genesis 25:28). Throughout his life Jacob is someone who cannot avoid favouritism and feud, and his first trick is to deceive his brother over a bowl of soup. Esau comes in from the fields hungry, and Jacob sees an opportunity to gain what is not rightfully his. But he does not steal Esau's birthright; he takes advantage of Esau's hunger. Jacob deceives him, but Esau is foolish to give away a double share of the inheritance and the rightful headship of the family, which was his birthright. It is unclear what circumstances put Esau in the position where his only source of food would be Jacob, and why he was too hungry to wait. Perhaps his impatience let him down.

Soon after, Jacob adds insult to injury by deceiving his father. Isaac calls Esau and sends him hunting, so that he can eat game and then give him his blessing. But Rebekah is more loyal to her second son than to her husband or elder son, and so she sets Jacob up to get a couple of goats, which she will prepare as game to fool Isaac. She has even worked out how to make Jacob feel and smell like Esau to his blind father. The plan works—just—Jacob lies about his identity and Isaac blesses Jacob, thus underlining the first trick that Jacob had played on Esau. On both occasions food plays a major part, and, as my grandfather used to say, 'there's no robbing bellies'. Like a meal eaten, the deed is done. Thus when Isaac realizes he has been deceived, he can do nothing. An oral blessing had legal validity, just like a verbal undertaking can have today.

Esau is furious and seeks to kill Jacob, but Rebekah advises him to flee, and persuades Isaac to send him away to stay with Uncle Laban, to find a wife, or two! (Genesis 27:43). On the way, Jacob stops at a place called Luz and sleeps, using a stone for a pillow. Like his future son, Joseph, Jacob is a dreamer, and envisions a ladder to heaven with angels ascending and descending. God speaks to him, promising him the very land on which he sleeps. Jacob renames the place Bethel, which means 'House of God', and marks the spot with his oiled pillow-stone (Genesis 28:18–22). In return for God's favour, Jacob invents the tithe, vowing to give ten per cent of everything to God.

The hymn 'O God of Bethel' relates directly to this incident, which happens quite early in Jacob's 147-year life. Philip Doddridge, who wrote the words, was more explicit in his allusion than the modern version we tend to use today. His first verse began:

> *O God of Jacob, by whose Hand*
> *Thine Israel still is fed...*

And the second was originally:

> *To thee our humble Vows we raise,*
> *To thee address our Prayer,*
> *And in thy kind and faithful Breast*
> *Deposit all our care.*

Jacob was no saint before his encounter with God at Bethel and, although touched by God, he continued to find himself at the centre of trouble. As a lovable reprobate, perhaps, Jacob gives us all hope, and it is that hope that Doddridge wants to convey. Just as God stuck with Jacob, even though he continued to make mistakes, God will stick with us and not let us down or abandon us, even if our own footsteps wander.

Doddridge's hymn does not have much of the element of discipline that Jacob was yet to experience. A deceiver himself, he is then deceived by his family for the rest of his life. His Uncle Laban cons him into working for seven years to get Rachel as his wife, but dresses Leah as Rachel, thus turning the tables on the trick that Jacob and Rebekah played on Isaac. Then Laban makes Jacob work for another seven years to get Rachel, whom he always wanted.

After many years, as God promised, and on God's instruction, Jacob takes his family back to Bethel and makes them reject their foreign idols, reminding them of how God has helped him in difficult times. God appears to him again, and tells him that he is to be known as Israel and no longer Jacob. (This is the second time this happens—the angel whom Jacob meets at the river Jabbok also gives him the new name.)

Jacob and his family do not stay at Bethel very long, though, moving on to Canaan, and it is from Canaan that we hear of the story of Joseph and his brothers.

Bethel by its very nature is the place, or house, of God, and it is where Jacob feels renewed and blessed. Thousands of years later, in our churches, we strive to maintain our 'houses of God'—our church buildings—as places of peace, rejuvenation and blessing. Sometimes, in busy cities or in rural areas, this can be very hard, for it can be difficult to get people to 'church-sit' for visitors. We are all too aware these days that the older traditions of leaving the church key under the mat, or even of leaving the church open all day, are not always practical or sensible. Even if we can open the doors of our church buildings to pilgrims and tourists, the main road outside can often hinder the sense of peace and quiet that we love to feel when in the presence of God.

It is, of course, the case that the 'church' is not a collection of buildings, but the collection of people—the body of Christ—who love God and meet together to worship. But we must not forget or lose sight of the proper sense of place that our church buildings, especially the older ones, can and do have. Architecture and history combine so that whether we are in St Paul's Cathedral or a Saxon village church in the north-east of England, we can be struck down by a sense of peace as we enter and remain within them in the presence of God. Quiet country churches and large cathedrals alike are Bethels—houses of God—and even if they were not put up to mark a particular site of revelation (as Jacob's oily stone was), in time they become the sites of particular revelation and spiritual encounter.

It is an interesting and nicely ironic fact that today the hymn 'O God of Bethel' has no single tune that claims to be 'the' tune. The words are in 'common metre' (the most usual poetic structure), which means that any number of tunes fit, and those that are often used are by no means identical in mood. Just as houses of God can be so different in size, style and shape, the way we sing this hymn can also be varied depending on the tune used. MARTYRDOM has a lilting beauty, rising and falling in curves that can remind us of cathedral arches. BURFORD, on the other hand, is in a different mood: it is in a minor key, and has a poignancy that emphasizes the plea for God's protection. STRACATHRO makes the hymn different again: very firmly in D major, it is bright and airy and clean, and conveys a sense of seeking God's protection as we journey on our good and happy way. SALZBURG (HAYDN) is by Michael Haydn, younger brother of Joseph Haydn (1732–1809), the famous Austrian composer. This tune is not to be confused with the tune SALZBURG which is often used for the Easter hymn 'At the Lamb's high feast we sing'. Haydn's SALZBURG is named after the Austrian town, and is perhaps the least fitting of the four tunes that the *New English Hymnal* and *Common Praise* offer us. It is quite a jolly tune, but doesn't seem to ring true with the idea of the 'weary pilgrimage' to which the words refer.

Whatever your preference, though, the variety of tunes reflects the variety of moods and intentions with which this hymn can be sung and, indeed, the variety of locations to which it might refer. As a congregation gathers in their own 'Bethel'—God's house in their community, be it large, small, old or new—they express the same sentiments that Jacob and countless others have felt over the ages, and they address them to the same God, the God of Abraham and Isaac, of Jacob, of Moses, the God and Father of our Lord Jesus Christ.

O God of our ancestors, hear us as we remember the incidents and events of our lives which have made us what we are. Help us to examine them in your presence with humility and courage, honesty and hope, so that all that we are may be turned by your Spirit to the good of all human kind. This we ask through Jesus Christ our Lord, Amen.

BE STILL, MY SOUL

✢

Be still, my soul: the Lord is on thy side.
Bear patiently the cross of grief or pain.
Leave to thy God to order and provide;
In every change, he faithful will remain.
Be still, my soul: thy best, thy heavenly friend
Through thorny ways leads to a joyful end.

Be still, my soul: thy God doth undertake
To guide the future, as he has the past.
Thy hope, thy confidence let nothing shake;
All now mysterious shall be bright at last.
Be still, my soul: the waves and winds shall know
His voice who ruled them while he dwelt below.

Be still, my soul: when dearest friends depart,
And all is darkened in the vale of tears,
Then shalt thou better know his love, his heart,
Who comes to soothe thy sorrow and thy fears.
Be still, my soul: thy Jesus can repay
From his own fullness all he takes away.

Be still, my soul: the hour is hastening on
When we shall be for ever with the Lord.
When disappointment, grief and fear are gone,
Sorrow forgot, love's purest joys restored.
Be still, my soul: when change and tears are past
All safe and blessèd we shall meet at last.

WORDS: KATHARINA A. VON SCHLEGEL (B. 1697), TRANS. JANE L. BORTHWICK (1813–97)

MUSIC: FINLANDIA, JEAN SIBELIUS (1865–1957)

·:·

The tune for this hymn has excellent credentials and is well-known worldwide as the main theme to Sibelius' tone poem of the same name. FINLANDIA was written in 1899, at a time when nationalism was gaining ground in Finland, which was then under Russian rule. Originally it was part of a six-movement work entitled 'Finland awakes', but when Sibelius was specifically asked for a 'nationalistic' overture, he separated the final movement and renamed it 'Finlandia'. The hymn tune is the central theme only, which means that a very large work has been distilled greatly for hymnodic purposes. This is not unlike what has happened to 'Land of hope and glory', a similar type of work with a similar function, which itself began life as the central theme of one of five symphonic marches. Now, even 'Land of hope and glory' is sometimes used as a tune for the hymn 'At the name of Jesus'.

For some people, the idea of a popular tune being used for a hymn is sacrilege. The 'Ode to Joy' from Beethoven's *Ninth Symphony*, the 'Trumpet Tune' by Jeremiah Clarke, 'Jupiter' from *The Planets* by Holst and other classical pieces have similarly been turned into hymn tunes, and often the words have been specially written to match the tune. In the popular music world, we sometimes encounter rewrites such as a setting of the *Gloria* to Mike Batt's *EastEnders* theme tune ('Glory be to God on high...'), and a hymn was even suggested for the theme tune to *Dallas*! On the other hand, as we have already seen, there are at least three successful hymn arrangements of the Irish tune 'Danny Boy' (LONDONDERRY).

There can be problems with these hymns, in that the original, popular or predominant use of a tune can heavily influence us when we sing different words. The associations we have for a tune may colour our thoughts or prayers in inappropriate ways. To use a theme tune from a television series can conjure up images associated with that series when we sing words to the tune, and this can hinder us in worship. Sometimes, of course, it works the other way around, and the use of a hymn in a film or television programme can change our associations and distract us!

While we need to be careful of this trend, it is not necessarily bad, nor is it a new phenomenon. Medieval and later composers such as Josquin Des Prés (c.1440–1521) and Guilaume Dufay (c.1400–74) were both writers of sacred masses and motets as well as secular songs, and sometimes the secular song would provide the melodic basis for the mass setting.

Ultimately, with any of these transferences of music from one realm to another, we must ask whether they work well, whether they are edifying, and most importantly whether they serve to glorify God and uplift our worship. Singing 'At the name of Jesus' to 'Land of hope and glory' may well conjure up all kinds of jingoistic images and may not be such a good idea, but this setting of 'Be still, my soul' to FINLANDIA is much more successful.

Unusually for a hymn of this kind, the words were written long before Sibelius was born. They were originally German (*Stille, meine Wille, dein Jesus hilft siegen*), and were written in 1752 by Katharina von Schlegel, who is thought to have been a nun in Cothen, the same city where J.S. Bach (1685–1750) had been *Kapellmeister*. It was not until 1855 that Jane Borthwick and her sister Sarah Findlater produced *Hymns from the Land of Luther*, in which her translation first appeared. While the hymn quite evidently takes its cue from 'Be still, and know that I am God' (Psalm 46:10), Jane Borthwick subtitled the hymn with Luke 21:19: 'By your endurance you will gain your souls.' This suggests that she felt it was a hymn extolling the virtue of patience in the face of pain or grief, yet also expressing the eternal hope that the faithful have in Christ.

The words themselves speak not only of hope and patience, but of God's steadfast love and of how we can rely on his power to bring us out of sorrow and fear. The same God who calms the storm is still in charge and will guide us tomorrow as yesterday, even if our worldly circumstances change. And even if we lose those whom we love, we will be reunited with them when we are 'for ever with the Lord'.

This hymn is said to have been the favourite of the Olympic runner Eric Liddell (1902–45). Immortalized in the film *Chariots of Fire*, (along with JERUSALEM), Liddell was an athlete who would not run on Sundays. After winning medals at the 1924 Paris Olympic Games, he went on to become a missionary in China, and was imprisoned during the Second World War. He died of a brain tumour while incarcerated at the Japanese prisoner-of-war camp at Weihsen, but not before sharing this hymn with his fellow prisoners.

The vision of sorrow forgotten and of a safe, joyful future in heaven, where all mysteries will be revealed, is one to which we can all relate, whether we are in dire straits in prison or suffering the pain, confusion or loneliness of old age. Unusually, we sing in this hymn to our own soul. This is something we also find in the Psalms, as in, 'Awake, my soul!' (Psalm 57:8), and 'Why are you cast down, O my soul, and why are you disquieted within me? Hope in God; for I shall again praise him, my help and my God' (Psalm 42:5–6).

As we sing to our souls, echoing the voice of the Psalmist to 'be still', we are reminded of the permanence of the soul—of the idea that it is the soul that survives, and that the soul is not affected by the ravages of illness or death. The soul is moved, however, moved in the events alluded to in the hymn, and indeed moved by this hymn, set as it is to such evocative music.

The tune itself is compressed, subdued perhaps, yet it is also expansive. It is confined to a small range, with the lowest note being E flat, and the highest C, and this compression makes the tune comfortable both to hear and to sing. There are no notes to strain for, nor any great leaps, making all smooth and calm. The harmonies are close, giving an intimate yet intense mood to the hymn, which can give us a sense of deeper channels flowing, channels that take us down to those levels of the soul where despair, hope, fear and joy reside.

It is 'down there', where 'deep calls to deep' (Psalm 42:7), deep in the centre of our being, that we encounter God at our most challenging and painful times. It is down deep that we find our souls resonating with the power and love of God to move us to weep, or to rejoice, and, in either case, to sing.

O God, our heavenly friend, be at the still centre of our souls, so that when we turn to you in the pain of grief or sorrow, the flurry of activity may be hushed and our worries calmed in the presence of your faithful will. Let nothing shake our confidence, nor make us deaf to hear your soothing voice as we journey onward to our promised rest in that heavenly city, where every tear shall be wiped away, and all joy restored, Amen.

WHAT A FRIEND WE HAVE IN JESUS

✣

What a friend we have in Jesus,
all our sins and griefs to bear;
what a privilege to carry
everything to God in prayer!
O what peace we often forfeit,
O what needless pain we bear,
all because we do not carry
everything to God in prayer.

Have we trials and temptations,
is there trouble anywhere?
We should never be discouraged:
take it to the Lord in prayer.
Can we find a friend so faithful
who will all our sorrows share?
Jesus knows our every weakness—
take it to the Lord in prayer.

Are we weak and heavy-laden,
burdened with a load of care?
Jesus is our only refuge:
take it to the Lord in prayer.
Do thy friends despise, forsake thee?
take it to the Lord in prayer;
in his arms he'll take and shield thee
Thou wilt find a solace there.

Blessed Saviour, thou hast promised
thou wilt all our burdens bear.
May we ever, Lord, be bringing
all to thee in earnest prayer.
Soon in glory bright unclouded
there will be no need for prayer.
Rapture, praise and endless worship
will be our sweet portion there.

WORDS: JOSEPH MEDLICOTT SCRIVEN (1820–86)
TUNE: CONVERSE (ERIE), CHARLES CROZAT CONVERSE (1832–1918)

✧

Friendship is one of the greatest gifts of God, whether we are thinking of friendship with God or of our own earthly friends. Without friends we would be significantly diminished, and we tend to pity those who are without friends. It seems to be church communities who foster and value friendship that thrive most, and Jesus himself described his relationship to his disciples as one of friendship:

No one has greater love than this, to lay down one's life for one's friends. You are my friends if you do what I command you. I do not call you servants any longer, because the servant does not know what the master is doing; but I have called you friends, because I have made known to you everything that I have heard from my Father.
JOHN 15:13–15

Our friends are very important to us, and are sometimes more significant in our lives than members of our families. We can choose our friends but not our relatives! Among friends there is often a sense of gentle yet unthreatening ownership. We are rightly wary of talking about 'possessing' other people, but we do use a language of 'having friends' and there is an important sense in which we do 'own' our friends, and they own us.

Jesus calls his disciples his friends because he has shared everything with them, pleasant and difficult experiences alike. Sharing is a kind of mutual owning, and so what we share in friendship we jointly own.

This can be immensely joyful: we can have the best fun with our friends. Jesus' own cousin John the Baptist says that his joy as friend of the Bridegroom is a perfect joy: 'He who has the bride is the bridegroom. The friend of the bridegroom, who stands and hears him, rejoices greatly at the bridegroom's voice. For this reason my joy has been fulfilled' (John 3.29). While we have our friends, we rejoice with them, not only because friendship is a gift from God exemplified in Christ, but also because, as Ralph Waldo Emerson (1803–82) put it: 'A friend may well be reckoned the masterpiece of nature.'

Jesus shared *himself* with the disciples: he gave them part of himself and they gave him parts of themselves. We can give one another parts of ourselves, and yet we rarely say, 'What have you done with that part of me I gave you?' We cannot and do not really ask this, because once a gift is given, the recipient owns it from then on. This is common sense and common law. We only cease to own the gift if we throw it away, and therein lies the vulnerability that comes with giving and sharing.

The origins of 'What a friend we have in Jesus' and its history are therefore rather ironic, for today, this hymn has few friends: it has been omitted from several major hymn books, and because it used to be popular it has been parodied. Although it is seldom sung today, the tune is widely known still. It is perhaps one of those hymns that everyone knows, but few sing any more.

Its author was an Irishman who emigrated to Ontario, Canada in 1846 following a tragic episode in which his fiancée drowned on the eve of their marriage. In Canada he devoted his energies to helping the poor, and became known locally as the 'Good Samaritan of Port Hope'. He found love again, becoming engaged to Eliza Roche, a relative of the Pengelly family to whom he was tutor. Unbelievably, Eliza fell ill and subsequently died before any wedding could take place. Scriven then joined the Plymouth Brethren until his own life ended when he drowned in Rice Lake, Ontario some years later. He is commemorated there to this day.

Scriven's own best friendships were tragically ended, but he was committed to his faith, and also to his mother. It was to comfort his mother that he wrote 'What a friend we have in Jesus' in 1855, and he was delighted to consider the hymn as a joint effort between himself and Jesus. Some hymn books wrongly attribute the words to the Scotsman Horatius Bonar (1808–69), who wrote 'I heard the voice of Jesus say'.

It is often the people closest to us that we hurt most often, which means that our friends are often the ones who have to endure our bad temper, selfishness or misery. The 'friendship' that this hymn enjoyed in the early 20th century led to its being parodied by soldiers, to sets of words such as 'When this bloody war is over / Oh, how happy I will be!' Much-loved hymns are often subjected to this unkindest form of flattery, which makes the hymn a victim of its own success.

The tune, so well-known then as now, was written by the American Charles Converse in 1868. Among Converse's friends were the Hungarian composer Franz (Ferencz) Liszt (1811–86), who took minor orders in the Roman Catholic Church. From Liszt, Converse learned about the composition of symphonies and oratorios, but he was also happy writing hymn tunes. Composition was always his hobby, though, and he pursued a successful career as a lawyer in Erie, Pennsylvania. In the United States the tune CONVERSE is known as ERIE for that reason. It is unlikely that Converse, who was multi-talented and successful, ever met the benighted Scriven, in spite of the fact that their words and music were put together in a hymn book called *Silver Wings* in 1870, while both men were still alive. Other tunes, among them BLAENWERN, have been tried, but CONVERSE remains the favourite.

Knowing Scriven's story, and knowing that the words were written for his sick mother many miles away in Ireland, makes the hymn all the more poignant and inspiring. Its message is simple and effective: offer everything to the Lord in prayer, no matter how bad it may seem (and Scriven knew how bad it could be). In spite of everything, we should never be discouraged, because even if our worldly friends disappear, Jesus remains faithful. The end of the third verse is particularly poignant:

> *Do thy friends despise, forsake thee?*
> *take it to the Lord in prayer;*
> *in his arms he'll take and shield thee*
> *Thou wilt find a solace there.*

We are reminded of the loss of his wives-to-be, but also of the everlasting arms into which they were welcomed, and into which Scriven, and we, hope to be enfolded in death. Here Scriven hints at the vulnerability found in friendship, the risk of rejection or abandonment to which all friends and lovers submit themselves when offering themselves to each other.

That same vulnerability was known by Jesus in his earthly ministry and upon the cross. Jesus had friends before whom he made himself vulnerable. In being the perfect friend, he gave and shared everything—he gave his life, even—and in doing so opened the gates of glory to all believers, so that we may all share his kingdom. This he did for us, for we are his friends.

O God our refuge, we give you thanks for those whom we love, and hold in prayer before you all those who have no friends. Help us to be servants of friendship, and give us strength to bear your love for others. Protect us in our vulnerability and keep us ever mindful of the friendship you have shown to us in the death and resurrection of Jesus Christ our Saviour, Amen.

DEAR LORD AND FATHER OF MANKIND

✣

Dear Lord and Father of mankind,
forgive our foolish ways.
Reclothe us in our rightful mind,
in purer lives thy service find,
in deeper reverence praise.

In simple trust like theirs who heard,
beside the Syrian sea,
the gracious calling of the Lord,
let us, like them, without a word,
rise up and follow thee.

O Sabbath rest by Galilee!
O calm of hills above,
where Jesus knelt to share with thee
the silence of eternity,
interpreted by love.

With that deep hush subduing all
Our words and works that drown
The tender whisper of Thy call,
As noiseless let Thy blessing fall
As fell Thy manna down.

Drop thy still dews of quietness,
till all our strivings cease:

take from our souls the strain and stress
and let our ordered lives confess
the beauty of thy peace.

Breathe through the heats of our desire
thy coolness and thy balm;
let sense be dumb, let flesh retire;
speak through the earthquake, wind and fire,
O still small voice of calm.

WORDS: JOHN WHITTIER (1807–92)

MUSIC: REPTON, CHARLES HUBERT HASTINGS PARRY (1848–1918)

❖

Hubert Parry's tune REPTON has now become almost exclusively associated with these very popular words by the American Quaker writer John Whittier. It was not always so, and while the marriage of tune and words has undoubtedly been successful, it was a rather strange coupling, of which neither author nor composer had any knowledge. While written in the same twenty-year period, the words and music were never intended for each other, and come together from rather dubious backgrounds.

Parry, who obtained an Oxford music degree aged only 18, joined the staff of the Royal College of Music at 35, after having worked in business. The Director at the time was George Grove (1820–1900), who, after working on *Smith's Dictionary of the Bible*, created the now famous *Grove Dictionary of Music*. At 46, Parry succeeded him as Director, and soon added a Professorship of Music and a Knighthood to his credit. In 1903 he was made a Baronet. His anthem 'I was glad', a setting of Psalm 122, written for the coronation of Edward VII in 1902 and used at subsequent coronations in 1911 (George V), 1937 (George VI) and 1952 (Elizabeth II) is well-known and much loved.

The tune REPTON was originally written in 1887 for an oratorio about the life of Judith. The book of Judith appears in the Old Testament Apocrypha, a collection of Jewish writings that exist only in Greek rather than Hebrew. In what is quite a violent story, Judith, a young, beautiful widow, visits the army camp of Nebuchadnezzar's general

Holofernes in order to get him drunk, in which state she cuts off his head and takes it to her own people as an inspiration to them to attack. Her mission and their subsequent assault are successful, and the Assyrians flee, leaving the book to conclude with Judith's song of thanksgiving. The story is not historically accurate (Nebuchadnezzar is described as king of Nineveh rather than of Babylon!), and there are geographical mistakes too, but it is well told, and can be understood as a tale of one woman's faith and courage leading to her saving of Israel and Jerusalem from invasion. It probably dates from the second century before the birth of Jesus, and is thought to have been written by a Palestinian Pharisee.

This story presented the composer with great potential for emotional expression within the context of a 'religious' text. Parry himself was not a very enthusiastic Christian, believing that the challenges of Darwinism were too great (unlike those today who accept that evolution and divine creativity are not in conflict). Thus, for him, Judith presented a text that could be explored emotionally, while also satisfying the Birmingham Festival organizers who commissioned the work. *Judith* was an instant success when first performed in August 1888 and it helped make Parry's name.

If Parry's Christian conviction was weak, then John Whittier's was unorthodox. Born near Haverhill, Massachusetts, he was descended from the Pilgrim Fathers who settled in there in 1638. He was Secretary of the American Anti-Slavery Society and won a seat in the State legislature in 1835. He was more of a poet and journalist than a hymn writer, and would probably not have wanted his poetry to be turned into a hymn.

The words of 'Dear Lord and Father' were adapted by William Horder, who published them in his *Congregational Hymnbook* of 1884. They constitute the last six verses of a long, narrative poem called 'The Brewing of Soma'. In it, Whittier describes the intoxicating effect of Soma, a drink made from fungi and milk, used in Vedic (Hindu) rituals. In some ways, the origin of this hymn is rather disconcerting, and it is surprising that it can have become associated with a gentle piety and prayerfulness. It is often associated with Elijah's hearing of the 'still, small voice' in the Old Testament:

He said, 'Go out and stand on the mountain before the Lord, for the Lord is about to pass by.' Now there was a great wind, so strong that it was splitting

mountains and breaking rocks in pieces before the Lord, but the Lord was not in the wind; and after the wind an earthquake, but the Lord was not in the earthquake; and after the earthquake a fire, but the Lord was not in the fire; and after the fire a sound of sheer silence.
1 KINGS 19:11–12

But while we can fruitfully be reminded of Elijah's experience, and indeed of the call of the disciples in Galilee, and can find good sentiments expressed in the idea that we should be calm in deep reverence and enjoy the beauty of God's peace, this is not quite what the author had in mind. Nor did Parry anticipate such words, for the aria in *Judith* is entitled 'Long since in Egypt's pleasant land'. Yet from this strange marriage of rather unorthodox artists comes a hymn that has very successfully been redeemed of its past and has become a modern-day favourite.

The tune is beautiful and lyrical, and the words fit wonderfully. Dr George Gilbert Stocks, of Repton School in Derbyshire, made the coupling in 1924 (neither poet nor musician lived to hear this hymn) and named his arrangement after the school. Who knows what Parry, who is buried in St Paul's Cathedral, or Whittier, who is buried in the Union Cemetery, Amesbury, Massachusetts would have made of it? The latter might have been very annoyed!

So what are we to make of it? Here is a hymn that demonstrates that we need not concern ourselves too much with the intentions or expectations of its creators. Here is a hymn that transcends its origins to lift our eyes to heaven in humble praise. The 'simple trust' and 'gracious calling' of verse 2 appeal to the busy 21st century, in which many are 'strained' and 'stressed' by the order of life. Here is a hymn that we can sing reverently and honestly, and even if the knowledge of its fiery history and evolution may be a bit earth-shattering, we can still sing it creatively as we prepare to hear God's still, small voice emerging from the storm of modern life.

Father God, who in Jesus' tender voice calls your disciples to abandon the strivings and stresses of this noisy world, breathe your Spirit upon us, that as we turn to you in quiet praise, our lives may be beautified by your peace, and hallowed by your love, Amen.

TAKE UP THY CROSS, THE SAVIOUR SAID

✣

Take up thy cross, the Saviour said,
If thou wouldst my disciple be;
Deny thyself, the world forsake,
And humbly follow after me.

Take up thy cross; let not its weight
Fill thy weak spirit with alarm;
His strength shall bear thy spirit up,
And brace thy heart, and nerve thine arm.

Take up thy cross, nor heed the shame,
Nor let thy foolish pride rebel;
The Lord for thee the Cross endured,
To save thy soul from death and hell.

Take up thy cross then in his strength,
And calmly every danger brave;
'Twill guide thee to a better home,
And lead to victory o'er the grave.

Take up thy cross, and follow Christ,
Nor think till death to lay it down;
For only he who bears the cross
May hope to wear the glorious crown.

To thee, great Lord, the One in Three,
All praise for evermore ascend;
O grant us in our home to see
The heavenly life that knows no end.

WORDS: CHARLES EVEREST (1814–77)

TUNE: BRESLAU, ARR. FELIX MENDELSSOHN-BARTHOLDY (1809–47)

✣

This hymn takes its cue from Jesus' words, 'If any want to become my followers, let them deny themselves and take up their cross and follow me' (Matthew 16:24).

To an occupied people, who saw criminals walking the way towards Golgotha (the *Via Dolorosa*) on a daily basis, the message would have been clear. The condemned one would be carrying the *patibulum*—the horizontal part of the cross, which, everyone knew, was the piece of wood to which he would be nailed or tied outside the city wall. Then the *patibulum* would be attached to a vertical plank or pole which would be already standing in the ground when he got there. The previous corpse would probably have been removed already. The condemned man would carry the crosspiece on his back, on his final journey—adding insult to injury.

Since the Romans executed thousands of men (and probably women and children too) in this way, the image used by Jesus was a very real one, a frightening one, which everyone dreaded happening to them or anyone they knew. It is this literal burden on the condemned man's back that Jesus refers to, and, of course, there is the ironic fact that he himself was to walk that way, although he was not to carry his own cross—Simon of Cyrene carried it for him.

The idea that carrying one's cross is like carrying a burden is a common one in Christian spirituality. We often talk of 'the cross we have to bear'—of each of us having our own cross to bear, even—where that 'cross' is some burden in our daily lives, such as a difficult relationship, a daily chore, or regular ill-health.

But this trivializes the cross, and misses the point, common parlance as it may be. Discipleship is not about having a spiritual or physical inconvenience that one endures for the sake of Christ. Christianity is not merely about enduring suffering with good grace. If it were, that grace would undoubtedly be cheap grace. Christ's Passion and death achieve more than that.

Dietrich Bonhoeffer (1906–45), who wrote a book called *The Cost of Discipleship*, deplores 'cheap grace' and says that Christ calls us to come and die—nothing less. For Bonhoeffer, death at the hands of the Nazis was the cost of his discipleship.

The key word in the hymn, then, is not 'cross' but 'follow'. In verse 1 we sing:

> *Deny thyself, the world forsake,*
> *And humbly follow after me.*

And in the last verse:

> *Take up thy cross, and follow Christ,*
> *Nor think till death to lay it down.*

This hymn is about discipleship; it is about the journey we make through life. Charles Everest, the author, writes in a direct style, never losing the point, which can be sharp:

> *The Lord for thee the Cross endured,*
> *To save thy soul from death and hell.*

Everest was American, and this hymn was one of only two American ones to be chosen for that first great English hymn book, *Hymns Ancient and Modern* of 1861. Everest is not influenced or affected by local English debates, or the increasingly secularized English culture, in the midst of which that hymn book landed. He is direct: 'Take up thy cross, and follow Christ'. If you do, and if you don't give up, Christ's strength will be with you: you won't go to hell but share in Christ's victory over death.

In the last verse we find the focus changing. Instead of instructing us in discipleship, Everest composes a prayer and directs it heavenward: grant us, he prays, to see the redemption towards which the cross points, and towards which we, following Christ's way, are heading. This kind of stylistic gear-change is not uncommon and often goes unnoticed, but it serves not only to offer God praise in a final doxology, but to remind us of whom, and ultimately *to* whom, we are singing. In a church service, the sermon is part of the worship even if it is very much directed to the congregation rather than being spoken by them. Thus, as a minister in church might face the congregation to welcome them or to preach, he or she might also turn and face east when directing prayers to God. Everest does this with his hymn: it is as though, having sung about the way of the cross, he turns his back on us and leads us towards God, the 'great Lord, the One in Three'.

As we turn to God in the final verse, we make the very move of which the hymn speaks. Jesus bids us shoulder our cross and follow him, and in the last verse, having heard the rallying cry, we can picture Everest leading the way, picking up his cross and setting us all off in that great cross-following journey that he has just told us will not be easy. As we set off on that Mount Everest of climbs with our cross, the author Charles Everest encourages and leads us.

We can make the picture of carrying Christ's cross fit into almost any context. Wherever there is suffering, injustice or hardship, we can imagine Christ carrying his cross in the midst of them. We can easily see how a portrait of Christ carrying a cross through any modern scene of violence or suffering can make the point that Christ suffers today as he suffered then, and we can also make a moral point about whatever context the artist places Christ in.

But carrying Christ's cross does not begin with suffering. It is almost too easy to relate Christ to the suffering of refugees and political prisoners today. It is widely believed that there were more martyrs in the 20th century than in any other century to date. Everest's hymn reminds us that cross-carrying can and does involve suffering, but suffering is not the end point, nor the starting point. Therefore, neither is it the case that any disciple of Christ (or anyone else, for that matter) can claim, if they are having a bad time, or finding life a little difficult, that this is truly the 'cross to bear'.

The Passion of Christ involves suffering, but it is not about suffering —it is about sin and redemption. It is easy to associate the pain of the cross with pointless suffering, and, God knows, there is plenty of pointless suffering in this world. But the cross was not pointless. The cross had four points—north, south, east and west—and it points to all the people for whom Christ died.

'Take up thy cross' is not about suffering, it is about discipleship; and discipleship is not about suffering but about repentance. In the first century, a criminal carried a cross because he was guilty and his guilt was plain to see. That is why the execution was public. It was not only to deter future criminals, or to satisfy a perverted interest in the pain inflicted, but to humiliate the criminal with his guilt.

Dying on a cross is about sin, guilt and repentance. We all have a cross to bear and we are all sinners. Taking up our cross is about acknowledging our sin, perhaps even in public, just as the condemned criminal had no choice but to witness to his own sins. Taking up one's cross is a confession of guilt, and carrying it is an act of repentance.

It is not very easy. But Jesus never said that carrying our cross and following him would be easy. Christ didn't come to make repentance and forgiveness easy. He came to make them possible.

Lord Jesus, give us grace, we pray, to take up our cross and follow you. Give us strength to acknowledge the weight of human sin, and to lay our burdens at your feet, who died and rose again so that we might be forgiven, and dwell with you and the Holy Spirit in the Glory of God the Father. Amen.

JESU, GRANT ME THIS, I PRAY

✜

Jesu, grant me this, I pray,
Ever in thy heart to stay;
Let me evermore abide
Hidden in thy wounded side.

If the evil one prepare,
Or the world, a tempting snare,
I am safe when I abide
In thy heart and wounded side.

If the flesh, more dangerous still,
Tempt my soul to deeds of ill,
Naught I fear when I abide
In thy heart and wounded side.

Death will come one day to me;
Jesu, cast me not from thee:
Dying let me still abide
In thy heart and wounded side.

WORDS: LATIN, 17TH CENTURY, TRANS. HENRY WILLIAMS BAKER (1821–77)

TUNE: SONG 13, ORLANDO GIBBONS (1583–1625)

✜

Orlando Gibbons was one of the greatest English musicians of the 17th century. He is mostly known not so much for his hymns as for his madrigals (choral secular songs) and other choral works. A fine setting of the first verses of St John's Gospel, 'This is the record of John', is often sung in the Advent season, and madrigals such as 'The Silver Swan' are fine examples of their genre. Orlando was one of three musical brothers: Edward and Ellis Gibbons were older than he, and all three were composers. Orlando Gibbons has become the most famous, even though he only lived to the age of 41.

Like his brother Edward (1570–1650), Orlando was a chorister at King's College, Cambridge (although he was born in Oxford). Aged 21, he was appointed by King James I as organist of the Chapel Royal, a post that he held until his untimely death. When King Charles I became engaged to Henrietta Maria, the daughter of Henry IV of France, Gibbons was told to travel with the king to Dover to meet her ship. In nearby Canterbury he was suddenly seized with some kind of fit, and died, and he still lies buried in Canterbury Cathedral.

Struck down himself without warning, one of his more melancholic madrigals, composed around 1612, contains the words, 'What is our life? a play of passion... our graves that hide us from the searching sun are like drawn curtains when the play is done. Thus march we, playing, to our latest rest. Only we die in earnest, that's no jest.'

There are echoes here of the hymn's final verse, 'Death will come one day to me'. As well as composing madrigals, Gibbons wrote several hymn tunes, or 'songs', of which this is one of the most exquisite. SONG 13 displays Gibbons' gift for simple melody, interspersed with rests between each line. These give the singer pause for thought, time to reflect on the line just sung, as well as opportunity for breath! The beautiful tune has also been married to a poem of W.H. Vanstone (1923–99), 'Morning glory, starlit sky', which is taken from his book entitled *Love's Endeavour, Love's Expense*. There too, the tune adds a delectable poignancy to the words. There is an unhurried nature to the tune that instils a reverential calm in singer and hearer alike.

The words of the hymn are a translation from the Latin 17th-century hymn *Dignare me, O Jesu, rogo te*. The Reverend (Sir) Henry Baker, the translator, was quite a character. He was both the squire and the vicar of Monkland in Herefordshire, and his main claim to fame consists in his tenacious role as secretary to the committee that produced the first edition of *Hymns Ancient and Modern*, in 1860. He was effectively the main editor of the book, and as such Baker displayed great shrewdness and commercial acumen. He invited clergy and musicians and other interested people to submit tunes and words for consideration, thus raising the profile of the book before it was published, and was quite open about the fact that his brown-covered hymn book was intended to replace all or any other hymn books currently in circulation. To a great extent, *Hymns Ancient and Modern* did so, and was a great success.

Baker's role in producing the new hymn book was significant, and he was particularly keen to see translations of Latin hymns. Many were commissioned from J.M. Neale (1818–66), who was a prolific translator, but Baker himself also translated a number of hymns, including this one. Set in rhyming couplets, the four brief verses entreat Jesus to protect us in times of temptation, and emphasize the desire to 'abide' in Jesus' love. A passage from St John's Gospel lies behind the verses: 'As the Father has loved me, so I have loved you; abide in my love. If you keep my commandments, you will abide in my love, just as I have kept my Father's commandments and abide in his love' (John 15:9–10).

The love of Christ in which we abide is seen as expressed by the wounds of the cross, particularly the spear-wounded side. There is a balance to the hymn in that the first and last verses are about everlasting life and the desire to be with Jesus for ever, whereas the middle two stanzas are about the earthly, sinful life in which we live. The relationship alluded to is almost one of a child to a parent. Just as the Father and the Son are one (John 10:30), here we are treating the Son like a loving parent in whose wounds we can take refuge against sin, the world and the devil. The text is perhaps childish, but we should not scorn it for being so. For here we approach the Father as little children, in the hope of gaining eternal life: 'Truly I tell you, whoever does not receive the kingdom of God as a little child will never enter it' (Mark 10:15).

Abiding in Christ is also mirrored by his abiding in us. Christ abides in us if we abide in him, and it is Christ's dwelling in us that makes us the body of Christ today. As God the Father and God the Son abide in each other, so both abide in us and we in them by the Holy Spirit. This interrelationship, this indwelling of the Spirit in us and in God, is essentially trinitarian and is what gives us our distinctive understanding of God. The Trinity is a Godhead of mutual relationship, which also extends outwards to the Church, the body of Christ, to you and me. As Christians we are involved with and in the Trinity, and God in us. Thus we strive to abide in the love of God the Father, who in love created us;

to abide in the love of Christ, expressed supremely on the cross; and to abide in the Spirit, to be filled with the Spirit, who makes us what we are and sustains us as we journey on.

O Jesus, grant us, we pray, always to abide in your love, so that when tempted in this world we may be sustained by your Holy Spirit and kept from sin, and may be led to the enjoyment of your heavenly Kingdom, where you reign with the Father and the same Spirit, ever one God, Trinity in Unity, now and for ever, Amen.

SING, MY TONGUE, THE GLORIOUS BATTLE

✛

Sing, my tongue, the glorious battle,
Sing the ending of the fray,
O'er the Cross, the victor's trophy,
Sound the loud triumphant lay:
Tell how Christ, the world's Redeemer,
As a victim won the day.

God in pity saw man fallen,
Shamed and sunk in misery,
When he fell on death by tasting
Fruit of the forbidden tree:
Then another tree was chosen
Which the world from death should free.

Therefore when the appointed fullness
Of the holy time was come,
He was sent who maketh all things
Forth from God's eternal home:
Thus he came to earth, incarnate,
Offspring of a maiden's womb.

Thirty years among us dwelling,
Now at length his hour fulfilled,
Born for this, he meets his Passion,

For that this he freely willed,
On the Cross the Lamb is lifted,
Where his life-blood shall be spilled.

To the Trinity be glory,
To the Father and the Son,
With the co-eternal Spirit,
Ever Three and ever One,
One in love and one in splendour,
While unending ages run. Amen.

WORDS: LATIN, VENANTIUS FORTUNATUS (530–C.609), TRANS. PERCY DEARMER (1867–1938)

TUNE: PANGE LINGUA (MODE III)

GRAFTON (*TANTUM ERGO* FROM *CHANTS ORDINAIRES DE L'OFFICE DIVIN*, PARIS, 1881)

✜

With this sometimes neglected but beautiful ancient hymn we find ourselves in the realms of plainsong and medieval devotional poetry. The '*Pange Lingua*' was a Passiontide hymn composed in the sixth century by Venantius Fortunatus. The plainsong tune, which is still used today, also takes us back to the sixth century, if not earlier. Venantius Fortunatus was a native of Treviso in Italy, who, around the year 565, after having an eye complaint cured, went on a pilgrimage to Tours in France. Being delayed on the way, he settled in Poitiers, where, towards the end of that century, he was elected bishop. He was a prolific poet, and is still known for two of his poems, '*Vexilla Regis*' and '*Pange Lingua*', both of which are sung in translation today.

The imagery he uses is one of battle, with which all his readers and singers would have been familiar. In this day and age, the idea of marching with banners, or of battle being glorious, has given way to the remembered horrors of two World Wars, but it is important not to let modern images obscure our understanding of this ancient poetry. The battle spoken of in the first verse is the battle against sin, the 'glorious' battle that ends on the cross, when Christ wins the day—but the ironic twist comes in the realization that it is as victim, as apparent loser, that he actually gains a victory over sin and death.

The second verse speaks of an all-observing God taking pity on humankind who, in Adam, fell. The tree of the forbidden fruit and the tree of life (the cross) are juxtaposed, so that we can see Christ, as the second Adam, associated with the cross, the second tree. The 'pity' here is not trivial, but refers to God's compassion and the desire to have mercy on human sin. But the third verse reminds us that it was a planned response—God always knew when to send Jesus—and that, as in the first chapter of Colossians, he was sent at the 'holy, appointed time':

He is the image of the invisible God, the firstborn of all creation; for in him all things in heaven and on earth were created, things visible and invisible, whether thrones or dominions or rulers or powers—all things have been created through him and for him. He himself is before all things, and in him all things hold together... and through him God was pleased to reconcile to himself all things, whether on earth or in heaven, by making peace through the blood of his cross.

COLOSSIANS 1:15–17, 20

This passage is very much a subtext for the third verse. The fourth verse continues the idea that the cross is the culmination and purpose of Jesus' earthly life, popularly supposed to be 33 years in duration. On the cross the Passover 'lamb' is lifted, with which Jesus is so often associated, not least because the crucifixion of Jesus undoubtedly took place at around the time of the Jewish festival of Passover. As the lambs were being slaughtered and prepared for that feast, Jesus, the 'Lamb of God' as John the Baptist called him (John 1:29), was taking away the sins of the world by his death. The hymn talks of 'life-blood' being spilled, which reminds us of the sacrificial nature of Jesus' suffering and death.

The final verse is what is known as a doxology, a verse of praise to God the Trinity. But here it is not simply a final rounding-off with theologically correct praise to God. The Trinity is understood in the death of Christ, as in Jesus' dying we see the grace of the Father's love for humanity and we also recognize that love by the action of the Holy Spirit in our lives today. The death and resurrection of Christ point to eternity, and in eternity ('while unending ages run'), we live and dwell with God—Father, Son and Holy Spirit—who are one in love and glory.

The subdued majesty of this hymn is well set to the tune GRAFTON. GRAFTON is a lovely flowing tune, which glides effortlessly through the six-line verses (it is also used for 'Word supreme, before creation'). It is appropriate that a hymn that speaks of singing should do so so melodically, and the languidity of its flowing melody is achieved by keeping note intervals very close together. Very rarely does the singer have to move up or down by more than one note. Exceptionally, right at the mid-point of the tune, there is a descent of a fourth, but it is a natural falling point, and acts as a pivot to the second half of the tune, which is almost a mirror image of the first part.

GRAFTON originates in medieval plainsong, being derived from the French tune used for the latter part of a different poem by St Thomas Aquinas (c.1225–74), the last part of which is called TANTUM ERGO. The tune that many prefer is in fact the original plainsong melody, PANGE LINGUA.

The name 'plainsong' means exactly that: 'plain' is to be contrasted with 'florid' or 'fancy'. Fancy music was frowned upon by the medieval Church, who, at the Council of Tours in 813, decreed that 'everything that can lead the ears and the eyes astray and can corrupt the vigour of the mind is to be kept away from God's priests, for it is by tickling the ear and beguiling the eye that the multitude of sins generally enters into the soul'. Thus the path of Western music was both set in motion, but also fixed, for many centuries.

Plainsong is important because in most of Europe it was the main form of liturgical music between the fourth and fourteenth centuries. Its roots are to be found, along with the beginnings of all Christian worship, in synagogues and temples. Early Christian liturgy was hardly different from its Jewish counterpart, and the use of the Psalms is still common to Christianity and Judaism. The forms of music are just as old.

In the fourth century, Bishop Ambrose of Milan decreed that four scales, or modes, could be used for liturgical singing. In the sixth century Pope Gregory supervised extensive liturgical revision, adding four more modes to the repertoire. PANGE LINGUA is set in the third of these modes. In modern Western music we generally use only two of the eight modes that Gregory authorized—which we call major and minor.

A mode is a type of scale, defined by the *intervals* between the notes rather than the notes themselves. It can be played in any key, as long as the strict set of intervals between the notes is maintained. The Western major scale happens also to be the Ionian mode, which has the following pattern of intervals between one note and the next: (in the key of C) tone (C–D), tone (D–E), semitone (E–F), tone (F–G), tone (G–A), tone (A–B), then semitone (B–C). In order to maintain the same pattern of intervals in keys other than C, we need to add sharps and flats. (For example, G major has to have an F sharp in its key signature, and this distinguishes it from other major keys.) All these major keys are in the same mode—the Ionian mode, which is defined by this distinctive set of intervals. Other modes have different sets of intervals defining them, and can still be heard today, espcially in plainsong. The modes were named after Greek cultures whose musical system they were supposed to emulate, but this is not founded upon any factual evidence. The third mode became known as the 'Phrygian' mode, but most hymn books refer to PANGE LINGUA simply as 'mode iii'.

Whether we sing 'Sing, my tongue' to plainsong or a modern tune, we find ourselves connected to a world of medieval spirituality. To use the plainsong undiluted can be very powerful, and emphasizes the sheer age of the sentiments expressed. Plainsong gives a certain austerity to singing, and it also conveys a simplicity that many today are seeking, both within and outside the churches. Recordings of plainsong have sold millions in recent years, and the use of plainsong in church can be surprisingly familiar to any who come in rarely!

This hymn, then, takes us right back to the days of the sixth-century Church, for whom the death and resurrection of Jesus were not so long past. The music, in its simplicity, takes us to their time but also frees us in our own, as we remember that we stand and sing in a tradition that takes us back to the events themselves, and which through many centuries has nourished our faith. The music hasn't changed and nor has the message: Christ has won for us the victory over the grave—to him be glory for ever!

Lord Jesus, who by your death and resurrection has won the victory over death and sin, by your mercy forgive us our sins, and keep us mindful of the long inheritance of faith in which we walk, so that we may be inspired and renewed in your service, to your honour and glory, Amen.

WHEN I SURVEY THE WONDROUS CROSS

✣

When I survey the wondrous cross
on which the Prince of glory died,
my richest gain I count but loss,
and pour contempt on all my pride.

Forbid it, Lord, that I should boast,
save in the death of Christ my God:
all the vain things that charm me most,
I sacrifice them to his blood.

See from his head, his hands, his feet,
sorrow and love flow mingled down:
did e'er such love and sorrow meet,
or thorns compose so rich a crown.

His dying crimson, like a robe
Spreads o'er his body on the Tree;
Then am I dead to all the globe,
And all the globe is dead to me.

Were the whole realm of nature mine,
that were a present far too small;
love so amazing, so divine,
demands my soul, my life, my all.

WORDS: ISAAC WATTS (1674–1748)

TUNE: ROCKINGHAM, EDWARD MILLER (1731–1807), ADAPTED FROM PSALM TUNES COLLECTED BY
SAMUEL WEBBE THE YOUNGER (1770–1843)

Like Samuel Crossman's 'My song is love unknown' (p. 133), this hymn draws its inspiration from St Paul's words to the Galatians: 'May I never boast of anything except the cross of our Lord Jesus Christ, by which the world has been crucified to me, and I to the world' (Galatians 6:14).

Here Isaac Watts speaks of being 'dead to the globe', but it is effectively a direct quotation, as is the opening of the second verse, 'Forbid it, Lord, that I should boast, Save in the death of Christ my God'. This hymn has a clear scriptural basis, and at the same time offers a reflection upon it, rather as a preacher might comment. Watts draws us in: 'See, from his hands…'. He invites us to examine the Passion of Jesus, and yet does so in a way that maintains his own humility and thus encourages our own. The emotional impact of this hymn is unmistakable, and this may account for its tremendous popularity over a great many years.

Like a lot of good seasonal hymns, though, it is rarely sung for more than one week of the year. This is a shame, because the cross of Christ lies at the heart of all our worship, and Isaac Watts never intended it to be solely a Passiontide hymn. It certainly does no harm to sing it in Lent. He wrote it for a collection of 1707, and designated it as a communion hymn, to be sung on any day, during or immediately after the distribution of bread and wine. In the eucharist we always recall Christ's death, and the link between Christ's body and blood and the bread and wine is uppermost in our remembrance. Watts uses the image of blood and wine when he talks of love and sorrow flowing, mingled, down, and this reminds us of the blood and water flowing from Jesus' side after he had died on the cross (John 19:34).

For some, the fourth verse is too graphic in this respect. It tells of Jesus' 'dying crimson', spreading like a garment over the cross, blood pouring from wounded limbs. It is a gory image, but one which, like some of the more grotesque paintings of Christ by Mathias Grünewald (1480–1528), represents a painful reality. And yet, in that depiction of horrible death, there is the overtone of life—not just the simple idea that Christ died that we might live, but also the idea that the 'Tree' referred to by Watts is also the Tree of Life. The cross of shame, an embarrassment and a foolish thing to Gentiles, becomes the tree of life, bearing the fruit of forgiveness, redemption and eternal life. The fourth verse may be bloody, but it is one of the most important verses, and contains, of course, the direct quotation from St Paul on which the hymn is based.

It is easy to see, then, why this communion hymn has been taken to the very heart of English-speaking Passiontide spirituality. All the elements are there, beginning with the intrinsic value of the crucifixion for our salvation. Watts lays out his theme with a secondary text, this time from Philippians 3:8: 'I regard everything as loss because of the surpassing value of knowing Christ Jesus my Lord. For his sake I have suffered the loss of all things, and I regard them as rubbish, in order that I may gain Christ.' We stand with Watts, with the whole globe even, at the foot of the cross, and we cast aside all the vain things that might prevent us fully understanding and feeling what our Lord has done for us. Thus as we stand there, weak and humble before Christ's sacrifice, we are on solid ground biblically. This is no soppy lament for the pain of the cross—this is theology living and breathing and bleeding. In few hymns or poems are love and sorrow held together so perfectly, both in the text and in the singer.

In the opening lines, Watts originally wrote:

> When I survey the wondrous Cross,
> Where the young Prince of Glory died...

He later changed it, perhaps because the newer opening scans a little better, but also perhaps to avoid belittling the man who is God, as he hangs there for our sake. His role as Son of God is made clear in the title 'Prince of Glory', which makes him, naturally, the Son of the King of Glory. Then, midway through the hymn, we are reminded of his kingship by the ironic 'richness' of his crown of thorns.

The final verse is the hardest in so many respects. At the end it demands everything of us. God's offering, or present, or gift of his only Son is such that we can only respond with all our human love, which hardly matches to the amazing divine love expressed in the giving of Jesus for the whole globe. Watts referred to this love as a 'present', although some versions have rendered it as 'offering', just in case anyone misses the point!

This hymn is not so popular just because of its words, though. The tune ROCKINGHAM, to which it is invariably sung in Britain and elsewhere, is an exquisitely lyrical, flowing tune, which illustrates that love and sorrow, flowing, mingled, down. Words and music mingle, and we are slowly but surely swept along on a gentle tide of contemplation and worship. The major key is used, perhaps surprisingly, but therefore with greater effect. There is no lugubriousness here, no wallowing in the minor key as we sing of what a shame it is that Christ died. This old and famous hymn tune does not want to say that, or make us say it; it wants us to boast in the death of Christ, because of the victory to which it leads. And yet this is not a proud tune either. The triumph of the cross is muted, and the direction of the hymn is not outward: we are telling it abroad, but rather internalizing our meditation on the suffering and the glory of the cross.

There is a form of meditation advocated by St Ignatius of Loyola, known as the Spiritual Exercises, which, if followed properly, brings us to the foot of the cross in the third week of Lent. Ignatius is most often associated with the Roman Catholic Jesuits, but the idea of cross-centred meditation, in which one imagines oneself as being present, is an ancient tradition that has continued to develop. Richard Baxter, a Puritan with whom Watts was in sympathy, wrote a work in 1657 entitled *The Crucifying of the World for the Cross of Christ*, in which he too employed this kind of imaginative technique. Edward Miller's version of the old Psalm tune sets a contemplative tone, which further encourages us to imagine the realities of the crucifixion scene, yet without pretentiousness or self-deception.

This ideal marriage of tune and words was not brought about until 1833, when a version of Tallis' *Canon* was abandoned as the tune in favour of Miller's arrangement, which he named after the Marquis of Rockingham, a personal friend and three-times Prime Minister of Great Britain. Although the tune had been set to other psalms previously, it settled down to its current position, and now it is hard to imagine any other tune fitting these words more successfully, nor this tune being used for any other hymn.

O Lord Jesus Christ, look upon us from your cross and have mercy on us. Forgive us our vanity, our pride and our contempt for your laws, and by your precious blood wash away our sins, so that by the grace of your divine love our souls may be made clean and worthy of the salvation you have won for us, Amen.

O SACRED HEAD, SORE WOUNDED

✙

O sacred head, sore wounded,
Defiled and put to scorn;
O kingly head, surrounded
With mocking crown of thorn:
What sorrow mars thy grandeur?
Can death thy bloom deflower?
O countenance whose splendour
The hosts of heaven adore.

Thy beauty, long-desirèd,
Hath vanished from our sight;
Thy power is all expirèd,
And quenched the light of light.
Ah me! for whom thou diest,
Hide not so far thy grace:
Show me, O Love most highest,
The brightness of thy face.

I pray thee, Jesus, own me,
Me, Shepherd good, for thine;
Who to thy fold has won me,
And fed with truth divine.
Me guilty, me refuse not,
Incline thy face to me,
This comfort that I lose not,
On earth to comfort thee.

In thy most bitter passion
My heart to share doth cry,
With thee for my salvation
Upon the Cross to die.
Ah, keep my heart thus movèd
To stand thy Cross beneath,
To mourn thee, well-belovèd,
Yet thank thee for thy death.

My days are few, O fail not,
With thine immortal power,
To hold me that I quail not
In death's most fearful hour:
That I may fight befriended,
And see in my last strife
To me thine arms extended
Upon the Cross of life.

WORDS: PAUL GERHARDT (1607–76), TRANS. ROBERT BRIDGES (1844–1930)
TUNE: PASSION CHORALE, HARMONY BY JOHANN SEBASTIAN BACH (1685–1750)

❖

This most famous of Passiontide hymns is often associated with Johann Sebastian Bach and his *St Matthew Passion* written in 1729. But Bach, like many composers of his generation, was not averse to pinching a bit of good music if he came across it, and the tune was originally a popular love-song melody composed in 1601 by Hans Hassler (1564–1612). In a similar way Bach adapted and rewrote concertos by Antonio Vivaldi (1678–1741), so we should not be surprised to notice some borrowings, even in a work as great as the *St Matthew Passion*.

The words have a long and varied history, and have travelled to English through Latin and German. A medieval hymn, 'Salve mundi salutare' ('Hail, Saviour of the world'), which may have been written by St Bernard of Clairveaux (1091–1153), was an extended meditation on the parts of Jesus' body as he suffered on the cross. The hymn we have here derives from the section on Jesus' wounded head and the crown of thorns. Paul Gerhardt, a Lutheran pastor and prolific hymn writer, translated the Latin into German under the title 'O Haupt voll Blut und Wunden' and the words soon found a home with Hans Hassler's tune. Hassler is well-known in Germany, in spite of the fact that his most famous melody was borrowed by the more famous Bach, who used it five times in the *St Matthew Passion*, and also in the Christmas oratorio. Hassler's tune was written for a secular choral song called '*Mein Gemuth ist mir verwiret*' ('My being is in turmoil'). The practice of taking a popular tune and using it as a vehicle for praising God is by no means a 20th-century phenomenon invented by those who would sing the *Gloria* to the *EastEnders* theme, or put Christian words to 'Finlandia' or the final movement of Beethoven's *Ninth Symphony*. Even before Bach's time it was acceptable to take a contemporary song tune and reuse it as the basis for a whole Mass setting. Josquin des Prés (1440–1521) and Orlandus Lassus (1532–94) are well-known for doing exactly this, and the original words of the tunes they used were often not the kinds of sentiments one would find decorous in church!

Musically, then, the use of the Passion Chorale followed a long and traditional path as it retained its popularity. But as people wanted to continue singing the words that speak so movingly of the death of Christ, those words were adapted. The ten verses of Gerhardt's German words are still to be found in modern German hymn books and are set to the original version of the tune, which was smoothed out by Bach and later editors. Bach and others make the first five syllables rest on notes of equal value, whereas Hassler's original tune used notes of different lengths, thus creating a less liquid impression. In England the words had to be translated, of course, and this was first done by the Reverend John Gambold (1711–71), whose German translations were less successful than those of his contemporary John Wesley (1703–91). Gambold's translation began 'O head so full of bruises', and was replaced in many hymn books by James Alexander's translation of 1830, although some hymn books still use Gambold's translation.

Robert Bridges (1844–1930) used the original Latin as the basis for his translation of 1899, and it is this version that adorns most performing editions of the *St Matthew Passion* and many hymn books today. Bridges was a fine poet who became Poet Laureate to King George V (1865–1936) in 1913. He was also a musician who directed the village choir of Yattenden in Berkshire where he lived. Frustration at the quality of available hymnody led him to produce the *Yattenden Hymnal* in 1899, in which 'O sacred head' appeared.

The popularity of the hymn accounts for its presence in Bach's masterpiece. Not only is the hymn part of a great musical and literary tradition, but its presence in the *St Matthew Passion* illustrates the great Christian tradition of reading or performing the Passion narrative in Holy Week. In many churches today we find a dramatic reading of one of the Gospel accounts of Jesus' death, either on Palm Sunday or Good Friday. Sometimes this reading replaces a sermon: not only does it take quite a few minutes to perform, but if it is done well it hardly needs comment. Other ways of performing the Passion are famous: the York Mystery plays, and those of Chester, take us back to a medieval tradition of performing a cycle of plays (of which the Passion amounted to only part), and the players would perform in the streets. In Germany such plays are performed every ten years at Oberammergau, and in northern Italy every five years at Sordevolo.

Music crept into these performances, and in some churches the Passion gospel was simply sung all the way through by the priest. By the 15th century, other priests were joining in, taking parts such as Narrator, Christ and Pilate. The congregation were given crowd parts. Martin Luther (1483–1546) and Johann Walther (1496–1570) produced the first Passion in vernacular German in the 1520s, and it was a great success. By the time of Bach, the Passion genre was well established, and Bach was able to insert chorales into the performance, which were intended as reflective interludes, commenting upon the action described. Thus it was only natural for him to include, just after the point where the Evangelist sings, 'and they smote him on the head' (Matthew 27:30), the chorale that everyone knew: '*O Haupt voll Blut und Wunden*'. Each time Bach uses it in the *St Matthew Passion*, he sets it in a lower key, emphasizing the descent towards death.

The words themselves are directed to Jesus, and begin with a rhetorical question: can this mocking mar the glory of the Son of God? No, of course not. And yet there is a resigned feeling that the power of God is dimmed as Jesus hangs on the cross. The singer in verse 2 petitions to see the brightness of Christ's face. As we look on our dying Lord, we look for some sign of transfiguration, some light amid the darkness of sin. We know it is there, but in this context it may be hard to see.

There is guilt, too, in the hymn. The third verse, often omitted, speaks of the guilt that we all have:

> *Me guilty, me refuse not,*
> *Incline thy face to me.*

And in the next verse there is the request to share the pain:

> *In thy most bitter passion*
> *My heart to share doth cry,*
> *With thee for my salvation*
> *Upon the Cross to die.*

And yet, it is hardly bearable to stand beneath the cross and reflect on the pain and injustice of it all. To sing that we would die there instead is not easy. This is a hymn which, if sung with feeling and invested with the sentiments it expresses, is very hard to sing. The death of Christ points to our death, but it does so, even amid the gloom, in a positive way. Christ's outstretched arms are seen as an embrace, and the cross not ultimately as a symbol of painful death, but of life. The cross of shame becomes the tree of life. The hymn expresses that theology but in a very human way acknowledges the pain, and the difficulty of making that connection, especially when it is made along the arms of God nailed to a tree trunk.

O God our Father, help us to see through the agony of Jesus' suffering to the greater light of your saving love; yet make us never forget the price he paid, as we rejoice in the salvation he won for us, Amen.

MY SONG IS LOVE UNKNOWN

✜

My song is love unknown,
my Saviour's love to me,
love to the loveless shown,
that they might lovely be.
O who am I,
that for my sake
my Lord should take
frail flesh, and die?

He came from his blest throne,
salvation to bestow;
but men made strange, and none
the longed-for Christ would know.
But O, my Friend,
my Friend indeed,
who at my need
his life did spend!

Sometimes they strew his way,
and his sweet praises sing;
resounding all the day
hosannas to their King.
Then 'Crucify'
is all their breath,
and for
his death
they thirst and cry.

Why, what hath my Lord done?
What makes this rage and spite?
He made the lame to run,
he gave the blind their sight.
Sweet injuries!
yet they at these
themselves displease,
and 'gainst him rise.

They rise and needs will have
my dear Lord made away,
a murderer they save—
the Prince of Life they slay.
Yet cheerful he
to suffering goes
that he his foes
from thence might free.

In life, no house, no home
my Lord on earth might have,
in death, no friendly tomb
but what a stranger gave.
What may I say?
Heaven was his home;
but mine the tomb
wherein he lay.

Here might I stay and sing:
no story so divine;
never was love, dear King,
never was grief like thine!
This is my Friend,
in whose sweet praise
I all my days
could gladly spend.

WORDS: SAMUEL CROSSMAN (1624–83)

TUNE: LOVE UNKNOWN, JOHN IRELAND (1879–1962)

This hymn is both a reflection on the Passion of Jesus and an account of it. The writer, Samuel Crossman, knew the difficulties of ministry and the dangers of causing offence to politically motivated religious leaders. He writes of Jesus' triumphal entry into Jerusalem, widely celebrated on Palm Sunday, and of the sudden turn of the religious leaders to the shout of 'Crucify'. In the space of one verse we move from praise to punishment, and that was a swift progression which Crossman himself endured.

He was ordained in 1660, after the end of the English Civil War, but soon found himself on the wrong side of the established Church when, in 1662, an Act of Uniformity was passed, insisting that all clergy accept the use of the *Book of Common Prayer*. This prayer book was derived from texts originally put together by Archbishop Thomas Cranmer (1489–1556) in the time of Henry VIII (1491–1547). After Henry's death, when Queen Mary restored the Roman Catholic Church, Cranmer was martyred for his reforming work, but Mary's successor Queen Elizabeth I (1533–1603), who reigned for 45 years, managed to stabilize the situation with a slightly revised version of Cranmer's Prayer Book of 1552. Thus, in 1559, a prayer book was brought into use which lasted until the period of the Civil War, round about 1642. King Charles I was publicly executed in 1649 and his son Charles II did not become king until the restoration of the monarchy in 1660. As part of the restoration, and in keeping with previous parliamentary decisions concerning the worship of the Church, the fourth Act of Uniformity was drafted, and to it was appended the *Book of Common Prayer* of 1662, which is still widely in use today. The service of Choral Evensong, sung daily in so many English cathedrals and chapels today, is drawn straight from that book.

Samuel Crossman, however, did not assent to the Act, and according to its conditions, which stipulated a deadline of St Bartholomew's Day, he was ejected from his ministerial living, along with some 2000 others who had not been formally ordained by a bishop. Crossman was in sympathy with the Puritan cause, and his publication *The Young Man's Meditation, or Some few Sacred Poems upon Select Subjects and Scriptures* acknowledged George Herbert (1593–1633) as an influence and inspiration. This book was published in 1664 and it contains the poem that makes up the hymn 'My song is love unknown'.

The poem was prefaced by a quotation from Galatians 6:14: 'May I never boast of anything except the cross of our Lord Jesus Christ, by which the world has been crucified to me, and I to the world.' Thus Crossman acknowledges his spiritual debt to the Passion of Christ, and underlines for us the irony that just as Jesus fell foul of the religious authorities of his day, so too did Crossman. Unlike Jesus, however, Crossman did subsequently conform, and he later became a Prebendary and then Dean of Bristol Cathedral.

The text of the poem, which, until John Ireland set it in 1919, was sung to a Psalm tune, is a meditative poem that the author, or singer, directs internally rather than outward to God or neighbour. This hymn, as we sing it, is 'my song': we are invited to own it, to sing it to ourselves, and thereby to reflect on what 'my dear Lord' has done. As a reflection on God's unknown love, it is unsurpassed in beauty, and makes for one of those rare cases where poetry and fine music combine to create a profound hymnodic experience.

In the hymn we follow a way of the cross; indeed, the hymn can work well in procession behind a cross, pausing to read the passages of the Holy Week narrative to which the verses refer. Thus the third verse speaks very clearly of Palm Sunday and the involvement of the fickle crowd, and the fifth verse resonates with Pilate's releasing of Barabbas. Verse 6 tells of Joseph of Arimathea 'giving' a tomb. Yet, with each verse, there is a questioning, an examining of one's own soul. 'Who am I, that the longed-for Christ should die for me?' 'What has he done that they (the crowd, the religious leaders, the Romans) should turn against him?' Then, as we near the end, we are invited to reflect upon the fact that if Christ died for us, then the tomb should really have been ours, but instead we are able to 'stay and sing' the praise of Jesus our friend.

In some of these questions are profound echoes of the human condition: 'Who am I?' Others seem so simple: 'Why, what hath my Lord done?' The answer, of course, is found in Jesus' innocence of crime, for all he has done is to make the lame walk and the blind see. The confusion is palpable as we sing of those 'sweet injuries'. Crossman, in two words, preaches that understanding of the cross that speaks of Christ's suffering as both beautiful and awful, sweet because of the salvation it achieves and awful because of the pain undergone. In this two-word line, the death of Christ is powerfully paraphrased.

Similarly, we sing of the tomb as being both Jesus' final resting-place and our tomb—the tomb that we sinners deserve. Thus we acknowledge that we are guilty—we have sent Jesus to his tomb—but we also give thanks that we are the beneficiaries of his death and resurrection. We might indeed do well to stay and reflect on these ironic facts of salvation. Never was there such love, nor such grief, and here we see them inextricably linked.

One of the reasons we might be inclined to 'stay and sing' lies in the superb specially written tune that John Ireland composed. The story goes that he was asked to set this poem to a new tune, to replace a tune by Henry Lawes (1596–1662), and that Ireland, who was a composer of some note in his own lifetime and still today, did so in about ten minutes. The scrap of paper on which he jotted the tune became the first edition of a tune that sent these words and their reflective power straight to the heart of Passiontide.

It is no surprise that a specially written tune by an eminent composer fits the words so well, or that it manages to combine those two elements of inward reflection and outward declamation. It is written in the key of E flat major, when we might expect a minor key, but it conveys a hint of melancholy in its distinctive use of downward suspended notes in the tenor part. Thus, in the first verse, at the end of the first line, the music appears to rest on the word 'unknown', and does so on what appears to be a major chord (A flat, the fourth of the scale), yet, as the tenor line moves from an A flat to a G, we realize that this is a C minor chord, and the colour has therefore changed, even on one word. The same kind of movement is found at various points in the tune, and is emphasized at the midpoint, at the end of every fourth line. Thus there is penitence built in to this tune, and the ambiguity and irony of Crossman's poem is reflected subtly and effectively.

This hymn is rich indeed, and here might we stay reflecting upon it and the personalized interpretation of the Passion that it affords. In the end, we must return to that 'unknown love' referred to in the titles of both words and tune, the love unknown to humankind, but bestowed upon a loveless world so that we might become lovely to each other and to God.

O God who revealed your unknown love in Christ, who himself suffered to save the world by his cross and Passion, renew us with your mercy, so that we may turn from sin to love, from guilt to joy and from death to life. Grant this for the sake of our friend, the same Jesus Christ, your Son, our Lord, Amen.

ALL FOR JESUS

✠

All for Jesus—all for Jesus,
This our song shall ever be;
For we have no hope, nor Saviour,
If we have not hope in Thee.

All for Jesus—Thou wilt give us
Strength to serve Thee, hour by hour;
None can move us from Thy presence,
While we trust Thy love and power.

All for Jesus—at thine altar
Thou wilt give us sweet content;
There, dear Lord, we shall receive Thee
In the solemn Sacrament.

All for Jesus—Thou hast loved us;
All for Jesus—Thou hast died;
All for Jesus—Thou art with us;
All for Jesus Crucified.

All for Jesus—all for Jesus—
This the Church's song must be;
Till, at last, her sons are gathered
One in love and one in Thee.

WORDS: W. JOHN SPARROW-SIMPSON (1859–1952)
TUNE: ALL FOR JESUS, SIR JOHN STAINER (1840–1901)

Appropriate as this might be as a communion hymn, it was never intended primarily for that use. The words and music come directly from the cantata *The Crucifixion* composed by Sir John Stainer in 1887. Stainer was organist and director of music at St Paul's Cathedral in London at the time, while the words were compiled and composed by the Reverend John Sparrow-Simpson, who was the son of the Reverend William Sparrow-Simpson, Succentor of St Paul's in the second half of the 19th century. He described his friend and colleague Stainer in one of his three books about St Paul's:

All have recognized his musical versatility and power. Genial, warm-hearted and amiable in character, he gained and retained the affectionate regard of the choir. As a composer, his Anthems… his Cantatas… must live as long as sweet melody and pure harmony are appreciated.
GLEANINGS FROM OLD ST PAUL'S, ELLIOT STOCK, 1889, P. 252

Stainer was writing the cantata very much in the tradition of J.S. Bach's *Passions*, in which the narrative of the story is interspersed with solo arias and congregational chorales. Felix Mendelssohn-Bartholdy, another German composer, who was a friend of Queen Victoria and who often played the organ at St Paul's, had also been inspired by this model of writing. The congregation join in at key points in the narrative to reflect upon the events described, and with Stainer's *The Crucifixion* the involvement serves to make those attending a performance feel part of the action. The dramatic reading of the Passion narrative (the account of Jesus' trial and death) is an ancient tradition, and such dramatized readings are often used on Palm Sunday in many churches today. Stainer and Sparrow-Simpson produced a musical version in the spirit, if not the style, of Bach, contributing several hymns to the English tradition, the most famous of which is 'All for Jesus'.

'All for Jesus' closes the cantata and serves as a final meditation immediately after Jesus dies on the cross. The connections between the death of Christ and this hymn are subtle, but they are crucial to an understanding of the whole work, of which the hymn acts as a summary.

The congregation sing five hymns during a performance of *The Crucifixion*, which lasts about one hour. Each hymn is a meditation sung at the foot of the cross. As the piece draws to a close, the choir address the congregation in a movement entitled 'The Appeal of the Crucified'. We are asked:

> *Is it nothing to you?*
> *Behold me and see: pierced through and through*
> *With countless sorrows—and all is for you;*
> *For you I suffer, for you I die,*
> *Is it nothing to you, all ye that pass by?*

and:

> *Oh! Men and women, your deeds of shame,*
> *Your sins without reason and number and name:*
> *I bear them all on the cross on high;*
> *Is it nothing to you, that I bow my head?*
> *And nothing to you that my blood is shed?*
> *O perishing souls to you I cry,*
> *Is it nothing to you?*

Then it is all finished, and Jesus commends his spirit into the Father's hands. Then and only then do we sing 'All for Jesus'. The hymn is a response to the questioning by Christ on the cross. Is it nothing to us? Indeed not! We respond by singing:

> *For we have no hope, nor Saviour,*
> *if we have not hope in thee.*

The words go on to speak of trust and love and power, and then, in that 'communion' verse, the connection is made. Christ has died, for us, and we are left. It does matter to us—matters so much that we will be contented when we continue to encounter Christ in the sacrament of bread and wine.

The fourth verse reiterates the phrase 'All for Jesus' and addresses it to Christ, saying, 'You have loved us, you have died for us, but you are with us still, and all because of the cross'. And because of that cross, and the resurrection it points to, God's Church will always sing of cross and Passion until that great day when all will be united in Godly love. It is a tremendous ending to an hour's worth of music and, of course, stands alone as a hymn linking the suffering of Christ with our need and desire to remain in communion with our Lord.

At the cross, then, this hymn speaks of a majestic triumph: it really is quite rousing, and is not the kind of hymn we might expect to sing when thinking of the crucifixion of Jesus. The tune is expansive rather than lyrical, and it is in the bright key of E major. It rises in the third line of each verse to an F sharp, which is beyond the height of many a voice. (For this reason it can be good to transpose it down to D major, but if it is taken to the halfway house of E flat major, the flatness of the key can make the tune more lugubrious than it is intended to be.) There is no wallowing in grief here but rather an assured commitment to the faith made possible by the cross. *The Crucifixion* ends with Christ's death, but that is not because there was any doubt or fear associated with continuing the story to the resurrection. The resurrection is prefigured, not only in the final words of the hymn, but also by the resoluteness and confidence of the tune. As the hymn draws to a close, there is a finality—the finality of being able to stop, but not the finality of death or despair. In that way, the hymn ends the cantata so well: having taken the congregation through an account of the terrible injustice and sacrifice of the cross, we have to be able to stop, to take our leave.

It is the same in many areas of life: philosophers have to be able to 'stop doing philosophy' as Ludwig Wittgenstein (1889–1951) said, which means that there comes a point when, fully aware that you haven't solved the meaning of life and the universe, you still take off your thinking cap and go and do something else. Similarly, when we engage in any practical activity, we are aware that in one sense the job is never finished. We could go on tweaking the nuts and bolts, putting on more paint, or adding more ingredients to the recipe; we can always find a part of the house that is not completely clean; but there comes a point when we have to stop.

It is the same with worship. In one sense we can and should worship God continually, but when we are in church, the service has to come to an end, and ideally it does so in a way that enables us to go home feeling that we have worshipped God, that we have learned something of God, and that we have had a chance to offer prayers and praises. 'All for Jesus' seeks to do just that for *The Crucifixion*, and it certainly does enable folk to depart in a reflective peace, yet also assured that this was not the end. Indeed it is hardly the end, but the beginning of a song that shall 'ever be', all for Jesus Christ.

And the Church's song should be and is 'All for Jesus'. Jesus is the Church's bride, the Church is all for him, and he is all for her. Without Jesus, we, the Church of Christ, are nothing, and without the people of God the Church is an empty shell, without love, hope or song.

O God, who so loved the world that you sent your only Son into the world that whosoever believes in him shall not perish but have everlasting life, mercifully grant that we, walking in the way of the cross, may find it none other than the way of life and peace, for the sake of the same Jesus Christ our Lord, Amen.

THIS JOYFUL EASTERTIDE

✣

This Joyful Eastertide,
Away with Sin and Sorrow
My Love, the Crucified,
Hath sprung to life this morrow:

Had Christ, that once was slain,
Ne'er burst his three-day prison,
Our faith had been in vain:
But now hath Christ arisen.

My flesh in hope shall rest,
And for a season slumber:
Till trump from east to west
Shall wake the dead in number:

Death's flood hath lost its chill
Since Jesus crossed the river:
Lover of souls, from ill
My passing soul deliver:

WORDS: G.R WOODWARD (1848–1934)

TUNE: THIS JOYFUL EASTERTIDE, CHARLES WOOD (1866–1926)

✣

The Church year is marked out not only by Holy Days and special readings and prayers, but also by particular hymns and songs. This means that as we approach Easter we look forward to singing those great Easter hymns, 'Thine be the Glory' and 'Jesus Christ is risen today'. The unfortunate flip-side of this is that, just as it is considered odd to sing Christmas carols between New Year's Day and December, the annual opportunity to sing Easter hymns is all too brief.

And yet, every day we celebrate Christ's resurrection, and every Sunday is a celebration and reminder of Easter Day, that day when the crucified Jesus 'burst his three-day prison', rising to life and declaring the death of death. The spirit of Easter can and should be sung all year round.

Some Easter hymns are date-specific, though, and Woodward's is one of them. Convention and calendars dictate for how long Easter hymns can be sung. We can think of the Easter period as being between Easter Day and Pentecost, but even so, 'Jesus Christ is risen today' can only really be sung on Easter Day, and 'This Joyful Eastertide' suffers similarly.

On the other hand, when you can only sing certain hymns at certain times, they take on more than just a flavour of the season. There is something very special about words of a hymn that speak of 'now'— 'but *now* hath Christ arisen'—not only has it happened, it has happened *now*: we have arrived, and the good news is particularly good now! Being able to locate ourselves in the moments we celebrate is a delight and a privilege, and brings us into special contact with our Lord, the events and significance of whose life we are particularly celebrating *today*.

It is the same at Christmas, when, either at the Midnight Service or on Christmas Day itself, we can sing those words from 'O Come all ye faithful' that liturgical convention forbids at any other time:

> *Yea, Lord, we greet thee,*
> *born this happy morning*
> *Jesus, to thee be glory given;*
> *Word of the Father,*
> *Now in flesh appearing*

And again, on Maundy Thursday, at the eucharist, there is a tradition of adjusting the Eucharistic Prayer such that the priest says of Jesus, 'Who on *this* night that he was betrayed, took bread and gave you thanks...'. The immediacy of the account brings us closer to those events of long ago, the implications of which are still very much with us.

So there is something special about Easter music, as there is about all seasonal music, and without Easter music the Easter season would lack something that enables us to relate to the events and truths of the resurrection in a very particular way.

Woodward's celebratory text, which is often sung by the choir as an introit (the first piece of a service of worship), states the Easter truth simply: Jesus is risen, thereby doing away with the causes of sorrow, and wiping away sins. He echoes St Paul's claim in 1 Corinthians 15 that without the resurrection our faith would be in vain, underlining the fact that the resurrection of Jesus lies at both the base and the centre of Christian faith. Without the resurrection, the whole story falls apart. And the resurrection is that singular act of God which contravenes all the laws that we may care to think of. We do not need to worry too much about whether God was able to raise Jesus but in fact didn't (as some have said); rather it is the other way around: God did it, and thus the question as to whether he is able to doesn't need asking!

Jesus, 'our Love', as Woodward calls him, did indeed spring to life. Woodward uses a very active verb in the first verse: 'rising' can suggest an ethereal, levitational, almost passive event, but no—here we have Jesus 'springing' to life. It is far more enthusiastic, more dynamic, more alive.

Referring to Jesus as 'Love' is not new: George Herbert (1593–1633) wrote in a poem entitled 'Love':

> Love bade me welcome: yet my soul drew back
> Guilty of dust and sin.

And Herbert, like Woodward after him, sees the resurrected Christ rejecting human sin in favour of a welcome:

> And know you not, says Love, who bore the blame?
> My dear, then I will serve.
> You must sit down, says Love, and taste my meat:
> So I did sit and eat.

Jesus rises, so that we may sit with him.

In the second verse of the Easter hymn, Woodward goes on to suggest that after death, the human soul rests, sleeping until the day of the last trumpet when great numbers of the dead shall be raised. Perhaps there are even hints of a trumpet fanfare in the refrain, as the word 'arisen' is repeated, each time rising up the scale before concluding each time with a descent all the way down the F major scale.

The music itself is based on a Dutch Psalm tune of 1687, which the Irish composer Charles Wood harmonized at the turn of the twentieth century. The tune begins with an upward rise, appropriate for a resurrection hymn, and, in spite of having a tremendous vocal range, is eminently singable. Some congregations prefer to leave it to the choir, though, as it does go up to a top F in the refrain! Most hymns have smaller ranges than this, confining themselves to an octave (eight notes), and it is partly for this reason that this piece, which is a hymn in the proper sense of the word, is more often performed as an anthem by choirs.

Finally, the last verse is worthy of comment. Woodward uses water imagery, speaking of Christ as having 'crossed the river'. Like Mr Valiant-for-Truth in John Bunyan's *The Pilgrim's Progress*, death is seen as another 'side' to which we all cross, the way having been led by Jesus. Again Woodward's idea is not new. Pre-Christian, Greek myths speak of the River of Death, the River Styx, which is crossed only by boat, steered by Charon, the mysterious boatman.

Yet for Christians, we may be more inclined to think of the river of life mentioned in Revelation 22, and of the waters of baptism, through which we pass from death to eternal life. In the early Church, and still today, there is a strong tradition of Easter baptism, the preparation for which takes place during Lent. Thus at Easter there would be a double celebration of newness—new life in baptism into the new life in Christ, symbolically and spiritually brought about through baptism in water.

So let us be joyful, because of the life we have, the new life we have gained, in the resurrection of our Lord Jesus, who springs us from the prison of sin and sorrow and gives us a sure ground for faith.

Give us your Easter joy, O Jesus, that we may be freed to be your people in this world, and inspired by your resurrection hope may look forward to that day when we shall sit and eat in your Kingdom, Amen.

THE DAY OF RESURRECTION!

✣

The Day of Resurrection!
Earth, tell it out abroad;
The Passover of gladness,
The Passover of God!
From death to life eternal,
From earth unto the sky,
Our Christ hath brought us over
With hymns of victory.

Our hearts be pure from evil,
That we may see aright
The Lord in rays eternal
Of resurrection-light;
And, listening to his accents,
May hear so calm and plain
His own 'All hail', and, hearing,
May raise the victor strain.

Now let the heavens be joyful,
And earth her song begin,
The round world keep high triumph,
And all that is therein;
Let all things seen and unseen
Their notes of gladness blend,
For Christ the Lord hath risen,
Our joy that hath no end.

WORDS: GREEK, ST JOHN OF DAMASCUS (C.675–C.749). TRANS. JOHN MASON NEALE (1818–66)

TUNE: ELLACOMBE, *MAINZ GESANGBUCH* 1833

✥

This early eighth-century hymn is reckoned to be by one of the greatest of Greek hymn writers. St John of Damascus was born in that city and, as the son of a wealthy Christian, succeeded his father as the *Logothete* (chief representative) to the Muslim Caliph. It was a post he was unable to fulfil adequately as a committed Christian, and some time around 716 he left Damascus (now in modern Syria), and went to join a monastic community at Mar Sabas, which is situated in the Kidron Valley, between the Dead Sea and Jerusalem. The monastery had been founded in 478 by St Sabas (439–532).

St John of Damascus was a musician as well as a poet, and is thought to have trained singers and developed a system of musical notation. As a liturgist, St John wrote canons, which were canticles used for worship on particular days of the week. The tradition of saying or singing distinctive canticles for each day of the week is preserved today by many churches. The Franciscan order have shared this practice widely with their worship book *Celebrating Common Prayer*, which itself has influenced the Anglican *Common Worship*. Originally there were nine canticles (or 'odes'), and one was reserved for use in Lent. As well as a canticle for each day, the Magnificat, or Song of Mary (Luke 1:46–55); the Benedictus, the song of Zechariah after the birth of John the Baptist (Luke 2:68–79) and the Benedicite, an invention expressing the praise of Shadrach, Meshach and Abednego as they were put into the burning fiery furnace (Daniel 3), were also added. These canticles are still very much in use today where prayer books are used: the Benedictus follows the New Testament reading at Morning Prayer; the Magnificat is sung or said at Evensong (Evening Prayer) every day, and the Benedicite is often used during Lent and Advent as the first canticle at Matins (Morning Prayer).

The canon was the highest form of Greek hymnody, and as well as daily canticles there were texts for special feasts and seasons. By the seventh century it was common practice to insert extra verses, or *troparia*, into the midst of these 'official' texts, and these were absorbed into the canon. St John of Damascus was one of the greatest writers of *troparia*, and the hymn we have here comes from the canon written for Easter Day. Thought by many to be the finest of the Greek canons, it is also known as the 'Golden' canon.

In many churches today, Eastertide officially begins at a vigil or evening service on Holy Saturday night. This ancient tradition takes us back to St John of Damascus, and to the composition of this ode, or canticle. Just before midnight, everyone would gather outside the church and, as a cannon shot announced to the whole city that Easter Day had arrived, the archbishop would shout 'Christ is risen!' and the crowd would respond, 'He is risen indeed'. Bells would be rung, drums beaten, candles lit and celebrations would begin to welcome the light of Christ, risen from the dead to conquer the darkness of sin and doubt. Then the Golden Canon would be sung, as it still is in Greek Churches today. In the Western Church we have largely replaced it with the *Exultet*, which dates from a similar period but comes from the Latin rather than the Greek tradition.

We have not lost the Golden Canon, though, thanks to the great English translator John Mason Neale, who, in his short life, made a very significant contribution to English hymnody in the 19th century. He was a Londoner who went to Cambridge in the years 1836 to 1840, where he was a founder member of the Cambridge Camden Society, who were particularly interested in church architecture and who took up the cause of church restoration in the 19th century. The style of architecture known as 'Victorian Gothic' dates from that period and can be attributed to their influence.

Neale was ordained in May 1842, but suffered from ill-health and spent the next few winters in Madeira. In May 1846 he became Warden of Sackville College, in East Grinstead, Sussex, where he devoted much time to the writing and translation of hymns. 'Good King Wenceslas' is one of his own compositions, but he is better known for his translations from Latin and Greek (it is said that he knew twenty languages). Neale had a particular interest in the Eastern Orthodox Church, writing three books on the subject. His linguistic skills produced hundreds of translations, and also a famous joke which he played on John Keble (1792–1866), who was a fellow hymn writer and friend. In 1827 Keble had published *The Christian Year*, a collection of his own hymns. Neale met him many years later while collaborating on another book, and challenged Keble's claim that all of his earlier work had been original by producing a Latin text which appeared to be almost identical to one of Keble's English language hymns. Keble was embarrassed and insisted that he had never seen this so-called 'original' Latin version. After a while Neale revealed that he had translated the hymn into Latin *from* Keble's English for fun!

Originating in eighth-century Damascus and brought to 19th-century England by Neale, 'The Day of Resurrection' is one of our most well-known and well-loved Easter hymns. It has a spacious German tune, which in most hymn books is distinctively set as alternating unison and harmonized lines. The opening halves of the first, second and third lines all have that sweeping phrase which opens out into harmony, almost depicting Christ's bursting forth from the tomb on Easter Day.

The words have an immediacy that echoes the desire expressed in the second line to 'tell it out abroad'. A reference to the Passover follows—the Jewish feast that we associate with Jesus. The Passover commemorates the Israelites' deliverance across the Red Sea, escaping from Pharaoh's soldiers (Exodus 14:21–31), and takes its name from the final plague that God sent among the Egyptians, when all the firstborn were killed, save for those who painted their doorposts with the blood of a newly killed (Passover) lamb (Exodus 12:21–24). In St John's Gospel, the moment of Christ's crucifixion coincides with the slaughtering of the Passover lambs (John 19:14), and in eucharistic services there is a long tradition of reminding ourselves of Christ's role as the 'Lamb of God who takes away the sins of the world'. Easter is, in a sense, a Christianized Passover feast, and its date is still determined in reference to the Jewish festival. At Easter, though, and in this ancient hymn, it is clear that it is Christ who has 'brought us over' the divided sea, which represents the gulf of sin between humanity and God. This is all made possible by the 'resurrection-light' in which Christ hails us, to which we can only respond with hymns of victory and jubilation.

In the third verse of the hymn we move to a wider dimension as all creation celebrates. St Paul describes the whole of creation as 'waiting with eager longing' for the redemption of the whole world (Romans 8:19). Here in the third verse, the heavens, earth, the round world and all therein rejoice. St John of Damascus would not have been sure about the world being round, but Neale, in translating, had a cartographical advantage which he put to good use!

Many of the traditions associated with the celebration of Easter have changed little over the years. After all, there have been fewer than two thousand Easters, and the message and meaning have not changed. As this ancient hymn reminds us, Easter is about Christ's resurrection, which points to and brings about the redemption of the past, the future and the present, and the salvation of all humanity.

O Christ our Risen Lord, shed your resurrection-light on all your faithful people, that as we celebrate your victory over death and sin, we may be inspired to sing your praise and share the good news of redemption and of the joy that begins at Easter and which has no end, Amen.

THINE BE THE GLORY

✤

Thine be the glory, risen, conquering Son,
Endless is the victory thou o'er death hast won;
Angels in bright raiment rolled the stone away,
Kept the folded grave-clothes where thy body lay.

Thine be the glory, risen, conquering Son,
Endless is the vict'ry thou o'er death hast won.

Lo, Jesus meets us, risen from the tomb;
Lovingly he greets us, scatters fear and gloom;
Let the Church with gladness hymns of triumph sing,
For her Lord now liveth, death hath lost its sting:

No more we doubt thee, glorious Prince of Life;
Life is nought without thee: aid us in our strife,
Make us more than conquerors through thy deathless love;
Bring us safe through Jordan to thy home above:

WORDS: FRENCH, EDMOND BUDRY (1854–1932), TRANS. RICHARD BIRCH HOYLE (1875–1939)

TUNE: MACCABAEUS, GEORGE FRIDERIC HANDEL (1685–1759)

✤

This is one of the few Easter hymns that have broken out of an Eastertide straitjacket. Other Easter hymns, so many of which are rightly popular, are confined to the Easter season, but this hymn manages to get an outing at other times of the year too, which has to be a good thing.

One of the reasons for this hymn's continuing favour is its rousing tune. With a triumphant refrain after each verse, repeating the first two lines of music, it is easy to learn and sing, and it can be played to great effect either by the trumpets on or with an organ in a large resonant church, or indeed with other instruments—even, dare I suggest, jazzing it up. Purists may exclaim with horror, but it has to be said that this hymn tune does work in various orchestrations, and Handel's music can take it. Like Easter itself, this hymn can still delight after so many years, and new presentations enhance rather than diminish it.

Hardly any of us play or sing it authentically, of course. Like so many good hymn tunes, it was pinched from somewhere else, and without the composer's permission (the words were written two hundred years after Handel's birth). The hymn is very popular in England, but it is worth noting that neither the words nor the music are really English. Handel emigrated to Britain in 1712, and became a naturalized Englishman in 1726, but he was originally German, from Saxony.

The words of the hymn, although originally in French, were written by a Swiss. Raymond Budry was from Lausanne, but after being ordained in the Free Evangelical Church in Vaud, spent 35 years as the pastor of Vevey on Lake Geneva. (Vevey is now the headquarters of the Nestlé chocolate-making empire.) Budry wrote the hymn in 1884 after his first wife died, and it was published a year later in *Chants Evangéliques* (Lausanne, 1885). It soon found its way into English, translated by a Baptist minister from Kingston-upon-Thames, Richard Hoyle, and it now exists in many languages, invariably set to Handel's magnificent tune.

The French words are:

> *À toi la gloire, O Ressuscité!*
> *À toi la victoire pour l'éternité!*
> *Brillant de lumière, l'ange est descendu,*
> *Il roule la pierre du tombeau vaincu.*
> *À toi la gloire, O Ressuscité!*
> *À toi la victoire pour l'éternité!*

> *Vois-le paraître: C'est lui, c'est Jésus,*
> *Ton Sauveur, ton Maître, Oh! ne doute plus!*
> *Sois dans l'allégresse, peuple du Seigneur,*
> *Et redis sans cesse: Le Christ est vainqueur!*

Craindrais-je encore? Il vit à jamais,
Celui que j'adore, le Prince de paix;
Il est ma victoire, mon puissant soutien,
Ma vie et ma gloire: non, je ne crais rien!

The translation is accurate, and in both versions there is a description of the events of Easter Sunday, all sung firstly back to Jesus, and then to ourselves. Thus we praise Jesus for the victory over death that the raising of 'thy body' has won, but then in the middle verse we sing not to Jesus but to each other as we describe Christ's return from the grave. In this second verse, we are the Church greeted by our Lord Christ, who has defeated death by resurrection. Death has now lost its sting (1 Corinthians 15:55–56), and we are released to sing God's praises. In verse three we address Christ directly again, as we declaim lack of doubt and ask for his continual blessing on our lives here and hereafter.

The River Jordan is mentioned as the crossing place to the promised land, in the same way that it is in 'Guide me, O Thou great redeemer': 'When I tread the verge of Jordan… land me safe on Canaan's side'. For the Israelites in the wilderness, the River Jordan was a boundary, and although Moses himself never crossed it, the Israelites did eventually cross into Canaan, where they settled. In Christian hymnody, the Old Testament account is used as an allegory of the modern journey towards heaven, so the idea of being brought 'safe through Jordan' is a reference to death and judgment. The message of this hymn is all about Jesus having broken down the barriers of sin that separate us from God, thereby enabling us to pass over the spiritual 'Jordan' into the promised land of heaven.

Handel's tune gives the hymn an appropriate confidence, even though it was hardly written with these sentiments in mind. It was originally written for his oratorio on the life of Judas Maccabeus, who was a war hero of the Jews, in a story found in the apocryphal literature of the Old Testament (1 and 2 Maccabees). The chorus 'See the conquering hero' was the big hit, of which MACCABAEUS was the tune. Handel apparently did not much care for the work himself, in which words and music had been adapted from the poet John Dryden. The chorus also appears in *Joshua*, another oratorio of 1747. *Judas Maccabeus* does not contain a love-interest, so Handel was never very enthusiastic about it! It was popular, however, particularly among the Jewish community of London, who were delighted at Handel's glorious portrayal of the Maccabees' rebellion, even though his original spur to writing had been a victory of the English over the Scots.

Battle is never far from this hymn, whether it is the battles of the past to whose glorification the music was intended, or the battle over sin won by Christ on the cross and in rising from the tomb. The music is evidently martial and triumphant, and the opening words rouse us to the glorification of Easter as the great Christian triumph over sin, fear and death.

Handel himself might have been bemused at the thought that this is now one of the world's most popular and well-known Easter hymns. He was a devout man who was an ardent supporter of the poor, composing and working for the foundlings of Thomas Coram's Hospital, and it is reported that he prayed twice a day. He was a regular attender of worship at Sir Christopher Wren's newly completed St Paul's Cathedral, where he also played the organ (sometimes without his shirt on!). There are few hymn tunes by Handel ('Rejoice, the Lord is King' to GOPSAL is another well-known one), but there is something very appropriate in the idea that this very devout and prolific musical genius should inadvertently be the composer of such an inspiring hymn.

The idea of a hymn extolling the virtues of a conquering hero becoming an Easter hymn may be strange, but there is a delightful irony in the fact that it is actually Christ who is the conquering hero, and it is he whom we see victorious at Easter. As St Paul puts it:

In all these things we are more than conquerors through him who loved us. For I am convinced that neither death, nor life, nor angels, nor rulers, nor things present, nor things to come, nor powers, nor height, nor depth, nor anything else in all creation, will be able to separate us from the love of God in Christ Jesus our Lord.
ROMANS 8:37–39

The reason why these words are so inspiring is that Jesus, the risen, conquering son, has opened the way to eternal life by innocently dying for the sake of the sins of the world, and earning a much-needed and long-awaited victory over death. To him be the glory!

To you be the glory, Jesus, for by your saving death and resurrection you have opened the gates of glory to all believers and reconciled the world to God the Father. By your infinite Spirit of love, renew us with your Easter joy each and every day, so that we may live in the hope and promise of eternal life that only you can bring. For you reign with the Father and the same Spirit, one God, now and for ever, Amen.

PRAISE TO THE HOLIEST IN THE HEIGHT

✢

Praise to the Holiest in the height,
And in the depth be praise,
In all his words most wonderful,
Most sure in all his ways.

O loving wisdom of our God!
When all was sin and shame,
A second Adam to the fight
And to the rescue came.

O wisest love! that flesh and blood,
Which did in Adam fail,
Should strive afresh against the foe,
Should strive and should prevail;

And that a higher gift than grace
Should flesh and blood refine,
God's presence and his very self,
And essence all-divine.

O generous love! that he who smote
In Man for man the foe,
The double agony in Man
For man should undergo;

And in the garden secretly,
And on the cross on high,
Should teach his brethren, and inspire
To suffer and to die.

Praise to the Holiest in the height,
And in the depth be praise,
In all his words most wonderful,
Most sure in all his ways.

WORDS: JOHN HENRY NEWMAN (1801–90)

TUNE: GERONTIUS, JOHN BACHUS DYKES (1823–76)

CHORUS ANGELORUM (SOMERVELL), SIR ARTHUR SOMERVELL (1863–1937)

RICHMOND, THOMAS HAWEIS (1734–1820), HARMONIZED BY SAMUEL WEBBE THE YOUNGER
(C.1770–1843)

✥

The Dream of Gerontius by Sir Edward Elgar (1857–1934) is one of the last great works of the 19th century. When it was first performed on 3 October 1900 after insufficient rehearsal, it was not a success, but ever since it has captured the hearts and minds of listeners, whether they be people of faith or not. Elgar, who was a Roman Catholic, chose as his text an inspirational poem by Cardinal John Henry Newman, a former Anglican priest who, after becoming involved with the Oxford Movement, became a Roman Catholic priest in 1848.

The poem, of which the hymn is just a small part, was written by Newman in 1865 in response to a request from the editor of *The Month: An Illustrated Magazine of Literature, Science and Art*. The words of two hymns contained in the poem soon became popular. 'Firmly I believe and truly' is sung by the dying man, Gerontius, as he approaches death. His name derives from '*gerontion*' which merely means 'old man' in Greek, as in gerontology, the medical study of old age.

As Gerontius approaches death, he encounters the torment of purgatory, judgment and finally redemption and eternal life in the presence of the 'holiest in the height'. Newman's poem led to a revival in interest in the doctrine of purgatory—the cleansing waiting-place in the outer courts of heaven, where souls are made pure before entering heavenly joy. In Newman's poem it becomes logical to pray for someone in such a place, but the doctrine has never been popular in the reformed churches, who prefer a more biblical expectation of judgment and eternal life. The hope of eternal life with God the Trinity, surrounded by saints and angels, is hardly contentious, and Newman's great hymn 'Praise to the Holiest' has remained popular ever since it was written.

The tunes we use for the hymn are not from Elgar's masterpiece, nor could they be. Elgar uses massive forces of choir and orchestra, and sets the poem at length. We hymn singers do have some choice, though, having two fine tunes, and even a satisfactory third choice. RICHMOND is sometimes used, but in England it has a fair hearing as the tune for 'City of God', and is often superseded by CHORUS ANGELORUM or GERONTIUS, both of which were composed for these words.

J.B. Dykes, who wrote GERONTIUS, was organist at St John's Church, Hull, where his grandfather was the vicar. He studied Classics at Cambridge, and in 1848 was ordained in the Church of England, serving at Malton, Yorkshire (the same year that Newman was ordained in the Roman Catholic Church). He was Precentor of Durham Cathedral from 1849 to 1862 and published sermons as well as over three hundred hymn tunes, among them NICEA (for 'Holy, Holy, Holy') and MELITA ('Eternal Father, strong to save'). GERONTIUS is an expansive tune, which brings out the joy of praise and gives the text a positive feel. It also has a lyricism that copes with the central verses of suffering and agony.

To my mind, Somervell's CHORUS ANGELORUM (sometimes known as SOMERVELL) handles this double purpose of the hymn even better. It sweeps through the words with a more subtle gesture, and contains harmonic suspensions (delayed lingerings) in the melody which remind us that praise and passion are closely connected. Arthur Somervell had been a student of Parry and Stanford and was knighted in 1929 for his services to musical education, carried out in his role as chief inspector of music on the National Board of Education. The other tune of his that is well-known is WINDERMERE, named after the place of his birth, which is used for 'O Lord our God arise'.

The text of 'Praise to the Holiest' is rooted in St Paul, and is all about the victory of Christ over death. The opening line is drawn from Psalm 148:1, 'Praise the Lord! Praise the Lord from the heavens; praise him in the heights!' and ever since the editors of *Hymns Ancient and Modern* first used these words in 1868, this whole verse has flanked Newman's meditation on redemption, being repeated entire at the end.

The second verse opens up the theology of St Paul, who writes:

Thus it is written, 'The first man, Adam, became a living being'; the last Adam became a life-giving spirit. But it is not the spiritual that is first, but the physical, and then the spiritual. The first man was from the earth, a man of dust; the second man is from heaven.
1 CORINTHIANS 15:45–47

Jesus is seen as the 'second' Adam, the true human who atones for the first human whose sin led to the fall of humanity in Eden. Jesus, unlike Adam, came from heaven, not from earth:

He is the image of the invisible God, the firstborn of all creation... the firstborn from the dead... and through him God was pleased to reconcile to himself all things, whether on earth or in heaven, by making peace through the blood of his cross.
COLOSSIANS 1:15, 18, 20.

God's wisdom, expressed in 'wisest love', consists in the Father's decision to send Jesus to make good the failings of Adam, from whom all sin is derived.

The fourth verse has sometimes caused problems because it has been misunderstood. There is not the suggestion here that there is something higher than the gift of God's grace, but rather the idea that incarnation, the coming of Jesus, making God's very essence real among us and making perfect the flesh and blood of our existence, is a sublime gift for humanity. Some have attributed allusions to the eucharist here, because 'flesh and blood' are mentioned, but this is Catholicizing the text too much, for what is referred to is human, physical flesh, not spiritual bread and wine.

Then follows a subtle reference to the 'double agony in man'. This refers to the spiritual and physical suffering of God-in-man Jesus Christ. On the cross, God suffers and humanity suffers, for Christ is truly both. Christ also, as the second Adam, is truly human, and so suffers as both, suffering privately in the garden of Gethsemane, and publicly on the cross. At the same time, Christ is defeating the 'old' Adam by redeeming sin in the suffering he undergoes. As St Paul puts it: 'For since death came through a human being, the resurrection of the dead has also come through a human being; for as all die in Adam, so all will be made alive in Christ' (1 Corinthians 15:21–22).

In another text he writes:

Sin came into the world through one man, and death came through sin, and so death spread to all because all have sinned… Adam, who is a type of the one who was to come… For the judgment following one trespass brought condemnation, but the free gift following many trespasses brings justification… Therefore, just as one man's trespass led to condemnation for all, so one man's act of righteousness leads to justification and life for all.
ROMANS 5:12–18

This complex text lies at the heart of the hymn. Christ's action of suffering, and resurrection, is the key to our forgiveness and eternal life, and for that God's holy name is praised, in heaven above and here below.

O God of heaven and earth, who sent your Son Jesus Christ to rescue us from the slavery of sin, we praise your glorious name and give thanks to you for your salvation freely given. By your gift of grace, renew us daily with your generous love until that day when we too shall rise to dwell with you in heaven, Amen.

HE WHO WOULD VALIANT BE

✣

He who would valiant be
'Gainst all disaster,
Let him in constancy
Follow the Master.
There's no discouragement
Shall make him once relent
His first avowed intent
To be a pilgrim.

Who so beset him round
With dismal stories,
Do but themselves confound—
His strength the more is.
No foes shall stay his might,
Though he with giants fight:
He will make good his right
To be a pilgrim.

Since, Lord, thou dost defend
Us with thy Spirit,
We know we at the end
Shall life inherit.
Then fancies flee away!
I'll fear not what men say,
I'll labour night and day
To be a pilgrim.

WORDS: JOHN BUNYAN (1628–88), ADAPTED BY PERCY DEARMER (1867–1936)

MUSIC: MONKS GATE, ADAPTED BY RALPH VAUGHAN WILLIAMS (1872–1958)

Both the words and the music of this hymn are adaptations of previous material. Ralph Vaughan Williams, as well as being one of England's greatest composers of the first half of the 20th century, was a keen collector of English folk music. Folk music lies at the root of all music, since it predates much that was written down and comes from a tradition that is both oral and aural. Before notated music, people sang, and they did so in most cultures of the world; and their music, along with the ballad-like words that accompanied it, was passed down from one generation to another. The peoples of the British Isles were no exception, and thanks to recent research we now have access to a great deal of folk music deriving from Celtic, Anglo-Saxon, Norman and other cultures.

The interest in folk music in Britain really took off in the Victorian period, and the Irishman Charles Villiers Stanford (1852–1924), the Australian Percy Grainger (1882–1961) and Vaughan Williams are the three people most famously associated with it. Mention should also be made of Cecil Sharpe (1859–1924), whose life's work was collecting English folk song material. Of the four, Vaughan Williams is distinctive in turning folk music into hymn tunes, mainly for the *New English Hymnal* of 1906, of which he was an editor. In all he provided 35 folk hymn tunes for that volume.

Bunyan's *The Pilgrim's Progress* was obviously a favourite of the composer's, since in 1951 he wrote an opera based upon it. John Bunyan wrote the book as an allegorical story, with the subtitle 'From this World to That Which is to Come'. It was published in two parts, in 1678 and 1684, and tells the tale of the transparently named Christian, who realizes that he is condemned to death and judgment unless he makes a journey from the City of Destruction where he lives, to the Celestial City where everlasting life is to be found. He sets off without his family, who refuse to accompany him, and passes through places with inventive titles such as the 'Slough of Despond', the 'Hill Difficulty', 'Vanity Fair' and 'Doubting Castle', until he reaches the final river which he must cross into the Celestial City. He meets various people on the way, among them Faithful, who is killed at Vanity Fair, and Hopeful, who accompanies him to the end. Other characters, such as Talkative or the evil Lord Hategood, have delightful cameo roles in this fine piece of storytelling. Unlike a parable, which generally has only one main message, an allegory is laden with meaning at many levels, and can therefore be an absolute joy to read. For this reason, Bunyan's story is a much-loved classic, which can be read by people of most ages, and on each reading new insights can be discovered.

Part Two is a kind of re-run, with Christiana, Christian's wife, his children and his neighbour, Mercy, following the same route. They are accompanied by Great-heart, and meet, among others, Mr Valiant-for-truth, who with them crosses over the river to the other side, to eternal life, with celestial trumpets sounding. It is Valiant-for-truth who introduces the song that has become the hymn.

The song is one of many in the book, although it is the only one that has become a hymn. As Christiana and he near the end of their pilgrimage, Valiant-for-truth declares that it is by faith that he has come so far, and in words that are sung to any who might hear, he invites those who would seek true courage to join him:

> *Who would true valour see,*
> *Let him come hither.*
> *One here will constant be,*
> *Come wind, come weather.*

The words are not quite as we find them in the hymn, because Percy Dearmer, a prolific writer and adapter of hymns, altered them for inclusion in the *New English Hymnal*. Some hymn books have returned to Bunyan's original words, replacing the lines 'No lion can him fright, He'll with a giant fight' with 'No foes shall stay his might, Though he with giants fight'. The meaning is much the same, but the original version refers to events in the story of which today's hymn singer may be unaware. On their journey, Valiant-for-truth and Christiana have encountered Giant Despair, who imprisoned Christian in Doubting Castle, but whom Great-heart manages to kill (along with various other monsters and giants).

Song and hymn both sum up the purpose of the book, which is to say that in being a pilgrim in the Way of Christ, we should not be discouraged. Indeed we should take inspiration from discouragement, thus confounding those who would put us down. No discouragement should make us give up because we know that whatever life throws at us, at the end of the pilgrimage is the promise of eternal life. That promise stands above and beyond any fanciful philosophy or delight with which any human may tempt us, and in the pursuit of this heavenly goal anyone has the right to proceed.

Just as Vaughan Williams' MONKS GATE tune is based on a folk tune, there is a lot in Bunyan's book that reads like a folk tale. Strange characters and a journeying theme are prevalent, and the idea that Christian is someone seeking Truth appeals widely. The story has extra poignancy when read alongside the story of Bunyan's life. He had humble beginnings, born in Bedfordshire in 1628, but was recognized as a preacher by 1657, having read little more than the Bible, the Prayer Book, and Foxe's *Book of Martyrs*. After the restoration of the monarchy in 1660, Bunyan found himself on the wrong side of the law and was imprisoned in Bedford jail for most of the period 1660–72. It was long thought that Part One of *The Pilgrim's Progress* was written during this time in prison, but it is more likely that he wrote it when he was returned to prison for a further six months in 1676.

To be imprisoned for one's beliefs or Christian actions is neither pleasant nor uncommon. History has many examples of brave men and women who have been so, and some of them have used their incarceration as an opportunity to write, read and pray with their torment. We may be reminded of the German theologian Dietrich Bonhoeffer (1906–45), who, while imprisoned by Hitler, wrote inspiring *Letters and Papers from Prison* before being executed by the Nazis. In our own time, we may think of Terry Waite (b. 1939), taken hostage in Lebanon while working for the Archbishop of Canterbury, who subsequently published memoirs upon his much-applauded release. While in Lebanon, somehow a postcard from a well-wisher got through to him, and he treasured it for the rest of his time in captivity. On it was a photograph of a stained-glass window commemorating John Bunyan.

Bunyan's story, and his own life story, resonate today. So too do his ideals. For him, this life is one beset with spiritual warfare. Fairy-tale dragons are symbolic of powers that would drag us down, take over our lives, or otherwise distract us from following a true lifelong pilgrimage towards our eternal home. In this day and age, one of the temptations of the Christian life is to ignore these dimensions completely. It is so easy to cruise through the life of faith, unaware of what is really happening in the spiritual realm around us, and paying it little attention. Bunyan's book and the hymn derived from it serve to remind us to keep alert, and keep walking in the way, confident of our Lord's guidance.

O God of our pilgrimage and master of our lives, as we seek to walk in your way and follow your paths of righteousness and truth, guide us through the dangers and difficulties that hinder us, and lead us at the end to your eternal city, where you reign, Father, Son and Holy Spirit, now and for ever, Amen.

THE HEAD THAT ONCE WAS CROWNED WITH THORNS

✠

The head that once was crowned with thorns
Is crowned with glory now:
A royal diadem adorns
The mighty victor's brow.

The highest place that heaven affords
Is his, is his by right,
The King of kings and Lord of lords,
And heaven's eternal light;

The joy of all who dwell above,
The joy of all below,
To whom he manifests his love,
And grants his name to know.

To them the cross, with all its shame,
With all its grace is given:
Their name an everlasting name,
Their joy the joy of heaven.

They suffer with their Lord below,
They reign with him above,
Their profit and their joy to know
The mystery of his love.

The cross he bore is life and health,
Though shame and death to him;
His people's hope, his people's wealth,
Their everlasting theme.

WORDS: THOMAS KELLY (1769–1854)

TUNE: ST MAGNUS, JEREMIAH CLARKE (C.1673–1707)

✥

Like most Ascensiontide hymns, this one bids us look up to heaven to see our ascended Lord seated at the right hand of God the Father. Liturgically speaking, Ascensiontide covers that period between the Ascension and Pentecost, and in some senses it is a very odd time. We think of Christ going to the Father in glory, and await the sending of the Holy Spirit.

That period of time must have been disconcerting for Jesus' disciples, who had lived through an emotionally draining period. Only six weeks earlier they were marching into Jerusalem behind their friend and Lord Jesus, shouting 'Hosanna'; and some of them were probably expecting to be in the royal palace by the end of the day, with Jesus sitting on a throne, giving out orders and elevating his friends to high places. It was not to be like that, though, and there was to be a lot of descending to do before any ascending.

Within a few days their friend was dead. He had been betrayed by Judas, who had then felt so guilty about it that he had hanged himself, and Peter had got himself in a terrible state because he denied knowing Jesus only hours before the Romans crucified him. That had been a dreadful time, and for three days they didn't know what had hit them; they just hid.

But then it got better, but also confusing. Mary and Peter came running back from the tomb that they had borrowed (and 'borrowed' really was the word) to say, first of all, that Jesus' body wasn't there, and then that they had met an angel, and that they had even seen Jesus himself, although Mary hadn't recognized him at first and wasn't allowed to touch him.

Thomas, that doubting Thomas, didn't believe them, saying that he wouldn't believe it unless he could touch the place where the soldiers had stuck a spear in Jesus to see if he was dead or not. And he was dead, for sure.

So it was good news, and confusing news, which needed a bit of explaining. It vaguely fitted in with things that Jesus had told them when he had been travelling with them, but there certainly were some gaps. Then Cleopas said that he and a friend had walked along the road to Emmaus with Jesus, although, like Mary, they hadn't recognized him, not until he broke bread with them at a meal to which they had invited him. Then he had opened their minds to the scriptures and explained a great deal about how the Messiah must suffer and die, and be raised again.

Thomas still didn't believe it, until that day when Jesus appeared to all of them and invited him to touch his wounds, which he did. He was sorry then, but also overjoyed. How stressful for them all—all this pain, this joy, this confusion, this fear, this hope.

And then, it was a bit like before, but better. Jesus was with them again, eating picnics on the beach, and he had forgiven Peter too, although he gave him a hard time first: three times he asked him if he loved him, once for each denial.

As those weeks rolled on, Jesus had to go. He told them to carry on his work and preach the good news to all nations, and then, in a wonderful but frightening movement he was gone, lifted up to heaven. And now, here they are. Jesus has gone again. While Jesus has gone on high, they suffer here below. He said he would return in a new way: a comforting Spirit would come to them and empower them to do his work, but until the Spirit does come, the disciples are alone again. It seemed appropriate to replace Judas, and so Matthias was appointed by casting lots, but still for a few days the disciples were uneasy. Jesus' first departing was very unpleasant and scary—a sudden, violent death which was a harrowing experience for all concerned. But this time it seemed different, more like those quiet, gentle deaths—some call them a good death, a death which, while sad, can still be celebrated because of the life that has been lived and because of the sure and certain hope prepared ahead. Nevertheless, Jesus is gone, and that is sad, as they await the coming of the Spirit who will make them glad.

While Jesus reigned above, the disciples were apprehensive down below, and returned to their upper room. The task before them was immense, and we can only admire their tenacity, their hope, their faith and their determination. They had descended to the greatest emotional depths and ascended to the highest spiritual heights in a relatively short space of time. Emotionally, they must have been exhausted.

So it was a strange time for them, and today it can be a strange time for us if we follow the order of events, spaced out as they are in the liturgical year. However, as with all liturgical seasons, we do know what will happen next. This hymn expresses that combination of experiences —the experience of having seen the ascension and not knowing what will happen next, but also of knowing what is to come, and being aware of the Holy Spirit, not only in the lives of the disciples, but in our lives today. Just as we can survive the pain of Good Friday because it points to Easter joy, so we can handle Jesus' ascension because we know that the Spirit will swiftly follow. The disciples could certainly survive the ascension departing better than Good Friday, because in the intervening time they had learnt so much, and seen with their own eyes and touched with their own hands the victory of life over death.

The emotional upheaval to which the hymn alludes, and which the disciples must have felt, can also be seen in the lives of both the composer of the tune and the author of the words of the hymn. The Church of Ireland priest Thomas Kelly, who was ordained in 1792, found himself censured by the Archbishop of Dublin, who believed him to be too much like a Methodist. Thus Kelly left the Church of Ireland but continued to be a prolific writer of long-lived hymns. To leave the Church that had called him and to which he had given his life would have been a wrench indeed.

Yet Jeremiah Clarke's agony was greater: he suffered here below more than Kelly did, eventually committing suicide. He was an accomplished organist whose 'Prince of Denmark's March' is widely used at weddings today. Clarke was organist of St Paul's Cathedral from 1699 until his untimely and sad death in 1707. The story goes that he was depressed over a love affair, and shot himself. Such a tragic end seems far removed from the joyfulness of his tune ST MAGNUS, which fits Kelly's words so well, and which emphasizes the joy of all those disciples of today who celebrate the death, resurrection and ascension of Christ in the light of the sending of the Holy Spirit at Pentecost. Yet we often find, not least in the life of Christ, that where there is such light and joy, there is often a poignant tinge of pain or suffering. So it was for the disciples at Ascensiontide, and so it is for so many since then, and today.

O Father in heaven, who reigns in glory with the Son and the Spirit, grant to all your people the comforting touch of your healing hands, so that those who suffer here below may be joined to those who raise a shout of triumph at the victory over death won by your Son. This we ask for the sake of the same Jesus Christ, our risen, ascended Lord, Amen.

HAIL THE DAY THAT SEES HIM RISE

✛

Hail the day that sees him rise, Alleluya!
Glorious to his native skies; Alleluya!
Christ, awhile to mortals given, Alleluya!
Enters now the highest heaven! Alleluya!

There the glorious triumph waits; Alleluya!
Lift your head, eternal gates! Alleluya!
Christ hath vanquished death and sin; Alleluya!
Take the King of glory in. Alleluya!

Lord, though parted from our sight, Alleluya!
Far above yon azure height, Alleluya!
Grant our hearts may thither rise, Alleluya!
Seeking thee beyond the skies. Alleluya!

There we shall with thee remain, Alleluya!
Partners of thine endless reign; Alleluya!
There thy face unclouded see, Alleluya!
Find our heaven of heavens in thee. Alleluya!

WORDS: CHARLES WESLEY (1707–88) AND THOMAS COTTERILL (1779–1823)

TUNE: LLANFAIR, ROBERT WILLIAMS (1781–1821)

✛

There is an apocryphal story about the period of earthly time between Ascension and Pentecost, the period when Jesus has ascended to the Father, but the Spirit has yet to descend. When Jesus arrives in heaven, the angels welcome him and take care of him. After a little while, one of them says to Jesus, 'So, my Lord, you did a great job down there, but now you are back up here, we were just wondering, what provision have you made for the continuation of your ministry, the proclamation of the gospel and the saving of humankind?' To which Jesus replies, 'Well, I have left a dozen or so of my friends to take care of things.'

'Right', says the angel, 'and, er, what will you do if they fail, or give up? What other provision have you made?'

And Jesus answers, 'I have made no other provision.'

'I have made no other provision.' It is not a quotation from the Bible, or even from a learned scholar, and in one sense it is not even true, because of course the Holy Spirit was to help them, and helps us still. But as the disciples waited between the ascension and Pentecost, they may well have been wondering what provision Jesus had made.

When we looked at 'The head that once was crowned with thorns', we considered how apprehensive the disciples were, and how strange a time it must have been for them. With this hymn, we get a glimpse of the triumphant joy that the Ascension represents. Just as the disciples may have had some worries between the Ascension and Pentecost, it must also be the case that they had great cause for joy and hope in their anticipation of the sending of the Spirit. They also had much to celebrate as they saw their Lord Jesus carried up to heaven to sit at the right hand of God the Father. It is in this hymn, perhaps of all Ascensiontide hymns, that we can join with them as we sing for joy at the final triumph of the Easter season.

The hymn is littered with Alleluyas, and rightly so. 'Alleluya', which can be spelt in various ways, is a Hebrew word, found in the Psalms, which means 'Praise Yahweh' or 'Praise the Lord'. It is found in many hymns and is used liturgically as an interjection of praise to God. Liturgically it is used during the Easter period as a way of emphasizing the praise that is due to God for his saving work wrought in Christ's death and resurrection. 'Alleluya', then, is a good word, and we do good to utter it! In 'Hail the day', we certainly get a lot of opportunity, although it is worth noting that Wesley's original hymn did not contain the word at all. Wesley's words, in fact, have been altered quite a lot, mostly by Thomas Cotterill, and today we tend to sing, at most, only seven of the ten verses that Wesley penned.

This verse is no longer sung:

> *Master (will we ever say),*
> *taken from our head today,*
> *See thy faithful servants, see*
> *Ever gazing up to Thee.*

Nor this one:

> *Ever upward let us move,*
> *Wafted on the wings of love,*
> *Looking when our Lord shall come,*
> *Longing, gasping after home.*

Both of these abandoned verses point us upward to heaven, and suggest that the Church spends her time gazing up to heaven all the time. Such is the popular perception perhaps, from outside the Church, that Christians have their heads in the clouds and are never mindful of earthly things. This is neither desirable nor an accurate description of the life of faith.

At the Shrine of Our Lady of Walsingham in Norfolk, there is a chapel that honours the Ascension, and in the ceiling we see the feet of Jesus disappearing through the roof. Underneath are two footprints indicating where Jesus might have been standing. It is a startlingly realistic recognition of Jesus' ascension, and it reminds us of the scriptural account of Jesus being 'taken up' (Acts 1:6–11; Luke 24:50–53). But like the apocryphal story, and like the words of Wesley's hymn, this 'going up' can tempt us into believing that God lives in the sky—and a misconceived idea that Christians believe that God lives in the sky can encourage people to believe that Christianity is about being other-worldly and out of touch with life 'down here below'.

What we need, and what this hymn helps us to achieve, is a balance. We look up to Jesus, in both senses of the word. We look up to him as our saviour and inspiration, whose path we hope to tread. And we look upwards to heaven, but the footprints of Christ are very much on the ground, and that is where we must walk. While Christ 'enters now the highest heaven', we remain below, striving to do his work and spread the gospel, ever mindful of his promise to us: 'I am with you always, to the end of the age' (Matthew 28:20).

While it is simplistic to think of Christianity as conceiving of God in the sky, this does not mean that it is wrong or childish to think of Jesus seated at the right hand of God 'up' in heaven. Wesley's words are far from childish: they express great truths about the continuing role of Christ in this and every age. Jesus is portrayed as still praying for us—praying to the Father—for just as he promised, 'If in my name you ask me for anything, I will do it' (John 14:14); and wherever or whenever heaven is, we are reminded of the promise Jesus makes, that 'I go to prepare a place for you' (John 14:2). These words form the basis of a simple yet hope-inspired faith, and it is that faith in which the hymn rejoices.

The tune too, composed by the little-known Robert Williams of Anglesey, is simple, expansive and joyful. Each line begins in a very similar way, and the Alleluyas all have the same dotted rhythmic structure, making this a very easy tune to sing. G major is usually used for LLANFAIR, the most preferred tune these days, and the brightness of the key, the small range (G–D) of the notes that make up the tune, and the repetitive nature of the melody all combine to make this one of the hymns in which we can 'let rip'. It is one of the most joyous hymns in the book, and is well suited to a procession or the opening of a service celebrating our Lord's Ascension.

Thus we sing the praise of God as we reflect upon Christ's Ascension, without worrying too much about where heaven is, and where Jesus is, for as we sing such a great hymn, making a joyful noise in unison and harmony with those around us, we can certainly feel that Christ is among us, receiving and directing our prayer, our praise and our song.

O Jesus Christ, although you are parted from our sight, reveal yourself to us in worship and in song. Send your Spirit upon us, that in all we say or do, we may be inspired from above, and from within, by the thought of your glory, and the music of your love, for you reign at the right hand of the Father, with the Holy Spirit, ever one God, now and for ever, Amen.

COME, HOLY GHOST, OUR SOULS INSPIRE

✛

Come, Holy Ghost, our souls inspire,
And lighten with celestial fire;
Thou the anointing Spirit art,
Who dost thy sevenfold gifts impart:

Thy blesséd unction from above
Is comfort, life, and fire of love;
Enable with perpetual light
The dullness of our blinded sight:

Anoint and cheer our soiléd face
With the abundance of thy grace:
Keep far our foes, give peace at home;
Where thou art guide no ill can come.

Teach us to know the Father, Son,
And thee, of Both, to be but One;
That through the ages all along
This may be our endless song,

Praise to thy eternal merit,
Father, Son, and Holy Spirit. Amen.

WORDS: LATIN TRANS. JOHN COSIN (1594–1672)

TUNE: *VENI CREATOR*, MELODY FROM *VESPERALE ROMANUM* (MECHLIN), MODE VIII

·❖·

This ancient hymn is associated both with Pentecost and with ordinations and coronations. At coronations it is sung after the Creed, before the anointing of the monarch. It almost goes without saying that before an anointing or before an ordination, it is not only traditional but also very right to call upon the Holy Spirit.

The VENI CREATOR, as it is known to many, dates from the ninth century and is said to have been written originally by the Emperor Charles the Fat—fat, that is, to distinguish him from his grandfather Charlemagne (742–814). Charlemagne is credited with having re-established what he called a 'Holy Roman Empire' in the year 800. From its earliest roots, therefore, this plainsong hymn which typifies Pentecost and is still used today at ordinations, consecrations and coronations was possibly written by a king.

At a coronation, the Holy Spirit is called upon in this hymn before the moment of anointing. This might remind us of the idea that rulers are appointed by God, that they have a 'divine right', which is emphasized by their being anointed with holy oil. King Charles I (1600–49) felt very strongly about this, believing that God had called him to be king, and that he was king of England by right. He fell foul of Oliver Cromwell (1599–1658) and was beheaded in 1649, but he nevertheless took the divine right of kings very seriously. For many, the execution of a king was a heinous crime, not only against the state but against God, who had chosen Charles to be king. Others, of course, felt that monarchy was useless and outdated, serving only the interests of the rich and the ecclesiastically complacent, and believed that the deposing of the king was the right and proper thing to do. Both parties claimed God on their side.

Cromwell's 'Commonwealth' of the 17th century did not last, and the monarchy was restored with Charles II (1630–85) in 1660. The British king or queen is still anointed, not just because he or she is God's chosen servant, but also as a sign of the indwelling presence of the Holy Spirit in his or her ministry as king or queen. Thus in 1953, the anointing was introduced with this prayer:

O Lord and heavenly Father, the exalter of the humble and the strength of thy chosen, who by anointing with Oil didst of old make and consecrate kings, priests, and prophets, to teach and govern thy people Israel: Bless and sanctify thy chosen servant Elizabeth, who by our office and ministry is now to be anointed with this Oil, and consecrated Queen: Strengthen her, O Lord, with the Holy Ghost the Comforter; Confirm and stablish her with thy free and princely Spirit, the Spirit of wisdom and government, the Spirit of counsel and ghostly strength, the Spirit of knowledge and true godliness, and fill her, O Lord, with the Spirit of thy holy fear, now and for ever; through Jesus Christ our Lord. Amen.

Then, appropriately, the choir sang Handel's anthem *Zadok the Priest*, which describes Solomon being anointed king (1 Kings 1:38–39).

It is important to note the order of events, because it is only *after* the anointing that the symbols of power are given over. The king or queen, having already been given a Bible, is anointed with holy oil, and only then are the spurs, sword, armills, royal bracelets and stole and robes, and the orb, given to him or her. Then the ring and the sceptre are given, and then, almost last, the rod with a dove on it. The dove is a symbol of the Holy Spirit, and in this case it is conspicuously associated with mercy, equity and peace. Only then, to crown it all (as it were), is the crown given.

The English translation of the words of the hymn was made by John Cosin, an Anglican priest whose career spanned the fall and rise of the English Crown in the 17th century. Originally published in 1627 in his volume *Private Devotions in the Practice of the Ancient Church*, Cosin wanted the words to be sung each morning, as a reminder of the presence of the Holy Spirit in church life. Cosin's was not the first translation of these words, for the *Book of Common Prayer* which Archbishop Thomas Cranmer (1489–1556) had produced in 1549 contained a translation. Cosin's translation replaced Cranmer's when the Prayer Book of 1662 was put together. This Prayer Book is still very much in use. Strictly speaking, Cosin's hymn is the only hymn officially authorized by the Church of England (a setting of the same text in responsorial form is found in the Service for the ordering of Priests).

The hymn summons the Holy Spirit, and does so according to the belief that if we call on God's name the Spirit will descend, just as at the baptism of Christ, and at Pentecost when the early Church felt the first tongues of spiritual fire, blessing and inspiring them for ministry (Acts 2:1–4). The way in which the ancient melody weaves its magic gives the hymn an ethereal feel, although we must not be tempted to suppose that the singing of this hymn at occasions such as ordinations or coronations is tantamount to the casting of some kind of spell. No part of the Bible, nor indeed of any hymn or prayer, is intended to conjure up God or the Holy Spirit. Instead, this is a mellifluous setting of a beckoning prayer, a request for the descent of the Holy Spirit, a request which is made in the confidence that God answers prayer rather than any confidence that God's Spirit can be conjured up.

The text seeks enlightenment and illumination through the fire of the Holy Spirit, and does so with a direct address to the Spirit, who is immediately associated with the seven gifts or spirits in the book of Revelation. In that book, St John the Divine writes to seven churches, referring to seven lampstands and seven stars (Revelation 1:4–12). In the letter to the church at Sardis we find: 'These are the words of him who has the seven spirits of God and the seven stars' (Revelation 3:1), and these seven spirits are associated with seven flaming torches (Revelation 4:5). The Lamb seen in the vision has seven horns and seven eyes, which are the seven spirits, and it is therefore only the Lamb who can open the seven seals (Revelation 5:5–6). There are also seven angels, with seven trumpets (Revelation 8:2–6), and there are seven thunders, a dragon with seven heads and seven diadems (Revelation 12:3) and seven angels with seven plagues and seven golden bowls (Revelation 15:1–7). There is also a seven-headed beast symbolizing seven mountains and seven kings (Revelation 17:9). The number seven, here and elsewhere, is the number of perfection, a divine number. Six is an imperfect number, because it is short of seven—hence the 'number of the beast' being 666 (Revelation 13:18), where six is short of seven, three times over, three also being a holy number. Thus to call on God's sevenfold spiritual gifts is to invoke the perfection of God, manifested in the seven spirits of God.

The hymn continues with requests for God's grace, protection, enlightenment, comfort and wisdom, so that our praise may be continuous and eternal, in full knowledge and adoration of the Trinity. 'Eternal merit' is perhaps an unusual phrase, and has value in rhyming with 'Holy Spirit', but it is clear that it refers to God's goodness, manifested in all three persons of the Holy Trinity.

Come, Spirit of God and enlighten us with the fire of your love, so that we may be inspired in your service, made wise in the knowledge of your salvation, and kept safe under the shadow of your wings, for you reign with the Father and the Son, ever one God, now and for ever, Amen.

I BIND UNTO MYSELF TODAY

✣

I bind unto myself today
The strong name of the Trinity,
By invocation of the same,
The Three in One, and One in Three.

I bind this day to me for ever,
By power of faith, Christ's Incarnation;
His baptism in Jordan river;
His death on Cross for my salvation;
His bursting from the spicèd tomb;
His riding up the heavenly way;
His coming at the day of doom;
I bind unto myself today.

I bind unto myself the power
Of the great love of Cherubim;
The sweet 'Well done' in judgment hour;
The service of the Seraphim,
Confessors' faith, Apostles' word,
The Patriarchs' prayers, the Prophets' scrolls,
All good deeds done unto the Lord,
And purity of virgin souls.

I bind unto myself today
The virtues of the star-lit heaven,
The glorious sun's life-giving ray,
The whiteness of the moon at even,

The flashing of the lightning free,
The whirling wind's tempestuous shocks,
The stable earth, the deep salt sea,
Around the old eternal rocks.

I bind unto myself today
The power of God to hold and lead,
His eye to watch, his might to stay,
His ear to hearken to my need.
The wisdom of my God to teach,
His hand to guide, his shield to ward;
The word of God to give me speech,
His heavenly host to be my guard.

Christ be with me, Christ within me,
Christ behind me, Christ before me,
Christ beside me, Christ to win me,
Christ to comfort and restore me.

Christ beneath me, Christ above me,
Christ in quiet, Christ in danger,
Christ in hearts of all who love me,
Christ in mouth of friend and stranger.

I bind unto myself the name,
The strong name of the Trinity,
By invocation of the same,
The Three in One, and One in Three.
Of whom all nature hath creation;
Eternal Father, Spirit, Word:
Praise to the Lord of my salvation,
Salvation is of Christ the Lord.

WORDS: 5TH–7TH CENTURY GAELIC, ATTRIBUTED TO ST PATRICK (372–466),

TRANS. MRS CECIL FRANCES ALEXANDER (1818–95)

TUNE: ST PATRICK'S BREASTPLATE/GARTAN (MELODY FROM THE *PETRIE COLLECTION OF IRISH MUSIC*, 1903)

EDITED BY CHARLES VILLIERS STANFORD (1852–1924)

✣

This great hymn is *the* hymn for Trinity Sunday, the Sunday after Pentecost when the Church adds up all we believe and devotes a Sunday to the doctrine of the Holy Trinity. Trinity Sunday is the day for theologians, and can be the undoing of preachers. Knowing just what to say on Trinity Sunday can be difficult, as we pick our way through twenty centuries of theology and credal statements, and try to avoid some of those simple but vaguely helpful analogies of water, ice and steam, or of candle, wick and flame, claiming that each have three parts but make one substance.

But whatever is *said* on Trinity Sunday, the hymns for the day are, or should be, dominated by this stupendous piece of ancient doctrine, sung to the magisterial tune St Patrick's Breastplate. The hymn can also be sung on 17 March, as it is reputedly by St Patrick, and this makes it one of the oldest texts in most hymn books.

The familiar text of today was arranged by Mrs Alexander (author of 'There is a green hill far away' and 'Once in royal David's city') at the request of the editors of *The Irish Church Hymnal* in 1889. The original 'breastplate' or *lorica* of St Patrick was not in metrical form, and it is not likely that St Patrick actually wrote it. The earliest recorded text is held by Trinity College, Dublin, and dates from the 11th century. An earlier, eighth- or ninth-century manuscript, known as 'The Book of Armagh', also containing an account of the life of St Patrick, mentions the text as being associated with a collection of hymns called *Canticum Scotticum* ('Scottish songs'). It is harder to date the hymn any earlier, although some hymn books place the original Gaelic text somewhere between the fifth and seventh centuries. However old it is, though, there is a universal desire at least to acknowledge the popular attribution of the text to St Patrick, the patron saint and evangelizer of the Irish people.

Patrick himself was not Irish, but Cornish. He first went to Ireland as a captive, and spent six years there before escaping back to Britain, where he trained for ministry, also visiting Gaul (now France). He returned to Ireland as a bishop, where he set up what became the Irish church at Armagh. The modern Irish church still has its Archiepiscopal base there.

The notion of the *lorica*, or breastplate, gives the text a Celtic feel. Literally the breastplate, as a piece of armour, was worn in battle, but a 'spiritual' breastplate gained popularity, believed to prevent disease, ward off danger and guarantee a place in heaven for its wearer.

The word also began to have a metaphorical meaning, derived in part from the prophet Isaiah, who wrote, 'He put on righteousness like a breastplate, and a helmet of salvation on his head' (Isaiah 59:17).

St Paul picked up the same idea: 'Stand therefore, and fasten the belt of truth around your waist, and put on the breastplate of righteousness' (Ephesians 6:14) and 'Let us be sober, and put on the breastplate of faith and love, and for a helmet the hope of salvation' (1 Thessalonians 5:8).

Thus the 'breastplate' became spiritual protection, a text to be recited and learned. In ST PATRICK'S BREASTPLATE (as we must call it) we find the three characteristic elements of a *lorica*: an invocation of God, Father, Son and Holy Spirit; a list of the protections sought, usually in reference to specific parts of the body; and a list of the risks from which protection was sought. The first verses are bound together, just as they seek to bind to the singer various spiritual powers and events. Christ's virgin birth, baptism, death, resurrection and ascension, and the second coming, are all specifically mentioned in the second verse, while the third verse invokes angels, saints, apostles, patriarchs and prophets in the cause of self-preservation. The fourth verse describes the whole realm of nature in its power and longevity.

Then God is called upon to assist in bodily form: eyes, ears, hands and voice are to be filled with God, and then, in verses which are hardly ever sung today, we find a list of threats and dangers from which protection is sought:

> *Against the demon snares of sin,*
> *The vice that gives temptation force,*
> *The natural lusts that war within,*
> *The hostile men that mar my course;*
> *Or few or many, far or nigh,*
> *In every place and in all hours,*
> *Against their fierce hostility*
> *I bind to me these holy powers.*

> *Against all Satan's spells and wiles,*
> *Against false words of heresy,*
> *Against the knowledge that defiles,*
> *Against the heart's idolatry,*
> *Against the wizard's evil craft,*
> *Against the death-wound and the burning,*
> *The choking wave, the poisoned shaft,*
> *Protect me, Christ, till thy returning.*

All human life, and death, is here. As we read the list of fears, we can see clearly what makes this kind of poem a 'breastplate'. These two verses, although usually omitted, should come between verses 5 and 6, which themselves precede the verse 'Christ be with me'.

The rather unusual structure of the poem is reflected in its musical setting. Charles Villiers Stanford, a great Irish composer, known for settings of texts often still used at Choral Evensong, arranged this hymn with two tunes. The first verse, which is only half-length, employs the first half of the tune St Patrick's Breastplate, which is then used in full for all the other verses except 'Christ be with me'. This creates a powerful change of emphasis towards the end of the hymn. If all the verses are being sung, this can be a relief, as the tune changes to Gartan, which, as a half-length tune, has to be sung twice through. Then, as a climax to the hymn, the now familiar first tune, with the first-verse words, returns in a final blaze of colour and praise, crowned by four final lines which emphasize the supremacy of Christ as the Saviour who unites us to God the Trinity.

Some people find that this hymn, like the Trinity itself, is hard work, and it is sometimes abbreviated or simplified. But a full rendition can be very rewarding and, tiring as it may be, this is a great hymn, which when sung can give the feeling of a summit climbed. But on reaching that summit, having explored the heights and depths of a wide-ranging text, the spiritual view can be tremendous as we survey the range, power and beauty of God, Father, Son and Holy Spirit, to whom we are related, at least partly through the offering of songs of praise.

O Holy God, Creator of all, Saviour of all, Sustainer of all, we give you thanks and praise for your great glory, revealed in the love of the Father, the redemption by the Son, and the freedom found in your life-giving spirit, for you reign, ever one God, Trinity in Unity, now and for ever, Amen.

ONWARD, CHRISTIAN SOLDIERS

✣

Onward, Christian soldiers, marching as to war,
With the cross of Jesus going on before.
Christ, the royal Master, leads against the foe;
Forward into battle see His banners go!

Onward, Christian soldiers, marching as to war,
With the cross of Jesus going on before.

At the sign of triumph Satan's host doth flee;
On then, Christian soldiers, on to victory!
Hell's foundations quiver at the shout of praise;
Brothers lift your voices, loud your anthems raise.

Like a mighty army moves the church of God;
Brothers, we are treading where the saints have trod.
We are not divided, all one body we,
One in hope and doctrine, one in charity.

Crowns and thrones may perish, kingdoms rise and wane,
But the church of Jesus constant will remain.
Gates of hell can never gainst that church prevail;
We have Christ's own promise, and that cannot fail.

Onward then, ye people, join our happy throng,
Blend with ours your voices in the triumph song.
Glory, laud and honour unto Christ the King,
This through countless ages men and angels sing.

WORDS: SABINE BARING-GOULD (1834–1924)
MUSIC: ST GERTRUDE, SIR ARTHUR SULLIVAN (1842–1900)

✛

There is much about this hymn that can be deceptive. The name 'Sabine' may appear to be a Germanic female name, but the author of these words was in fact the Anglo-Indian curate of Horbury Bridge, near Wakefield, in Yorkshire, when he wrote them in 1864.

A more significant misconception is that this hymn is about war. Like many scriptural passages, it employs imagery of war and marching as metaphors for the life and journey of faith, but it does not extol the virtues of war. Sadly, in Victorian times, as in many periods of history, war was never far away, and its language and imagery were familiar, although the emotions that war aroused were not always fully appreciated or acknowledged.

The Napoleonic Wars, the Crimean War and the Boer War in the 19th and the First and Second World Wars in the 20th centuries have increasingly brought closer to home the realities of war, which has made many experience something of its horror. This in turn has bred a determination to avoid war. When those at home are less aware of the difficulties and pains of conflict, they are more likely to send their sons away to fight, and to treat their loss as in some sense honourable. For this reason, hymns that draw on Victorian war imagery, of which 'Onward, Christian soldiers' is perhaps the most famous, are often accused of glorifying war, presenting it as a noble Christian activity.

Some have associated this hymn with a quotation from the story of God giving Jahaziel the Levite a promise of victory for King Jehosaphat: 'Do not be afraid or discouraged because of this vast army. For the battle is not yours, but God's' (2 Chronicles 20:15, NIV). This does not really help the modern cause of the hymn, although in our day and age we may be helped into interpreting such a promise as evidence of God guiding his people in the face of adversity, where the equivalent modern battle may be against the forces of despondency, peer pressure or the challenges to human integrity in a contemporary world. But even a cursory reading of the words of this hymn, combined with a little knowledge of its context, reveal quite a different use of warlike imagery, and a purpose far removed from battle or violence.

The hymn was written for children to sing at Pentecost, in outdoor procession. Its purpose was far from promoting war, although perhaps cleverly employed a theme and manner of activity that appealed to children. In every age, many children have enjoyed marching around and playing soldiers, no matter how much their parents and elders lament such an activity! The hymn was written for an occasion when the local school was to join forces with that of a neighbouring village, and was for the children to sing while marching from one to the other. Baring-Gould could not think of an appropriate hymn, so, writing late into the night and having in mind the tune of the slow movement of the *Fifteenth Symphony* by Joseph Haydn (1732–1809), he wrote the hymn.

As the children marched from one village to the next with their banners, they sang of marching behind the cross of Christ. Baring-Gould was drawing upon a very ancient tradition of banner-bearing. In pre-Christian times banners emblazoned with the king's coat of arms preceded troops into battle, and this idea was picked up by the Church, who would put at the front of their street processions standards bearing a cross and red streamers, and march while singing the ancient hymn 'Vexila Regis prodeunt' ('The royal banners forward go'). Such processions were celebratory acts of witness. Baring-Gould undoubtedly had the same kind of approach in mind, as do many ecumenical processions of witness that occur in towns and cities today.

The words themselves, which are not gender-inclusive and employ the language of battle, are actually celebrating the victory of Christ over death and hell (verses 2 and 4), and the need for Christian unity (verse 3), and are a rallying cry to unite under the single banner of Christ (verses 1 and 5). Then, as now, there were divisions in the Church, particularly with the mutual suspicion of High Church Anglo-Catholics and Low Church Evangelicals at its height in the mid to late 19th century, but this hymn extols the virtues of unity of hope and doctrine in the face of division.

There is a verse that is rarely sung today:

What the saints established, that I hold for true.
What the saints believed, that I believe too.
Long as earth endureth, men the faith will hold,
Kingdoms, nations, empires, in destruction rolled.

Faith will triumph, as 'earth's proud empires pass away' (see 'The day thou gavest', p. 211) and the Church of God marches onward against 'sin, the world and the devil'. It is not entirely clear *where* the march will end, as there is no indication of a heavenly home at the end of the journey, but the defeat of hell can be taken to infer this. Rather than pointing to an eternal future, Baring-Gould concludes with a verse of praise to Christ, which is not a bad way to end, but had he had more time, he might have done it differently. We must not forget that he wrote it in the middle of the night on the day before it was needed!

Because the words were written very quickly, and yet gained such widespread popularity, the author was persuaded that some of the words or rhymes ought to be changed, and so various amended versions began to circulate, although most reputable hymn books have returned to his original words, reprinted here. Haydn's symphonic theme did not survive as the tune, for in 1871 the up-and-coming composer and son of a military clarinettist, Arthur Seymour Sullivan, wrote the tune that will always be associated with 'Onward, Christian soldiers'.

Sullivan, like Henry Purcell (1659–95), composer of 'Christ is made the sure foundation' (p. 243), was a chorister at the Chapel Royal and later studied at the Royal Academy of Music in London. He was organist of various London churches, the Director of what was to become the Royal College of Music, and was knighted by Queen Victoria in 1883. His greatest fame comes from his alliance with William Schwenck Gilbert (1836–1911), who outlived him but never got a knighthood. Between them they wrote many popular English operettas, among them *HMS Pinafore* (1878) and *The Mikado* (1885). Sullivan's knighthood, it was said, came not just because the Queen had a greater respect for his music than for Gilbert's lyrics, but for his wider services to British music.

Sullivan's hymns were a very small part of his output, although St Gertrude and Lux Eoi (used for the Easter hymn 'Alleluya, Alleluya') are very much in use today, as is his arrangement of Noel, the tune for 'It came upon the midnight clear'. St Gertrude was reputedly named after a lady in the congregation of a church where Sullivan was organist. It was used in the 1942 Academy Award-winning movie *Mrs Miniver*, and it was sung at the funeral of American President Dwight D. Eisenhower (1890–1969) at the National Cathedral, Washington.

The onward march of the hymn itself has to some extent been halted due to the offence it causes to political correctness. Though less popular now, it still speaks of church unity and of the power of the cross to lead and inspire; and for that, and its rousing tune, it should never be forgotten.

Christ our royal Master, as we march onward in the way of your love, grant that we may tread in the footsteps of the saints, and come at last to the greater glory of your eternal Kingdom, where you reign with the Father and the Holy Spirit, now and for ever, Amen.

BE THOU MY VISION

❖

Be thou my vision, O Lord of my heart,
Be all else but naught to me, save that thou art,
Be thou my best thought in the day and the night,
Both waking and sleeping, thy presence my light.

Be thou my wisdom, be thou my true word,
Be thou ever with me, and I with thee, Lord,
Be thou my great Father, and I thy true son,
Be thou in me dwelling, and I with Thee one.

Be thou my breastplate, my sword for the fight,
Be thou my armour, be thou my true might,
Be thou my soul's shelter, be thou my strong tower,
O raise thou me heavenward, great Power of my power.

Riches I heed not, nor man's empty praise,
Be thou mine inheritance now and always,
Be thou and thou only the first in my heart,
O Sovereign of heaven, my treasure thou art.

High King of heaven, thou heaven's bright Sun,
O grant me its joys after vict'ry is won,
Great Heart of my own heart, whatever befall,
Still be thou my vision, O Ruler of all.

WORDS: IRISH, C. 8TH CENTURY, TRANS. MARY BYRNE (1880–1931),
VERSIFIED ELEANOR HULL (1860–1935)
TUNE: SLANE, TRADITIONAL IRISH MELODY

Like 'I bind unto myself' (p. 163), this Irish hymn draws on a great deal of battle imagery, and we find a reference to the spiritual breastplate again. Dating from a similar period and the same culture as 'St Patrick's breastplate', this old Gaelic hymn has been restored to us after many centuries of neglect, yet it is as relevant today as it must have been all those centuries ago.

The tune SLANE, which is invariably used (but is also used with other words, such as 'Lord of all hopefulness'), is now so tied to the words that we can hardly imagine singing them to any other tune. It is a beautifully lyrical tune, symptomatic of the Irish gift for melody, and it is a favourite hymn for many, appearing at baptisms, weddings and funerals alike. It is appropriate for all these occasions because its text seeks God's presence in all events and, like the *lorica* or 'breastplate' in ancient Celtic spirituality, the singers feel bound to God and God to them, as they involve the presence and power of God as protector and inspiration.

The tune has no known author, and in some hymn books even the harmony is not attributed to anyone. The tune is an old one which came to attention in a collection of Irish airs and hymns in 1920. In 1919 Dr Eleanor Hull had taken Mary Byrne's 1905 translation of the Gaelic '*Rob tu mo bhiole, a Comdi cride*' and put it into a regular but uncommon verse format. In the *New English Hymnal*, for example, there are no other hymn tunes with this metre. When Joyce Placzek (1901–53), writing under the pen-name of Jan Struther, wrote 'Lord of all hopefulness' in 1931, and when Jack Copley Winslow (1882–1974) wrote 'Lord of creation, to thee be all praise!' in 1961, they both wrote words in that metre specifically with the intention that they be sung to SLANE. Such is the popularity of the tune that people want to use it more than only for these ancient words. The most recent attempt to pair new words to SLANE is to be found in the *New Start* hymn book, specially published for the millennium, in which the tune is paired as a second option to 'Come wounded healer' by Martin Lekebusch (b. 1962). For that hymn, Richard Lloyd (b. 1933) wrote the tune DEEPCAR, thereby adding a second tune to the repertoire for hymn texts in this metre. SLANE will never be replaced, though, even if we are hearing new words and new tunes in that rare metre.

Each of the four lines of SLANE are different, yet they are recognizably unified by the use of repeated notes and a reliance on a very simple but effective harmonic structure. The melody gently ascends through an octave range, reaching a top E flat early in the third line, and then takes us back down to rest, very much where we started, at the end of the fourth line. Even though the tune ascends quite high, it never leaves the gentle mood it establishes at the outset, and perhaps this is why so many people find this hymn tune so comforting and pleasing. The gentle mood of the tune also renders it useful for the occasional offices of baptism, marriage and funeral.

The words form a personal prayer, and have a rhythm that chimes both at the beginning and the end of each line. The first four verses are full of 'be thou's, the repetition of which creates an almost other-worldly, mantra-like intensity. The influence of the ancient breastplate or *lorica* structure is plain to see, and, combining form with content, we find at the very centre of the poem, in verse three, a reference to God as breastplate—armour for the spiritual fight. This self-referential line indicates the key to the hymn, right at its heart.

The text of the hymn, even when translated and versified, is a little archaic, although this hardly detracts from its popularity, and there has been no successful attempt to 'modernize' the text by replacing 'thou' with 'you'. The very thought of doing so is alarming, and as well as ruining the familiarity of the piece, the aura of an ancient tradition would be killed. It has to be admitted that at the time Mary Byrne made the translation, 'thee' and 'thou' were hardly in daily use, but she very likely chose to use that form because of its resonance with the past, and also perhaps for its succinctness, which has no equivalent in modern English. 'Be thou' can at best be translated as 'God be', but then that phrase introduces an ambiguity as to whether a second- or third-person pronoun is being used to address, or refer to, God.

In this hymn, therefore, we are committed to older forms of langu- age. This is not a bad thing, and it is foolish to suppose that modern congregations cannot handle the 'thou' form for God. Most people prefer the traditional form of the Lord's Prayer, after all.

The second line of the first verse is rather unusual, however, and needs a little unpacking. At first glance, 'Be all else but naught to me, save that thou art' is rather odd, and can seem meaningless. 'Naught' rhymes with 'thought' in the next line, but this isn't really the reason why it is there. The line does make sense if we consider that 'be all else but naught to me' really means 'nothing matters to me', and thus that the meaning is 'nothing matters to me save for your being'.

Other lines are clearer. In the first verse we find petitions for God to be inspiration for thought and an ever-present light. The second verse alludes to our relationship with God as Father, and the desire to be a 'true son' refers to a passage in 2 Corinthians: 'I will be your father, and you shall be my sons and daughters, says the Lord Almighty' (2 Corinthians 6:18). Verse 3 has strong imagery of battle, with allusions to St Paul's description of 'the armour of God' in Ephesians 6 (see 'I bind unto myself'). The fourth verse eschews wealth in favour of the spiritual wealth of faith, and we might be forgiven for wondering whether there is a little Victorian pun buried in the last line of the fourth verse: the 'sovereign' of heaven is not just the King of heaven but, in a verse about wealth, may be a slightly tongue-in-cheek reference to the coin of that name! It is, of course, the Sovereign God, not the sovereign coin that is our treasure!

The final verse continues the theme of kingship, but it is the realm of heaven that we are now concerned with, and it is the joys of heaven that are sought in the second line. But then, to conclude, there is the more down-to-earth request that in whatever happens, we need and seek God's guiding power and protection.

O Sovereign God, the wealth of whose love is beyond all human understanding, yet whose light and warmth reach beyond the vision of our faltering sight, be the strength and salvation of our lives, be wisdom and inspiration to us, that in all we do, we may ever lift our eyes to your great glory, O King eternal, Father almighty, Ruler of all, Amen.

GLORIOUS THINGS OF THEE ARE SPOKEN

✣

Glorious things of thee are spoken,
Zion, city of our God;
He whose word cannot be broken
Formed thee for his own abode.
On the rock of ages founded,
What can shake thy sure repose?
With salvation's walls surrounded,
Thou may'st smile at all thy foes.

See, the streams of living waters,
Springing from eternal love,
Well supply thy sons and daughters,
And all fear of want remove.
Who can faint while such a river
Ever flows their thirst to assuage:
Grace, which like the Lord the giver,
Never fails from age to age?

Round each habitation hovering
See the cloud and fire appear
For a glory and a covering
Showing that the Lord is near.
Thus they march, the pillar leading,
Light by night and shade by day;
Daily on the manna feeding
Which he gives them when they pray.

Saviour, if of Zion's city
I through grace a member am,
Let the world deride or pity,
I will glory in thy name.
Fading is the worldling's pleasure,
All his boasted pomp and show;
Solid joys and lasting treasure
None but Zion's children know.

WORDS: JOHN NEWTON (1725–1807)

MUSIC: AUSTRIA, FRANZ JOSEPH HAYDN (1732–1809)

ABBOT'S LEIGH, CYRIL TAYLOR (1907–91)

✛

It is said that in 1809, when Vienna was under bombardment by Napoleon's troops, the great Austrian composer Haydn, then old and frail, was carried to his piano, where he solemnly played through his own composition, the 'Emperor's Hymn' (later to be called AUSTRIA). He had composed it for Emperor Franz II of Austria for the occasion of his birthday on 12 February 1797. The composer never touched the piano again, and a few days later he died, aged 77.

Haydn had never liked Napoleon, being a great royalist, favouring both Austrian and English royal families. In 1796 he had written a setting of the Latin Mass, intended for liturgical use, entitled *Missa in tempore belli* ('Mass in time of war'), which became known as the 'Pauken', or 'Kettledrum' Mass, because of its ominous drum beats; and then in 1798 the more famous *Missa in angustis* ('Mass in time of anxiety') or 'Nelson' Mass was composed. Both works reflect Haydn's (and Austria's) dislike and fear of Napoleon, and the recognition of Admiral Nelson's resistance to Napoleonic expansionism was tribute indeed. Nelson was defeating Napoleon at the Battle of the Nile while the work was being composed, and then in 1800 was a visitor to the court of the Esterhazy family, who were Haydn's employers and patrons.

The hymn tune dates from the same time, and while today it has three famous uses, its first, Austrian use was as a national anthem, composed to imitate the English 'God save the King' which Haydn had encountered in various successful trips to London. The original words, which were eventually replaced, were commissioned by Count von Sarau, probably with an eye to the revolution in France and the prevention of such a catastrophe in Austria, and were written by Lorenz Leopold Haschka (1749–1827). At the time, the Count explicitly referred to the lack of an anthem for Austria, who needed 'like the British, a national song calculated to display to all the world the devotion of our people to the king'. He also said of Haydn, 'I consider him alone capable of writing anything approaching in merit the English "God save the King".'

Thus, the words of the Austrian anthem, '*Gott erhalte Franz den Kaiser*' ('God preserve Kaiser Franz'), were written first and Haydn found a tune from his childhood days, which was probably a Croatian folk tune, and turned it into a great national anthem, which later became a string quartet movement and a hymn tune. Haydn was himself very pleased with the tune, and in 1799 composed a set of variations on it for the second, slow, movement of his Opus 76, no 3, String Quartet, which is now universally known as the 'Emperor Quartet'. Haydn was probably the finest and most prolific composer of string quartets that ever lived, and yet he was not averse to taking the theme for what, by then, had already become the national anthem, and using it in a piece of chamber music. It was an unusual move perhaps, but undoubtedly a successful one, as it is probably Haydn's most famous and popular string quartet.

The tune was later taken up by the Germans, when August Heinrich Hoffman von Fallersleben (1798–1874) wrote the *Deutschlandslied*, with the opening words '*Deutschland über alles*' ('Germany before everything'). Through various word changes and much political upheaval, the tune has survived as the German national anthem, but in 1946 the Austrian government abandoned it, adopting a new anthem with words written specially to a piece of Mozart's music.

The tune was first adopted in England in 1805, when John Newton's words were first allied to it. Thus when Emperor Franz, who was the grandson of Queen Victoria, visited her at Windsor, he quite likely sang his own national anthem tune but with unknown, foreign words written by a converted slave trader called John Newton!

Newton himself is well-known for having written the words of 'Amazing grace' (p. 202) and for his remarkable conversion, experienced while in danger at sea on a slave ship. This hymn takes its first line from Psalm 87: 'Glorious things are spoken of you, O city of God' (Psalm 87:3), but also draws explicitly on a text from Isaiah:

Look on Zion, the city of our appointed festivals! Your eyes will see Jerusalem, a quiet habitation, an immovable tent, whose stakes will never be pulled up, and none of whose ropes will be broken. But there the Lord in majesty will be for us a place of broad rivers and streams, where no galley with oars can go, nor stately ship can pass.
ISAIAH 33:20–21

Here are allusions to the river of life, the heavenly water that flows through the heavenly city, referred to as Zion:

Then the angel showed me the river of the water of life, bright as crystal, flowing from the throne of God and of the Lamb through the middle of the street of the city. On either side of the river is the tree of life with its twelve kinds of fruit, producing its fruit each month; and the leaves of the tree are for the healing of the nations.
REVELATION 22:1–2

And yet, in spite of this heavenly vision filled with flowing water, redemption and praise, there is a tell-tale note of caution in the third verse, where Newton writes:

Saviour, if of Zion's city
I through grace a member am...

'If' is the key word and it betrays the Calvinist theology that Newton adopted. John Calvin (1509–64), whose ministry was largely based in Geneva, held a doctrine of absolute predestination, which meant that one's place in heaven was already determined by God: 'No one can enter into the glory of the heavenly kingdom unless he has been in this manner, called and justified...'.

Calvin held that no one can lose their status among the elect, but as we do not know our destination, every Christian should live as though they are members of the elect. Not all Calvinists hold this rather strong line today, but Newton did, and it explains his doubtful 'if', which acknowledges that in spite of his conversion, good works and, above all, faith in Jesus Christ, he felt that his place in heaven was not guaranteed, nor was the knowledge of it available to him. In some hymn books the word 'if' has been changed to 'since', but that expresses a distinctive certainty alien to Newton, albeit while the original version expresses an uncertainty not well-known to us today.

Today we tend to speak more confidently of faith and salvation, and those who doubt do not so much doubt whether they are saved as question the existence of God. Newton's words, combined with the confidence of Haydn's tune, do not put God's existence, or his saving power, in any doubt whatsoever. It is rather that he lives his life in the hope and with the constant prayer that he may be saved. Many Christians today do not hold with the Calvinistic doctrine of predestination (although some do), but it is still very important that we do not take our salvation for granted.

Yet for all this, Newton's hymn is a very positive one, which speaks of the Church as the new Jerusalem (Zion) where God abides. God protects, God promises to supply our needs and he leads us into the promised land, just as he led the Israelites with a fiery and cloudy pillar. In him we trust.

O God our rock, nourish us with the living waters of your eternal promises, and warm us with the fire of your love, so that your Church may be continually blessed with your unfailing grace, and in her be found people worthy of the service to which you call them and open to the presence of your Holy Spirit, Amen.

HOW SWEET THE NAME
OF JESUS SOUNDS

✤

How sweet the name of Jesus sounds
In a believer's ear!
It soothes his sorrows, heals his wounds,
And drives away his fear.

It makes the wounded spirit whole,
And calms the troubled breast;
'Tis manna to the hungry soul,
And to the weary rest.

Dear name! The rock on which I build,
My shield and hiding-place,
My never-failing treasury filled
With boundless stores of grace.

By thee my prayers acceptance gain,
Although with sin defiled;
Satan accuses me in vain,
And I am owned a child.

Jesus! my Shepherd, Brother, Friend,
My Prophet, Priest, and King,
My Lord, my Life, my Way, my End,
Accept the praise I bring.

Weak is the effort of my heart,
And cold my warmest thought;
But when I see thee as thou art,
I'll praise thee as I ought.

Till then I would thy love proclaim
With every fleeting breath;
And may the music of thy name
Refresh my soul in death.

WORDS: JOHN NEWTON (1725–1807)
TUNE: ST PETER, ALEXANDER REINAGLE (1799–1877)

✣

This well-loved hymn gives us much to consider because it helps us reflect on the person of Jesus. John Newton, who wrote the words, was someone who had lived a somewhat chequered life, and in whom the flame of faith had first flickered, then died, and then roared with passion. Many know of Newton for 'Amazing grace' (p. 202), but this hymn is just as fine, although the fourth verse is invariably omitted.

After a torrid youth, John Newton was converted to Christianity, the faith of his early childhood. He left his seafaring career, and under the influence of the Wesleys and other non-conformists spent nine years training for the ordained ministry in Liverpool. Due to his early life of debauchery he found it hard to find a bishop who would ordain him, but was eventually ordained in 1764, becoming curate of Olney in north Buckinghamshire. While there, he befriended William Cowper (1731–1800), and between them they wrote hymns for the weekly prayer meetings at Olney church. In 1779 they published *Olney Hymns*, which contained 280 hymns by Newton and 67 by Cowper. Other hymns by Newton in that collection include 'May the grace of Christ our Saviour', 'Amazing grace' and 'Glorious things of thee are spoken'.

After sixteen more years at Olney, Newton moved to one of London's city churches, St Mary, Woolnoth, where he remained until his death at the age of 82. He and his wife Mary were originally buried there, but their bodies were transferred to Olney in 1893. In St Mary, Woolnoth

Church where he was originally buried, there is an epitaph, written by Newton himself, which reads:

John Newton, Clerk,
Once an infidel and libertine
A servant of slaves in Africa,
Was, by the rich mercy of our Lord and Saviour
Jesus Christ,
restored, pardoned, and appointed to preach
the Gospel which he had long laboured to destroy.
He ministered,
Near sixteen years in Olney, in Bucks,
And twenty-eight years in this Church.

Towards the end of his life Newton became frail and nearly blind, and had to be helped when he preached. In his final year, he preached a sermon which contained the phrase 'Jesus Christ is precious'. Probably due to his failing sight, he read the sentence aloud twice in succession, and his amanuensis whispered to him that he had already said it twice. Newton, responding, shouted out, 'I have said it twice and I shall say it again—JESUS CHRIST IS PRECIOUS.' Not in anger were these words uttered, but in faith, hope and joy. He wrote at the time, 'My memory is nearly gone, but I remember two things, that I am a great sinner and Jesus is a great saviour.'

'How sweet the name of Jesus sounds', written nearly 30 years earlier, expresses the same sentiment. We are so lucky to have Jesus to call upon, to hear us, to save us. Although all about Jesus, it draws its inspiration from a text in the Song of Songs: 'Your anointing oils are fragrant, your name is perfume poured out' (Song of Songs 1:3). Song of Songs provides the inspiration for the use of the word 'husband' in verse 5, which is most often changed to 'brother' these days. In Song of Songs we find the origins of the doctrine of Christ being 'married' to the Church, and this is still emphasized at most wedding services. The Church has long been seen as the 'bride of Christ', and thus Newton was merely turning this around in describing Christ as her 'husband'. Such language is unfashionable today, and so we tend to sing of Christ as our 'brother' rather than as our husband. Such a shift in meaning may well say as much about changes in attitude to marriage as about the understanding of this doctrine of the Church!

Other titles for Jesus abound in that verse. We sing of Jesus as shepherd, echoing Psalm 23 and the parable of the lost sheep (Luke 15:3–7). Jesus is our friend, as in John 15:15 ('I do not call you servants... I have called you friends'), and he is our king. The idea of Jesus as prophet is not so common within Christianity, and presumably recognizes the fact that Jesus comes after the great line of prophets, headed by John the Baptist. It was not in Newton's mind, of course, but it tends to be Islam that speaks of Christ as a prophet, but for Christians that is not sufficient. These other titles are very necessary for the man we believe to be the Son of God, Saviour of the World. Thus, Newton reminds us that Jesus is the 'way' and the 'life', surely echoing: 'I am the way, and the truth, and the life. No one comes to the Father except through me' (John 14:6). Jesus is also Lord (the title used so often of him in the New Testament), and finally is described as the 'end', the finishing point (*telos* in Greek). The last book of the Bible also reminds us that 'I am the Alpha and the Omega, the first and the last, the beginning and the end' (Revelation 22:13; also 1:8 and 21:6). In all, ten names are given for Jesus, and all in one praise-packed verse!

Alexander Reinagle was organist at St Peter's Church in Oxford, and the tune St Peter (named after the church) comes from his *Psalm Tunes for the Voice and the Pianoforte*, composed in 1830. The sweetness of the tune is certainly appropriate, and its straightforward melodic line is easily learned and remembered. The tune can easily be used for other sets of words, but is so wedded to these that it is best reserved for Newton's hymn.

Newton was a musician as well as a hymn writer and one hymn tune he wrote (Wonders) survives today as a setting of words by Samuel Davies (1723–61), but is seldom sung. The words of 'How sweet the name' show a sensitivity to music, firstly because they are all about the 'sound' of Jesus' name—to hear his name is a joyful thing. Secondly, we notice that in the final verse all is summed up in the description of Jesus' name as being like music to our ears, refreshing our soul in life and in death. The music of heaven, no doubt, will consist largely of songs of praise to Jesus and the Lamb!

O Lord Jesus Christ, friend of sinners and shepherd of our souls, soothe our sorrows, heal our wounds, and drive away all our fears, so that our lives may be filled with boundless stores of your grace and our hearts warmed by the thought of your love which you show to us each and every day. This we ask for the sake of your own dear name, Amen.

ALL PEOPLE THAT ON EARTH DO DWELL

✣

All people that on earth do dwell,
Sing to the Lord with cheerful voice;
Him serve with fear, his praise forth tell,
Come ye before him and rejoice.

The Lord, ye know, is God indeed,
Without our aid he did us make;
We are his folk, he doth us feed
And for his sheep he doth us take.

O enter then his gates with praise,
Approach with joy his courts unto;
Praise, laud, and bless his name always,
For it is seemly so to do.

For why? the Lord our God is good:
His mercy is for ever sure;
His truth at all times firmly stood,
And shall from age to age endure.

To Father, Son and Holy Ghost,
The God whom heaven and earth adore,
From men and from the angel host
Be praise and glory evermore.

WORDS: WILLIAM KETHE (D. 1594), PSALM 100 IN THE *ANGLO-GENEVAN PSALTER* OF 1561
TUNE: OLD HUNDREDTH, LOUIS BOURGEOIS (1510–61), *GENEVAN PSALTER*, 1551

In the year 959, King Edgar of Mercia and Northumbria also became king of Wessex, and soon appointed St Dunstan (909–88) to be Archbishop of Canterbury. Between them they reformed the affairs of church and state, including the rite of coronation, which was revised for Edgar's own coronation, which did not take place until 973. That same service has been used virtually unchanged since that date, save for obvious modifications necessitated by changing times. Hymns, poems and anthems have been composed by great British and Commonwealth composers through the ages, but the basic format of the service has remained unaltered for over a thousand years.

At Queen Elizabeth II's coronation in 1953, the eminent English composer Ralph Vaughan Williams (1872–1958) arranged this hymn with fanfares for choir, congregation and orchestra, and it received a splendid debut at that royal event. Ever since, the arrangement has been popular, and is often heard at festive occasions.

The Coronation Service (of which the coronation itself forms only a part) is a deeply spiritual and prayerful occasion, akin to an ordination. It was conceived in this way by Dunstan in the tenth century, and just as the words have hardly changed, neither has its deep spiritual significance been undermined.

For example, the first object that the new Queen was given in 1953 was the Bible. Passed through the hands of the Dean of Westminster and the Moderator of the Church of Scotland, the then Archbishop of Canterbury, Geoffrey Fisher, gave the Bible to the Queen with the words:

Our gracious Queen: to keep your Majesty ever mindful of the Law and the Gospel of God as the Rule for the whole life and government of Christian Princes, we present you with this Book, the most valuable thing that this world affords.

The sentiment that the word of God is the 'most valuable thing that this world affords' is an admirable one, which reminds us of the authority of scripture and its centrality to human life, revealing 'all things necessary for salvation'.

Enthronement and the swearing of oaths of allegiance followed, all being accompanied by sumptuous choral music by Redford, Gibbons,

Byrd, Samuel Sebastian Wesley and the Canadian composer Healey Willan. Then followed 'All people', as the offertory hymn accompanying the presentation of the gifts for communion. Vaughan Williams' lovely anthem 'O taste and see' was also used that day.

Before landing up at the coronation in 1953 (and still being sung today), the hymn, which is a metrical setting of Psalm 100, had an even longer liturgical history. The words themselves take us well back into Jewish temple worship, and they also have an English history under the title 'Jubilate'. The tune is as old as Kethe's words, but was not originally placed with them. In the French language edition of the *Genevan Psalter* of 1551, the tune which has become known as the OLD HUNDREDTH (as in the 100th Psalm) was originally set to Psalm 134. The composer Louis Bourgeois was a Parisian based in Geneva who contributed several tunes to the *Genevan Psalter*.

Psalm 100, the Jubilate, is a hymn of praise found in the fourth section of the Psalter (Psalms 90—106), and concludes a series of seven psalms which extol the kingship of Yahweh. The Psalm is titled as a 'Song of Thanksgiving', and even without a majestic tune such as the OLD HUNDREDTH, the joyful nature of the text is plain to see. Vaughan Williams' fanfares reflect the 'joyful noise' of the Psalm's opening line (the fourth line of this metrical version), as the Psalmist is bidding the gathered assembly to hail the Lord God as king.

Verse two draws on the translation of Miles Coverdale (1488–1568) which is largely preserved in the 1662 *Book of Common Prayer*: 'It is he that hath made us and not we ourselves'. Other, modern translations want to say that the Hebrew really means, 'It is he that has made us and we are his'. The hymn's 'Without our aid he did us make' errs towards the former. Either way, the sentiment is clear: God made us, and so to him we owe praise and thanksgiving.

There is a poignancy to these lines when they are read in an age that has witnessed the cloning of Dolly the sheep, and which may proceed further. *We* are God's flock, his folk, and he created us, and did so 'without our aid'. It is so easy to forget that we are creatures, not creators. We can create marvellous music and art, but we ourselves are made by God. If we have children, we are pro-creating, creating with God. We are involved in a creative process, and it is not just down to us if new life is produced. As society pushes the boundaries of medical technology, we must keep reminding ourselves that life is God's gift to us, and that it is he that made us, and not we ourselves.

As we would expect, Psalm 100 does not conclude with a doxology as the hymn does. It was not added by Kethe, but by the Methodist Church, for whom this was a popular hymn to sing when someone was converted to Christ.

William Kethe is one of our earliest hymn writers, and it is significant to notice that he wrote 'All people that on earth doe dwell' (his spelling) in Geneva, where he fled during the reign of the Roman Catholic Queen Mary (1553–58). In that period, Archbishop Cranmer, Bishops Ridley and Latimer and countless others were burned for their Protestant reforms perpetrated by and under Henry VIII (1491–1547), the main crimes of which consisted in the rejection of the Pope's authority and the use of the vernacular English in worship and scripture. Kethe, a Scot, went to Geneva where John Calvin (1509–64) was based, and while there, in 1561, he produced a book of Metrical Psalms entitled *Fourscore and seven psalms of David*. It was published in London almost simultaneously with *The Genevan Psalter*. Kethe's text reveals his Protestant leanings. For example, in the very first line we have 'all people that on earth', whereas the Psalm does not have this phrase, and even Coverdale's translation has 'lands' rather than 'people'. But surreptitiously, Kethe is welcoming all comers to the profession of faith and the expression of praise. 'All people' is inclusive language, which invites everyone to enter the courts of God, not only the clergy. We may not feel the need to make this distinction today, but we must remind ourselves of a period when the role of clergy, their material and spiritual powers and their necessity were all under debate. And those who found themselves on the wrong side of that debate, in the wrong place at the wrong time, went to the stake. In a manner of speaking, Kethe was sticking his neck out here as he advocated a religion for all, a people's faith.

Still today, this hymn, although perhaps old-fashioned in its language, is an all-embracing clarion call to praise. Just as the Psalmist bid the people to praise God with thanksgiving, so today we are called to the same worship of the same God. And still today, that invitation to worship and praise is one that is issued to all people, by and on behalf of God.

O God our creator, let all the world come before you in praise and thanksgiving, for we are your people and you are our God. You alone are good and gracious to your people, and your promises of mercy and salvation stand from one generation to another. To you be praise and glory, Father, Son and Holy Spirit, now and for ever, Amen.

CITY OF GOD

✤

City of God, how broad and far
Outspread thy walls sublime!
The true thy chartered freemen are
Of every age and clime.

One holy Church, one army strong,
One steadfast, high intent;
One working band, one harvest-song,
One King omnipotent.

How purely hath thy speech come down
From man's primeval youth!
How grandly hath thine empire grown
Of freedom, love and truth!

How gleam thy watch-fires through the night
With never-fainting ray!
How rise thy towers, serene and bright,
To meet the dawning day!

In vain the surge's angry shock,
In vain the drifting sands:
Unharmed upon the eternal Rock
The eternal City stands.

WORDS: SAMUEL JOHNSON (1822–82)

TUNE: RICHMOND, THOMAS HAWEIS (1734–1820), HARMONIZED BY SAMUEL WEBBE THE YOUNGER
(C.1770–1843)

❖

The Livery Companies of the City of London have a tradition dating back to a time even before the Norman Conquest of 1066. Other European cities also had guilds, known sometimes as 'mysteries' (from the Latin *mysterium* which means 'professional skill'). In London, the particular crafts and trades tended to live and operate near to one another, so that streets became named after them. Milk Street, Wood Street and Poultry are still to be found in the heart of the City of London today.

In the Middle Ages much of England's trade was controlled and supervised from London, where guilds established themselves. The Worshipful Company of Weavers is the oldest, with a Royal Charter dating from 1155. In some sense the Liveries (who began as guilds) operated monopolies in their particular trades, but in so doing they ensured quality control and acted as a kind of early trade union for their members. They imposed fines for bad work, and held tribunals in their halls, where they also met socially. The guilds also looked after the sick and needy, providing almshouses, and each had its own church, chaplain and patron saint. Each guild was distinctive in its dress, or livery, hence the name now in use of 'Livery Companies'.

To become a member of a guild, an apprenticeship had to be served. A special contract, known as an 'indenture', was signed by a member of the guild and the apprentices, who committed themselves to a period of service. Afterwards, they gained their freedom, enabling them to serve any master or become independent. Without this 'freedom', they could not operate in the City. Even today men and women become Freemen of the City of London, and to join a Livery Company the Freedom of the City is a prerequisite.

Today there are many more Livery Companies than the original 'great twelve', which include the Goldsmiths, Fishmongers, Mercers, Grocers and Drapers. Each has a long tradition and is very proud of its history, and still to this day the Merchant Taylors and the Skinners cannot decide which of them is older. They fought over their precedence, and in 1515 the Lord Mayor of London intervened, and declared that they should alternate annually as sixth and seventh in importance. Thus we have the origin of the phrase 'at sixes and sevens', meaning not to know where you stand.

The rivalries of trade are less formal now, and the Liveries now represent a great tradition, exerting a qualitative influence, defining the best of their respective trades. The Worshipful Companies serve other functions too, including, significantly, the raising of money for charity. Some, such as the Coopers, Merchant Taylors and Haberdashers, are still very much involved with educational trusts, and schools still bear their name.

It has to be acknowledged that not everyone admires these traditions, just as some people are deeply suspicious of the hymn 'City of God'. The hymn makes no mention of Christ, and seems to be extolling the virtues of power and influence exerted by a ruling élite. For some, the City of London represents that élite, many of whom work within its square mile. The link between the City of God and the City of London need not be couched in uncharitable terms, though, and both the hymn and the financial heart of London can take on spiritual significance.

The American Samuel Johnson, who wrote the words, was a fairly unorthodox man who refused to ally himself with any denomination and whose beliefs might well have made him more of a Unitarian, as he did not accept the doctrine of the Trinity, nor the divinity of Christ! The hymn was written while he was visiting Nice, in the south of France, and was first published in 1864 in a liberal-minded hymn book called *Hymns of the Spirit*. He is not to be confused with the Samuel Johnson of English literature (1709–84), who wrote a great dictionary and, with James Boswell (1740–95), travelled widely.

Just as some Christians have difficulty reconciling the holding of extreme wealth or power with the faith of Jesus, who had no place to call home, there is a case for having qualms about this hymn. But in both cases, we are presented with a reality that we wish to turn for good, rather than ignoring or abolishing it. The traditions of the City of London make it wealthy and influential, but it is surely the call of every Christian to steward the resources of wealth for the good of those in need and for the furtherance of the kingdom of God. A bit of money can be very useful in this regard!

Similarly, there are no words of this hymn that are heretical or offensive to the Christian faith. There are various ways to understand the 'city of God', even if they are not quite what Johnson may have had in mind. It seems that he is advocating a society in which all are free and equal (he was a campaigner for the abolition of slavery), and in which all look to a universal God as advocate of 'freedom, love and truth'. It is not clear in the hymn what that truth might be, but if we sing it as Christians, we bring our own values to it, and there is nothing in the hymn that a Christian cannot or should not sing.

When we think of Johnson's quasi-Unitarian doctrinal stance, we can remember with irony the origin of the phrase 'city of God'. The city of God is Jerusalem, the site of the temple, the heart of the Jewish faith, and it is also heaven: 'I will write... the name of the city of my God, the new Jerusalem that comes down from my God out of heaven' (Revelation 3:12). Later, St John the Divine sees heaven as 'the holy city, the new Jerusalem, coming down out of heaven from God' (Revelation 21:2). When we sing 'City of God', we can think of the 'eternal city' as the new Jerusalem, which emerges after the tribulations in the apocalyptic literature of the Bible.

We might also be reminded of *City of God*, written in 410 by St Augustine of Hippo (354–430) after the fall of Rome. The foundations of that eternal, yet complacent city were shaken, and shockwaves went around the world, and some believed that the catastrophe was due to the abolition of heathen worship in Christianized Rome. *City of God* is a reply to this claim, and is the first attempt at a Christian philosophy of history, using the idea of two rival cities, the eternal city of God and the declining city of the world.

The hymn 'City of God' can speak directly to those who live or work in commercialized cities. Its language is urban, and is all too poignant in the light of the destruction of the World Trade Center in September 2001. 'How rise thy towers, serene and bright' made me stop and think when we sang it in St Paul's Cathedral six days after that tragic event (I had selected it many weeks earlier), and yet there is a resilience in the final verse: 'in vain the surge's angry shock': the City stands 'unharmed upon the eternal Rock'.

Our hymns are changed by the contexts in which they are sung, often surprising those who wrote them. 'City of God' may well have been intended by Johnson to espouse a radical cause of some sort, but, now combined with a popular tune, it has found its way into the realms of civic, Christian worship. Long may it stay there, pointing us to that eternal city of God to which we all aspire, and of which we are all freewomen and freemen, yet still apprenticed in the service of our Lord and Saviour Jesus Christ.

Father in heaven, who has prepared for us a place in the eternal city, help us to further your kingdom on earth, that in the midst of the wealth and poverty of our society, your word of truth, freedom and love may be heard far and wide, and the faith of your Church remain unharmed upon the rock of our salvation, Jesus Christ our Lord, Amen.

COME O THOU TRAVELLER UNKNOWN

✣

Come O thou Traveller unknown,
Whom still I hold but cannot see!
My company before is gone,
And I am left alone with thee;
With thee all night I mean to stay,
And wrestle till the break of day.

I need not tell thee who I am,
My misery and sin declare;
Thyself hast called me by my name;
Look on thy hands and read it there:
But who, I ask thee, who art thou?
Tell me thy name and tell me now.

In vain thou strugglest to get free;
I never will unloose my hold!
Art thou the man that died for me?
The secret of thy love unfold:
Wrestling, I will not let thee go
Till I thy name, thy nature know.

Yield to me now; for I am weak,
But confident in self-despair;
Speak to my heart, in blessings speak,
Be conquered by my instant prayer;
Speak, or thou never hence shalt move,
And tell me if thy name is Love.

'Tis Love! 'Tis Love! Thou diedst for me!
I hear thy whisper in my heart;
The morning breaks, the shadows flee,
Pure universal love thou art;
To me, to all, thy mercies move:
Thy nature and thy name is Love.

WORDS: CHARLES WESLEY (1707–88)

TUNE: WRESTLING JACOB, SAMUEL SEBASTIAN WESLEY (1810–76)

DAVID'S HARP, ROBERT KING (1676–1713)

✣

This hymn, like 'O God of Bethel' (p. 72), is based on a story in the life of Jacob. Jacob was a deceitful patriarch, who began his dubious early career by conning his brother Esau out of his birthright as eldest son by exchanging it for a bowl of lentil stew (Genesis 25:29–34). Esau was annoyed at the trick, of course, but becomes more enraged when Jacob plays a similar trick on their father Isaac (see 'O God of Bethel'). Esau is dispossessed and, according to his mother Rebekah, wants to kill Jacob. Jacob flees and, on the way, encounters God in a dream at Bethel.

Jacob moves on from Bethel, marries the daughters of his Uncle Laban, Leah and Rachel, and, after various disputes with his father-in-law about sheep, leaves with his family and heads for Canaan. Rachel, Jacob's favourite wife, steals the family idols, and Laban pursues them. Laban doesn't find the idols, they all make their peace and Jacob and his family proceed on their journey.

In order to get to Canaan, though, Jacob is faced with the prospect of encountering Esau once more. He sends ahead to tell Esau he is coming, but Esau sends four hundred men to meet him. Jacob is afraid, sends presents to Esau, and sends his family to safety across the Jabbok river. It is at this point in Jacob's life, as he awaits his enemy brother, that the hymn picks up the story.

While Jacob waits alone, a stranger wrestles with him and injures him, dislocating his hip—but the stranger cannot overcome him. Jacob asks his name and demands his blessing. The stranger asks Jacob's name in return, and Jacob tells him, but the stranger will not reveal his own name. Jacob is now to be called Israel, which means 'he strives with God'. Jacob is now convinced that he has seen God 'face to face'. He has seen God and lived—a fearful prospect. He names the place 'Peniel', which means 'the face of God' (Genesis 32:22–31).

Wesley's hymn is about far more than this encounter, although it takes the meeting as its spiritual base. A pre-Christian understanding of God finds any real encounter frightening. Yet in Christ, humanity has seen God face to face, and we are all promised that day when 'we will be like him, for we will see him as he is' (1 John 3:2). Seeing the face of God is not something we think of as life-threatening, nor do we often think of our journey of faith as a wrestling match.

And yet, on our earthly pilgrimages, just as on Jacob's, there are or will be times when we do wrestle—wrestle with our faith, even wrestle with God. And we certainly wrestle with our families and colleagues from time to time. Conflict is, for better or worse, an inevitable part of all of our lives, but while it can be damaging, it can also be creative. For Jacob, it was both.

He was damaged in the hip-socket, although not seriously enough to stop him living to the ripe old age of 147! And, out of his wrestling, there was the creation of Israel, not just the new name for the new man but the new name for the nation of Israel, the children of Israel—the Jewish race.

We all have our struggles, and it is these to which the Methodist pioneer Charles Wesley was alluding when he wrote:

> *I need not tell thee who I am,*
> *My misery and sin declare;*
> *Thyself hast called me by my name…*

The wrestling of Jacob with God is overturned and Wesley Christianizes the event: we do not need to tell God who we are because he knows us intimately, and therefore knows of our weakness, our occasional despair, and our constant sin. The wrestler here—you or I, perhaps—seeks God's blessing, which is the prize. It cannot be won or earned, it must be given, and that is why this hymn has an imploring tone. We might wrestle for days, but ultimately the blessing must be given, not stolen or won; nor for Jacob can it be conned out of the Other.

But the Christian slant on the story is emphasized for Wesley by its denouement. In a creative juxtaposition of Old and New Testaments, we, the wrestler, do not need to reveal our name, but God does reveal the name of Love. In Jacob's story, it is the other way around—God remains ineffable, unknowable—but after Christ, God is known, as Love. This is the mystery of God revealed, for if we struggle with faith, God reveals his Son, who by nature and name is love.

The original version of Wesley's hymn contains twelve verses, the last four of which move us away from Jacob's story, referring directly to Jesus as Saviour, as 'Sun of Righteousness', and specifically associating Jesus with the stranger who wrestled Jacob. Verse 9 contains:

> *I know thee, Saviour, who thou art,*
> *Jesus the feeble sinner's friend.*

Verse 10 reminds us of Charles Wesley's 'Hark the herald angels sing':

> *The Sun of righteousness on me*
> *Has risen with healing in his wings.*

And the final verse 12 concludes with a positive response that has moved us on from the weary Jacob:

> *Lame as I am, I take the prey,*
> *Hell, earth and sin with ease o'ercome;*
> *I leap for joy, pursue my way,*
> *And as a bounding hart fly home,*
> *Through all eternity to prove*
> *Thy nature and thy name is Love.*

It is a shame that this hymn is not better known, and it is missing from some notable hymn books. Samuel Sebastian Wesley's tune kept the hymn in the family, for he was the son of Samuel Wesley, the son of Charles Wesley, who wrote the words. Samuel Sebastian never knew his grandfather Charles, who is best known in church circles, with his brother John, as a founder of Methodism. To musicians, S.S. Wesley is probably the best known of the family. For this reason alone it makes sense to prefer his tune, which was written for these words. Some editors prefer DAVID'S HARP, by Robert King, about whom we know very little. There is some question as to when King died, although we do know that he was awarded a Cambridge Bachelor of Music degree in 1696.

Either tune will do, for in a way neither can do justice to the poetry and vision of the words. It is sometimes said that a good poem makes a bad song, and that what a really good songwriter needs is some mundane words which can be raised by good music. Charles Wesley's 'Come O thou Traveller unknown' stands alone as poetry, and it is those words that speak of the inspiration and reward to be had in faith. Even if that faith be hard, it is those words that best reward our humble grapplings.

O God, whose strength is supreme and whose name is love, guide us on our journey as we encounter danger, doubt or despair, and reveal to us your loving nature as we wrestle with the world around us. Protect us and our loved ones, that as we lamely walk in your ways, we may meet you in your crucified Son, and leap for joy at the call of your Holy Name, for the sake of the same, Jesus Christ our Lord, Amen.

AMAZING GRACE

✤

Amazing grace! How sweet the sound
That saved a wretch like me.
I once was lost but now am found,
Was blind but now I see.

'Twas grace that taught my heart to fear,
And grace my fears relieved.
How precious did that grace appear
The hour I first believed!

Through many dangers, toils and snares
I have already come.
'Tis grace hath brought me safe thus far,
And grace will lead me home.

The Lord has promised good to me:
His word my hope secures.
He will my shield and portion be
As long as life endures.

Yea, when this flesh and heart shall fail,
And mortal life shall cease,
I shall possess, within the veil,
A life of joy and peace.

The earth shall soon dissolve like snow,
The sun forbear to shine;
But God, Who called me here below,
Shall be forever mine.

When we've been there ten thousand years,
Bright shining as the sun,
We've no less days to sing God's praise
Than when we'd first begun.

Words: John Newton (1725–1807) and others
Tune: Amazing Grace, Scottish/American traditional

✣

It can be so easy to see the life of faith as a progressive journey towards eternal life. We talk so often of a journey of faith, holding to the idea that our life on earth is some kind of voyage towards a heaven over the horizon. We know it is there but we cannot see it. So often we come across this kind of image in those pithy texts that appear on those cards we send to encourage one another, such as 'Lord, the ocean is so vast and my boat is so small'. There is also a passage of prose attributed to the Canadian Bishop Brent, but possibly borrowed from *Toilers of the Sea* by Victor Hugo (1802–85), which reads:

A ship sails and I stand watching till she fades on the horizon and someone at my side says, 'She is gone.' Gone where? Gone from my sight, that is all; she is just as large as when I saw her. The diminished size and total loss of sight is in me, not in her, and just at the moment when someone at my side says 'She is gone', there are others who are watching her coming, and other voices take up the glad shout, 'There she comes', and that is dying.

It is a passage which many find comforting, and which is often read at funerals. Another similar passage begins, 'Sometime at eve, when the tide is low, I shall slip my moorings and sail away'. In all these cases, we encounter the idea that life is like a sea journey ending in a safe port, which is the haven of heaven. The idea is derived from St Paul, who writes: 'As for me, I am already being poured out as a libation, and the time of my departure has come. I have fought the good fight, I have finished the race, I have kept the faith' (2 Timothy 4:6–7).

Mythology and Christianity are rich in 'death-as-journey' imagery and descriptions of earthly life as a journey before a journey. In ancient Greek culture the final journey to Hades involved a crossing of the river Styx, ferried by Charon, the mythical boatman.

In spite of all this, we must not be misled into considering the life of faith as some kind of simple linear progression. Most of us have ups and downs, times when we are more faithful than at other times, times when the path seems smooth, and other times when it is very rough. Sometimes on our 'journey' we may feel that we have slipped back, or even that we *want* to go back. The journey of life, if we call it that, is not a neat progression from A to B, and we often find that not only are we unable to take short cuts, but that some of the detours we take prove to be long and tortuous. The journey of faith is a narrow and winding way.

The journey motif is strong in 'Amazing grace', which is one of the most famous hymns ever written, and is still very much a favourite on both sides of the Atlantic. It was written after a voyage across that very ocean, a journey which was to change John Newton's life.

Newton's adult journey began at age 11 when he found himself in the Navy, following in his father's footsteps. He fled the Navy in 1746, was flogged for it, and for over a year was virtually a slave in Africa. In 1747 he became a slave trader himself, plying the route between Britain, Africa and the West Indies. It was while crossing the Atlantic in 1750 that Newton's journey took a new course, turned around in a serious storm that had his slave ship mercilessly tossed in the waves. Newton was terrified and found himself calling to God for help, so much so that when the storm had abated, and from the safety and distance of a few years later, he was convinced that the beginnings of his conversion experience had happened on that deck amid the stormy blasts of wind and rain.

'Amazing grace' is certainly his most famous hymn, and it is the one most associated with his tempestuous early life and conversion. It has been translated into many languages, among them Afrikaans, Cherokee, Choctaw, Creek, Kiowa and Navajo. The first four verses speak directly and personally of Newton's experiences on that beleaguered slave-ship, while the fifth verse moves him and us on to a vision of that safe haven where storms shall cease and all is joy and peace. The last two verses printed here are almost certainly not by Newton, admirable as they are.

The tune for 'Amazing grace' is an American traditional melody, which probably originated in Scotland. There are many slightly different versions of it, and it has been used to set many other words, including a version of the Magnificat. The most general confusion over the tune concerns the use of triplets (three notes together on one syllable), so that some people will sing three notes on the end of 'amazing', and others will sing two. Both versions seem to hold sway, which can create an unsatisfactory effect when the hymn is sung by a congregation! In a way, this confusion points to the diversity of the Christian life, for while we all strive to 'sing from the same hymn sheet', we all do so in our subtly different ways. But whichever way we sing it, the intention to praise God and the truth of the message we proclaim are unaffected by the imperfections and diversities of our offering. For we are all pilgrims on a journey which may or may not have begun with a conversion experience as tempestuous as Newton's, and only when we reach our final, heavenly destination will the praise of God be perfect and unified.

O God by whose amazing grace we are created, sustained and redeemed, we give you thanks for the earthly life we enjoy, and for the privilege of being your people. Lead us in the paths of righteousness, and as we progress through life, bless us with discernment, wisdom and compassion, so that our eyes may be always open to your light, for the sake of our Saviour Jesus Christ, Amen.

MINE EYES HAVE SEEN THE GLORY

✤

Mine eyes have seen the glory of the coming of the Lord:
He is trampling out the vintage where the grapes of wrath are stored;
He hath loosed the fateful lightning of his terrible swift sword:
His truth is marching on.

Glory, glory, hallelujah! Glory, glory, hallelujah!
Glory, glory, hallelujah! His truth is marching on!

I have seen him in the watch-fires of a hundred circling camps;
They have builded him an altar in the evening dews and damps;
I can read his righteous sentence by the dim and flaring lamps:
His day is marching on.

He has sounded forth the trumpet that shall never sound retreat;
He is sifting out the hearts of men before his judgment seat;
O, be swift, my soul, to answer him, be jubilant, my feet!
Our God is marching on.

In the beauty of the lilies Christ was born across the sea,
With a glory in his bosom that transfigures you and me:
As He died to make men holy, let us live to make men free,
While God is marching on.

WORDS: JULIA WARD HOWE (1819–1910)

TUNE: BATTLE HYMN OF THE REPUBLIC ('JOHN BROWN'S BODY'), AMERICAN TRADITIONAL

On Tuesday 11 September 2001 most of the clergy of the City of London and Hackney areas of the Diocese of London were in Oxford on a conference, entitled 'Urban ministry at a time of change'. The three-day conference had begun on the Monday, and on the afternoon of the Tuesday we all had some free time to explore Oxford. At about 2.15 in the afternoon, I was browsing in a second-hand bookshop (as you do in Oxford) when I overheard on the radio that two planes had crashed into the World Trade Center in New York.

The unfolding of the events that followed hardly needs retelling, but they did signal the beginning of a very moving and hectic few days for me personally. When I returned to London the following day, the similarities between Wall Street and the City of London had already subdued the City, and by lunch-time it had been decided to hold a large-scale service in St Paul's Cathedral on the Friday. So with less than 48 hours to go, we sat down to plan what was to become 'A Service of Remembrance with the American Community in London'. The Cathedral is accustomed to planning large services: in the last few years we had done the Millennium Service for England and the Queen Mother's 100th birthday service. The service to mark the Queen's Golden Jubilee had by then (nine months in advance) been virtually sorted out, and of course various contingency plans were safely in place for occasions of national importance that could be anticipated.

But no one had, nor could they have, anticipated the events of the previous day, and so we sat down with a blank piece of paper on which to do a year's work in one day—to draft readings, hymns and music that might help to express or alleviate some of the intense feelings of confusion, pain, grief and doubt that many were feeling.

The planning group included Cathedral clergy, musicians, and US Embassy representatives. It was agreed to begin the service with the American National Anthem and conclude with 'God save the Queen'. A symbolic candle-lighting would follow the American anthem, then silence, and the choir would sing 'Hear my prayer, O Lord', a setting by Henry Purcell (1659–95) of the first verse of Psalm 61. The Dean would welcome the congregation and the Lord's Prayer would be said, followed by the singing of that great Welsh hymn, 'Immortal, invisible'. It was anticipated that the American ambassador would read the first reading, which was chosen as Isaiah 61:1–4, with verse 11 added; and the Duke of Edinburgh would read the second reading. The Queen would also be attending. Romans 8:31–39 was suggested, and it was agreed that Psalm 23 be sung by the choir. In virtue of its simplicity and flowing melodies, the version by the French Roman Catholic priest Joseph Gellineau (b. 1920) was preferred. The choir would also sing Edgar Bainton's 'And I saw a new heaven', a most beautiful setting of words from Revelation 21. The sermon was to be preached by Dr George Carey, the Archbishop of Canterbury, while the prayers were to be written that afternoon. The printers, Barnard and Westwood, had already promised a proof copy for checking by midnight. The oil in the wheels of St Paul's had been liberally applied, and all was running smoothly.

One of the hardest decisions concerned the final hymn, over which we took a risk that not everyone thought wise (but which, we believe, was right). The question was how to end such an event, which was attended inside and out by ten thousand British and American people. Some wanted 'America the beautiful', which is a fine hymn, and works tremendously well at the Annual Thanksgiving Day service held in the Cathedral each year. But there was also a feeling that after such tragedy, even though it was so close at hand, there had to be a note of hope—even an uplifting end. And that is why we chose, and stuck with, 'Mine eyes have seen the glory of the coming of the Lord'.

The Americanness of this hymn is hardly in doubt. Julia Ward Howe was a lay preacher, appropriately from New York. Her husband was a doctor who campaigned against slavery, and who knew the man called John Brown on whom the famous folk song was based. John Brown was executed in Virginia for his anti-slavery activities. Julia Ward Howe was an admirer of the tune of the folk song, and in 1861 took up a suggestion to write alternative words for it. When it was first published the following year, Julia Ward Howe was paid only four dollars. It had also gained the title 'The Battle Hymn of the Republic'.

The biblical allusions of the hymn are specific. The opening line resonates with Simeon's song in the temple:

> *Master, now you are dismissing your servant in peace,*
> *according to your word;*
> *for my eyes have seen your salvation,*

which you have prepared in the presence of all peoples,
a light for revelation to the Gentiles
and for glory to your people Israel.
LUKE 2:29–32

The second line of the hymn refers to the 'grapes of wrath' found in Isaiah:

'Why are your robes red, and your garments like theirs who tread the wine press?'
'I have trodden the wine press alone, and from the peoples no one was with me; I trod them in my anger and trampled them in my wrath; their juice spattered on my garments, and stained all my robes.'
ISAIAH 63:2–3

The 'lightning swift sword' sounds like the sword guarding the Garden of Eden after Adam and Eve are evicted (Genesis 3:24), and in a less-popular verse there is a reference to the crushing of the serpent in Genesis 3:15:

I have read a fiery gospel, writ in burnished rows of steel;
As ye deal with my contemners, so with you my grace shall deal:
Let the hero born of woman crush the serpent with his heel…

The rather unusual description of Christ being born amid the 'beauty of the lilies' actually derives from the Song of Songs, where twice is written 'he pastures his flock among the lilies' (Song of Songs 2:16; 6:3). We may also be reminded of Christ's words: 'And why do you worry about clothing? Consider the lilies of the field, how they grow; they neither toil nor spin, yet I tell you, even Solomon in all his glory was not clothed like one of these' (Matthew 6:28–29).

The hymn is bold and uplifting, although it may be accused of being a bit militaristic in virtue of its origins in the American Civil War, and its march-like style. It may have been a controversial choice in the midst of the fear and grief of those early days after the carnage of the World Trade Center's collapse. Yet it speaks of hope, of Christ winning through, and of his return. The version printed here is as we used it in St Paul's on Friday 14 September 2001. It incorporates a frequently made, small but significant change in the last verse. In the original, fighting version the penultimate line reads, 'Let us die to make men free'. Nowadays we want to sing, 'Let us *live* to make men [all people] free', and that seemed most of all appropriate on that unique occasion in London, when all eyes were tearfully filled with the images of burning tower blocks and rubble, and yet desperately seeking to look heaven-ward in hope for their loved ones missing, and for the future of the world, which had just entered a new era.

O God, in whom we trust, in whom we invest our confusions and our hopes, our life and our death, hear our cries of disbelief and pain as we reflect upon the hardness of evil hearts, and the insufferable pain and shock of grief. Grant that in the midst of death, there may be life; in despair, hope; in danger, safety; in fear, assurance; and in agony, comfort. This we ask for the sake of your broken, risen Son, Jesus Christ our Lord, Amen.

THE DAY THOU GAVEST, LORD, IS ENDED

✣

The day thou gavest, Lord, is ended,
The darkness falls at thy behest;
To thee our morning hymns ascended,
Thy praise shall sanctify our rest.

We thank thee that thy Church unsleeping,
While earth rolls onward into light,
Through all the world her watch is keeping,
And rests not now by day or night.

As o'er each continent and island
The dawn leads on another day,
The voice of prayer is never silent,
Nor dies the strain of praise away.

The sun that bids us rest is waking
Our brethren 'neath the western sky,
And hour by hour fresh lips are making
Thy wondrous doings heard on high.

So be it, Lord; thy throne shall never,
Like earth's proud empires, pass away;
Thy Kingdom stands, and grows for ever,
Till all thy creatures own thy sway.

WORDS: JOHN ELLERTON (1826–93)
TUNE: ST CLEMENT, CLEMENT SCHOLEFIELD (1839–1904)

John Ellerton wrote this missionary hymn in 1870, and it immediately found its way into a number of Victorian hymn books. For many it is an archetypal evening hymn, and is often used at funerals, because it is easy to think of our brief lives as a metaphorical day; and as the hymn speaks of God's people spread out across the world, it also reminds us of the family of God stretching both forward and backward in time.

In 1897, Queen Victoria (1819–1901) chose this hymn to be used at the celebrations of her Diamond Jubilee, when it was sung in thousands of churches on 20 June of that year. At that time, the British Empire was at the height of its power, and indeed it was an empire proudly created and maintained.

And yet, this is a hymn that speaks of the missionary work of the Church, and which serves to remind those who sing it, today as then, that the ultimate empire is God's kingdom, of which we, and our brothers and sisters across the seas, are a part. And in that kingdom of God, both above and below, in darkness and in light, God's praise is ceaseless. As we turn in after evening praises (having also praised God in the morning), others are waking in distant lands to offer their praises. And indeed it is literally true: on a Sunday, for instance, we can certainly envisage a service finishing in the evening in New Zealand just as we in Britain are waking to go to church. In the winter, 6.30 in the evening in London is 7.30 in the morning of the next day in Auckland, while 'at the same time', the morning worship in Dallas is coming to an end, and the morning service in Vancouver is just beginning. This phenomenon is largely a product of human resourcefulness in response to night and day, but it has a wider, more profound impact when we consider the vast distances and the differences of culture, language and climate involved. And in each one, says Ellerton, our Lord is praised. That is comfort to us, and glory to God.

As each day passes, Ellerton reminds us, the earth does not sleep, and people somewhere are watching with God hour by hour. The hymn rolls onward towards the bright light of the main truth it seeks to express—which is that, no matter how proud we may be of the fact that God's praise is sung in some corner of the world that is for ever British, the material power of a human empire will always be superseded by God's kingdom. Whatever may come of the castles and kingdoms we build on the sand that covers this earth, there is only one kingdom of God, which is constant. It is towards that kingdom that the climax of this hymn points.

There is a sense in this hymn of time and history rolling on, but with purpose. Into that context we place all human power, all our joys and all our disappointments. The tune that is almost universally used, St Clement, conveys the sentiments of this hymn superbly, and has the added advantage of being both memorable and eminently singable. Scholefield is known for hardly any other tune, there are few tunes that could be used instead, and Ellerton's words fall into a 9.8.9.8 metre, which is very rare. These words and music are made for each other, and as the music rises and falls in waves, we can picture our 'brethren 'neath the western sky' singing the very same hymn, perhaps to the same tune. These days, pop songs and sporting anthems travel the globe and unite groups, and it was little different at the time of Queen Victoria's Jubilee—although without the internet and worldwide television rights, the process did take a little longer!

The tune is so singable because it relies on a musical pattern that is simple, and repeated, and, of course, of great beauty. The first and third lines of each verse are set to the same musical phrase. The fourth line echoes the second but brings us back home, whereas the second line takes us to the halfway resting place of the dominant chord of the scale. Thus midway there is repose, but it brings us straight back to restate the first line of the tune again. Because of this, a relaxed satisfaction is reached at the end of each verse as we feel the tune going where we have already half-expected it to go. This is the stuff of classic hymn tunes, both in its form and in its beauty. Such music certainly does 'sanctify our rest', and is most fitting at the end of Evensong, or some other evening worship.

This hymn is neither quiet nor gentle, neither rousing nor strident, and yet it seems to be made up of a little of each of these moods. The last verse can rise above the others as we sing of proud empires and God's kingdom, but at the same time the hymn has to descend into silence: it can hardly be sung as the opening hymn in a service, for it is so hard to follow. There is an irony here, of course, for just as the hymn speaks of God's praise never falling silent, the hymn does very firmly close at the end. We stop, but others take up the tune in another part of the world, yet under the same sky. Thus the praise of God never ends.

The day you have given us, Lord, is over, and the night draws in. We thank you that your Church is ever awake, and all the world over, your people are always watching the hours with you. As dawn breaks in each corner of the world, and a new day begins, wake us all to the joys of your eternal kingdom, so that on the last day, when heaven and earth pass away, we with all creation shall be redeemed by your saving love, Amen.

FIGHT THE GOOD FIGHT

✥

Fight the good fight with all thy might,
Christ is thy strength, and Christ thy right;
Lay hold on life, and it shall be
Thy joy and crown eternally.

Run the straight race through God's good grace,
Lift up thine eyes, and seek his face;
Life with its way before us lies,
Christ is the path, and Christ the prize.

Cast care aside, upon thy Guide
Lean, and his mercy will provide;
Lean, and the trusting soul shall prove
Christ is its life, and Christ its love.

Faint not nor fear, his arms are near,
He changeth not, and thou art dear;
Only believe, and thou shalt see
That Christ is all in all to thee.

WORDS: JOHN SAMUEL BEWLEY MONSELL (1811–75)

TUNE: DUKE STREET, ATTRIBUTED TO JOHN HATTON (D. 1793)

RUSHFORD, HENRY LEY (1887–1962)

PENTECOST, WILLIAM BOYD (1847–1928)

SHEPTON-BEAUCHAMP, ENGLISH TRADITIONAL MELODY, ARR. RALPH VAUGHAN WILLIAMS (1872–1958)

✥

Some people are deterred from this hymn by its opening line, which is misleading. This is not a hymn about battle, and nor is it as inappropriate for a wedding as modern humour would have it! It is all about setting Christ before us as our helper, the goal towards whom we strive, and in whose help we trust.

The first line gives us a clue as to the hymn's true origin, which is to be found in 2 Timothy:

As for me, I am already being poured out as a libation, and the time of my departure has come. I have fought the good fight, I have finished the race, I have kept the faith. From now on there is reserved for me the crown of righteousness, which the Lord, the righteous judge, will give me on that day, and not only to me but also to all who have longed for his appearing.
2 TIMOTHY 4:6–8

Parts of the hymn quote more directly from the New Testament. In the first verse we also recognize 'Fight the good fight of the faith; take hold of the eternal life' (1 Timothy 6:12). In the second verse we may recognize 'I press on toward the goal for the prize of the heavenly call of God in Christ Jesus' (Philippians 3:14) and 'Let us also lay aside every weight and the sin that clings so closely, and let us run with perseverance the race that is set before us' (Hebrews 12:1), which echoes 'Do you not know that in a race the runners all compete, but only one receives the prize?' (1 Corinthians 9:24). The prize is Christ, whose face we seek: '"Come," my heart says, "seek his face!" Your face, Lord, do I seek' (Psalm 27:8).

In the third verse, we encounter St Peter's advice: 'Cast all your anxiety on him, because he cares for you' (1 Peter 5:7), and are advised to 'lean' on the Lord just as the Israelites did in time of trouble: 'On that day the remnant of Israel and the survivors of the house of Jacob will no more lean on the one who struck them, but will lean on the Lord, the Holy One of Israel' (Isaiah 10:20).

In the last verse of this short hymn, we find resonances of the last things and of the fear that comes from doubt: 'People will faint from fear and foreboding of what is coming upon the world, for the powers of the heavens will be shaken' (Luke 21:26). The runner of the race may grow faint from exertion, but the everlasting arms of Christ are ready to support the weary spirit, now and always, for 'Jesus Christ is the same yesterday and today and for ever' (Hebrews 13:8). Finally, if we have faith, we realize that in Christ 'there is no longer Greek and Jew, circumcised and uncircumcised, barbarian, Scythian, slave and free; but Christ is all and in all!' (Colossians 3:11).

From the many quotations on which this hymn draws, we can see that it is a very rich text indeed. John Monsell, its writer, was an Anglican priest of Irish birth, who was Vicar of Egham in Surrey from 1853 to 1870, and then Vicar of the parish of St Nicholas in Guildford. He was tragically killed there in 1875, when he fell from the church roof while inspecting repair work.

The text of the hymn first appeared in *Love and Praise for the Church Year*, published in 1863, and it was subtitled 'The fight for faith'. Monsell was an advocate of strong, vibrant congregational singing, and encouraged it among his congregations. As with other hymns, and with St Paul's writings, the idea of fighting is metaphorical, but for Monsell it went hand in hand with uplifting, morale-boosting singing.

DUKE STREET, the tune that is most commonly used for the hymn, would probably have met with Monsell's approval. It is a straight-forward tune, mostly moving one note at a time, except that it concludes with a climax that enhances the phrases 'thy joy and crown', 'Christ is the path', 'Christ is its life' and 'That Christ is all'. The hymn is all about Christ, and both words and music emphasize this. Little is known of composer John Hatton, not even his date of birth, although he is thought to have come from St Helens, then in Lancashire. The tune was originally set to Psalm 19 in a Scottish Psalter of 1793.

There are other tunes which are sometimes used for this hymn, but they are not so successful. Shepton-Beauchamp is an English traditional melody notated by Cecil Sharp (1859–1924) and adapted by Vaughan Williams for these words in 1906. PENTECOST is a rather plain tune, originally composed for the words of 'Come Holy Ghost'; Sir Arthur Sullivan (1842–1900) used it for 'Fight the good fight' when editing *Church Hymns*. The composer of PENTECOST, William Boyd, was rather taken aback to find that his tune had been so allied with these words, for even he thought the match was unsuitable, but he seemed to change his mind later. As he wrote in the *Musical Times* of 1908: 'When I saw the tune I was horrified to find that Sullivan had assigned it to "Fight the good fight"! We had a regular fisticuffs about it, but judging from the favour with which the tune has been received, I feel that Sullivan was right in so mating words and music.'

English use has not borne out the partnership, but the pairing is still popular in North America, and it is rather amusing to imagine two Victorian hymnologists fighting about which tune 'Fight the good fight' should be sung to!

Henry Ley's RUSHFORD is the preferred tune in the *New English Hymnal* of 1986. One of the quirks of that hymn book was to introduce new tunes for familiar hymns and realign the well-known tune as a 'second' tune, and this is what happened to DUKE STREET in relation to 'Fight the good fight'. In the *New English Hymnal*, DUKE STREET is assigned to 'Pour out thy Spirit from on high', a hymn specially intended for the ordination of priests. By comparison, RUSHFORD is quite a complex tune, written in D flat major, and it includes some unusual harmonies. It is not particularly easy to learn, and it has not usurped DUKE STREET as was perhaps intended.

The message of the hymn, for all its possible tunes and multiple quotations, is fairly clear: pursue a Christ-centred life, live for him, and you will gain the crown of eternity. By God's grace we can pursue a holy life, looking ever before us to the way in which Christ leads us, and if we trust in him in the course of our lives, he will care for us as he always has done, and will continue to do so. Christ is everything to us, our life, our faith, our hope.

Be our guide, O Father, as we run the course of our lives, and help us to follow the path of your Son Jesus Christ, so that whether we run with confidence, or faint with fear, we may always believe and trust in him, and that by the grace of your Holy Spirit we may at the last attain the prize of everlasting life which you promise us in the same, Jesus Christ our Lord, Amen.

COME, YE THANKFUL PEOPLE, COME

❖

Come, ye thankful people, come,
Raise the song of harvest home!
All be safely gathered in,
Ere the winter storms begin;
God, our maker, doth provide
For our wants to be supplied:
Come to God's own temple, come;
Raise the song of harvest home!

We ourselves are God's own field,
Fruit unto His praise to yield;
Wheat and tares together sown,
Unto joy or sorrow grown;
First the blade and then the ear,
Then the full corn shall appear:
Grant, O harvest Lord, that we
Wholesome grain and pure may be.

For the Lord our God shall come,
And shall take His harvest home,
From His fields shall purge away
All that doth offend, that day,
Give His angels charge at last
In the fire the tares to cast,
But the fruitful ears to store
In His garner evermore.

Then, thou Church triumphant, come,
Raise the song of harvest home;
All be safely gathered in,
Free from sorrow, free from sin,
There for ever purified
In God's garner to abide:
Come, ten thousand angels, come,
Raise the glorious harvest home!

WORDS: HENRY ALFORD (1810–71)

MUSIC: GEORGE ELVEY (1816–93)

⊹

Harvest is traditionally a time of thanksgiving and rejoicing, and a time for taking stock, both literally and metaphorically. We rejoice in the gifts of creation, arable and animal, and we celebrate the God-given privilege and ability that we have to steward the resources of the planet. We give thanks for good harvests, for healthy beasts and good weather, all of which are prayed for in churches in the spring, at Rogationtide. We have reaped the crops sown months back, and at harvest time (which can fall between late July and late October!), we come with those who farm, as thankful people, to sing the song of harvest-home.

In recent years there has been cause for some gloom as we feel so close upon us the distress, despair and death brought by problems of infection and disease. British agriculture has suffered cruelly from problems over BSE and Foot and Mouth Disease. We cannot, nor should we, avoid or deny the real difficulties of diseases that have tormented and haunted the farming community, and continue to do so.

As we take stock mentally and emotionally, we reflect upon the passage of time. As another harvest, another season, passes, time and the world have moved on, and some crops that were sown in times of hope may later be harvested in doubt, confusion or fear. While the seeds have germinated and grown, the earth has turned, and for many it may have turned in the wrong direction. The crops have emerged and matured in a world in which they were not sown.

It is easy for us to take the fruits of the harvest for granted. It is just as easy to fail to notice disease in advance. Thus, when we think of the farming community at harvest time, we must remember some of the hardships that have been experienced in that industry over the last few years. Farmers have suffered a great deal, at cost of money, security, family relationships, sometimes even loss of life, as some farmers, equipped with the resources to do so, have taken their own lives when faced with bankruptcy and loss of livelihood. England's green and pleasant land has seen much tragedy these last few years. Farmers, families and livestock have all suffered. The bell still tolls for the animals killed and the farmers affected.

And yet we must not, and need not, despair. The poet and former Dean of St Paul's, John Donne (1571–1631) famously wrote, 'No man is an Iland, intire of itselfe'. No one is independent of the events that take place around us. Whether we are farmer or city dweller, we stand united in common humanity with those who have suffered. As Donne wrote, 'Any mans death diminishes me, because I am involved in Mankinde; And therefore never send to know for whom the bell tolls; It tolls for thee.' The language may be old-fashioned, but the sentiments are timeless.

Whichever way the world turns, for better or worse, we are involved in and with each other, and God in Christ is truly involved in and with us. All the world is God's own field: our Creator provides for us, but in Christ our God stands with us if and when we suffer. Our sowing and reaping, our hoping and fearing, are all known intimately by God, whose Spirit dwells in and with us whether we rejoice or lament.

Sometimes at harvest time we have cause for both, but also have cause to remember that it is the same Spirit of God that brings new life and hope even where there has been death and despair. Even if the year has been gloomy, we truly can give thanks to God as we reflect on his renewing power to give us the hope of a better world, here and hereafter.

This archetypal harvest hymn points us forward to God's harvest, as well as the harvest of crops before the winter sets in. It draws upon two of Christ's parables, the story of the wheat in the midst of which weeds are sown (Matthew 13:24–30), and also the story of the seed that grows unbeknown to the sower (Mark 4:26–29).

In the first of these two parables, a sower sows good seed in his field, but in the night an enemy strews weeds. Both kinds are allowed to grow up, until, like the sheep and the goats, they are separated in the end. In the second story, we hear of a sower who is amazed at how seeds grow, for they do so without intervention, according to an unseen plan. At the end, the sickle is raised and the harvest gathered in. Both agricultural parables are about the ultimate harvest, the harvesting of souls, a future event which has found its way into popular modern mythology in the form of the Grim Reaper. The reality, of course, is that in the end-time, God will gather together his own in the heavenly harvest, and it is this spiritual harvest-home to which Henry Alford refers in the last verse.

Alford, an Anglican clergyman, wrote the hymn in 1844 and altered it a few times, and the hymn also underwent extensive revision when it appeared in *Hymns Ancient and Modern* in 1861. The version here is as it appears in the *New English Hymnal*, but there is an alternative version of the final verse which reads:

> *Even so, Lord, quickly come;*
> *Bring thy final harvest home:*
> *Gather thou thy people in,*
> *Free from sorrow, free from sin;*
> *There for ever purified,*
> *In thy garner to abide:*
> *Come, with all thine angels, come,*
> *Raise the glorious harvest-home.*

In either case, we see a combining of the physical realities of gathered crops and harsh climate with the spiritual realities of heaven. The allusions to the two parables express thanks for material provision and the wonder of creation, seed-time and harvest, with an acknowledgment of God as creator, sustainer and redeemer of the whole world.

In one sense this is not a harvest hymn at all, as it is not really so much about giving thanks for safely harvested crops as about the eternal hope of heaven, brought about when God, the sower of the word in Christ, reaps the harvest of faithful souls. In that sense it is not relevant whether the material value of a harvest is good or bad, for when the Lord comes he will draw the world to himself and purge sin and suffering. In the meantime, however, it is right and proper to give thanks for the gifts of the earth and for the skills and dedication of those who steward them on behalf of all of us and to the glory of God. It is also right and good to stand beside them when their calling becomes a difficult one, for we are united with them in the task of earthly stewardship, and our gratitude to them is united with our gratitude to God, who through their labours sustains us.

O God our maker, we confess our failure to share the fruit of the earth with those in need. We remember before you all those places too numerous to name where hunger and poverty are the staple diet of your people. Forgive us, O God, for thinking of ourselves more than others and for consuming too much too readily. Hear our prayers for those who work in agriculture: provide for them, as they provide for us, and unite us all in the vision of that day when you gather all your people together, free from sorrow and sin, to dwell with you, Father, Son and Holy Spirit, now and evermore, Amen.

JUST AS I AM

✤

Just as I am, without one plea
But that thy blood was shed for me,
And that thou bidd'st me come to thee,
O Lamb of God, I come.

Just as I am, though tossed about
With many a conflict, many a doubt,
Fightings within, and fears without,
O Lamb of God, I come.

Just as I am, poor, wretched, blind;
Sight, riches, healing of the mind,
Yea all I need, in thee to find,
O Lamb of God, I come.

Just as I am, thou wilt receive,
Wilt welcome, pardon, cleanse, relieve:
Because thy promise I believe,
O Lamb of God, I come.

Just as I am (thy love unknown
Has broken every barrier down),
Now to be thine, yea thine alone,
O Lamb of God, I come.

Just as I am, of that free love
The breadth, length, depth and height to prove,
Here for a season then above,
O Lamb of God, I come.

WORDS: CHARLOTTE ELLIOTT (1789–1871)

TUNE: SAFFRON WALDEN, ARTHUR HENRY BROWN (1830–1926)

✣

The late 18th century was a time of revolution and change. 1789, the year of hymn writer Charlotte Elliott's birth, saw the French Revolution, yet at the same time another kind of revolution was taking place in ecclesiastical circles in England. Henry Venn (1725–97), Vicar of Huddersfield from 1759 to 1771, began what has become known as the evangelical revival in England. Following in the wake of the Wesley brothers, Venn was one of the founding fathers of a group known as the Clapham Sect. As well as being instrumental in the campaign to abolish slavery, led by William Wilberforce (1759–1833), parishioners and clergy of Clapham Church also founded the Church Missionary Society (CMS) and the British and Foreign Bible Society. Henry's son, John Venn (1759–1813), became Vicar of Clapham in 1792. Both Henry and John were relatives of Charlotte Elliott: Henry was her maternal grandfather, and John was her uncle.

The young Charlotte was a good poet, but her wit, talent and musical ability brought her into contact with some adventurous people, of whom her family disapproved. In 1821, when she was 32, she suffered a nervous breakdown. A crisis of faith followed, during which time she met a Swiss pastor, Henri Abraham César Malan (1787–1864) who, when she asked him how she could be saved, told her that to come to Jesus, she should 'just come to him as you are'.

Charlotte suffered for the rest of her long life, and it was a surprise to herself as well as everyone else that she outlived her brother Henry Venn Elliott (also a vicar) and her sister Eleanor. She had bouts of depression, and in modern terms may well have suffered from schizo-phrenia. Even as a permanent invalid, she was deeply committed to Christ, but could find little outlet for her fervour other than by writing poems and hymns. In 1834 she published *The Invalid's Hymn Book*, in which 'Just as I am' is to be found.

Another collection, *Hours of Sorrow Cheered and Comforted*, published in 1836, opened with a quotation from John Keble (1792–1866), the Anglo-Catholic author of many hymns:

> *The world's a room of sickness, where each heart*
> *Knows its own anguish and unrest;*
> *The truest wisdom there, and noblest art*
> *Is his whose skills of comfort best.*

Of her own condition, Charlotte Elliott wrote: 'My Heavenly Father knows, and he alone, what it is, day after day, and hour after hour, to fight against bodily feelings of almost overpowering weakness and languor and exhaustion.'

Like Keble's collection of hymns, written by a churchman whose perspective was so far apart yet so close to her own, Charlotte's hymn books were very popular and were reprinted many times. 'Just as I am' is probably her most famous hymn, and is deeply personal.

The opening verse states the theme of the hymn—the sinner approaching Jesus at his own invitation. Just as Malan had instructed her, Elliott passes on the wisdom that the best and only way to approach the merciful throne of God's grace revealed in Christ is 'just as I am'. Each verse begins with this half-line, and every verse concludes with 'O Lamb of God, I come', which, in a style characteristic of her poetry, is shorter than the other lines, adding emphasis. With her, we approach God, solely by virtue of Christ's redeeming work wrought on the cross.

There is a second verse that is rarely sung today, but which speaks very much of Elliott's desire to be saved and made clean by the blood of Christ:

> *Just as I am, and waiting not*
> *To rid my soul of one dark blot,*
> *To Thee whose blood can cleanse each spot,*
> *O Lamb of God, I come.*

Blemishes in ourselves can be washed away by his blood, as can doubts, fears, spiritual poverty and blindness, as mentioned in the other verses. With the final exclamation ending each verse of the hymn, there is a temporary release from these admittedly negative feelings. The final verse is special, turning as it does to the 'free love' of Christ, which opens the way to freedom in heaven, leaving the singer to express the anticipated and guaranteed joys of heaven above.

In all this, the poet is laying her burdens at Christ's feet. Jesus, the 'Lamb of God' (John 1:29, 36) helps those who come to him: 'Come to me, all you that are weary and are carrying heavy burdens, and I will give you rest' (Matthew 11:28). Charlotte Elliott knew these words from the Communion Service in the *Book of Common Prayer*, in which, after the words of absolution, the priest recites the 'comfortable words' —passages of scripture designed to reassure the communicant that 'all who truly repent' receive genuine forgiveness of their sins. Moments later the priest and people say, 'We are not worthy so much as to gather up the crumbs from under thy table.' This hymn therefore has eucharistic overtones which vibrate with the idea that in Christ's offering we are made whole, no matter how spiritually or physically sick we may be. Ultimately, 'all have sinned and fall short of the glory of God' (Romans 3:23), and thus Charlotte Elliott's own illness becomes a metaphor representing the sinful sickness of all humanity. In the more modern communion services, another phrase is added, which reminds us of the Roman centurion's words to Jesus when he seeks healing for his servant: 'Lord, I am not worthy to receive you, but only say the word and I shall be healed' (see Matthew 8:8).

In a day and age when lines of churchmanship are often drawn according to one's attitude to the eucharist, Charlotte Elliott's words are refreshingly inclusive. For her, as for John Keble, the eucharist is central as a memorial of salvation. Keble was an Anglo-Catholic, as was the writer of the tune SAFFRON WALDEN, which is the most popular tune for the hymn today. Arthur Brown, the composer, was a church organist in Essex and was a member of the London Gregorian Association, which used to meet for an annual service in St Paul's Cathedral, for which Brown prepared the service booklet each year. In this much he was a key figure in the English plainsong revival of the 19th century. He wrote some 800 hymn tunes and choral works.

Brown was also a keen supporter of John Keble's 'Oxford Movement'. In 'Just as I am', therefore, the Clapham Sect and the Oxford Movement join hands. The former focused on personal commitment to Christ and good works, while the latter was keen to provide a liturgical and spiritual alternative to the Roman Catholic Church, legalized in 1829, and wanted to preserve the apostolic succession of the Church of England. William Wilberforce, already mentioned, was a keen supporter of both the Oxford Movement and the Clapham group.

In 'Just as I am' many unlikely paths meet, but they all point to Christ. Barriers are breached, and through the words of an evangelical lady and the music of an Anglo-Catholic man we are reminded of the singular, unique journey to salvation which we all tread, in sickness and in health.

O Lamb of God, to whom we come for healing and relief, break down the barriers of sin and division that wound your Church, and give to all your people the comfort of your grace and the power of your Spirit to convince us of the breadth, length, height and depth of your everlasting love, given just for us, Amen.

JERUSALEM

❖

And did those feet in ancient time
Walk upon England's mountains green?
And was the holy Lamb of God
On England's pleasant pastures seen?
And did the countenance divine
Shine forth upon our clouded hills?
And was Jerusalem builded here
Among those dark satanic mills?

Bring me my bow of burning gold!
Bring me my arrows of desire!
Bring me my spear! O clouds, unfold!
Bring me my chariot of fire!
I will not cease from mental fight,
Nor shall my sword sleep in my hand,
till we have built Jerusalem
In England's green and pleasant land.

WORDS: WILLIAM BLAKE (1757–1827)

MUSIC: JERUSALEM, CHARLES HUBERT HASTINGS PARRY (1848–1918)

❖

'Jerusalem' is better known by the name of its tune, rather than by its first line. It is a fine tune, eminently singable, world famous and invariably associated with the Victorian Britain of its composer. For some, this is not a hymn because it is not addressed to God, nor is it really about God, and it has such a jingoistic feel to it that it ranks barely above 'Land of hope and glory' as a community song, hardly redeemed by Blake's rather suspect reference to the 'holy Lamb of God'. After singing it, some are tempted to mutter under their breath, 'No', as the little-doubted answer to the question raised by Blake in the first verse. No, Jesus did not walk in the green fields of England, and neither were they very pleasant in those days; and neither is England described as being very pleasant in the poem, as part of the country is described as being under Satan's influence.

Practising Christians can get wound up by this 'hymn' and take umbrage. The second verse, with its warlike imagery, can offend, even though the reference to a 'chariot of fire' comes from the account of Elijah being taken up in a whirlwind (2 Kings 2:11). Ironically, those who are more traditionally minded may dispute the cry for social justice found in this hymn, whereas those who are less nationalistic despise the song for its popularity among the more conservative-minded. Because 'Jerusalem' is so popular, it is unpopular.

'Jerusalem', words and music, then, cannot win. And yet it is known by just about everyone, many of whom can sing it off by heart. You can't keep a good tune down, even though there have been attempts within the hymn-singing community to apply Parry's stupendous tune to different words. Michael Perry (b. 1942) has written a paraphrase of Psalms 149 and 150, beginning 'Bring to the Lord a glad new song', but no matter how good a pedigree the words have, they don't stand a chance in the face of 'And did those feet in ancient time'. It is not a case of good or bad, better or worse: JERUSALEM wouldn't be JERUSALEM without Blake's words, and Blake's words wouldn't be the same without JERUSALEM. When the Poet Laureate Robert Bridges (1844–1930) asked Parry to set the words in 1915, he made an unbreakable match. The tune alone makes the words ring in our heads, and it would be very hard to make other words override their resonances and associations.

Parry himself was a noted English composer, the son of Thomas Gambier Parry (1816–88), who had been responsible for the painting of the nave roof of Ely Cathedral. As well as being one of the most prolific composers of his age, he was also a fine athlete, a fact which may or may not have influenced the producers of that Oscar-winning film *Chariots of Fire*, whose soundtrack owes so much to this very hymn.

The hymn itself was composed, at Bridges' suggestion, for a meeting of the women's suffrage group 'Fight for the Right' held at the Queen's Hall in London in 1916, and Parry himself conducted it again in early 1918 at the Royal Albert Hall, at a meeting which brought the suffrage campaign to a climax. British women won the right to vote in 1918, and the Women's Institute adopted the song as their anthem. Thus the words and music entered the British psyche, where they are still firmly embedded for better or worse.

Whatever we think of the words, and whatever we make of William Blake's rather unorthodox theology, the words do originate in and speak of the kind of social action and reform which, many years after their composition, led to the achievement of women's suffrage in February 1918. Blake, who was also a painter (like Parry's father), was the son of a London hosier. At 14 he was apprenticed to become an engraver. By 1783, when Blake was 26, his poetry was also being recognized, and in 1789 he published *Songs of Innocence*, a collection of gentle poems. In a poem entitled 'Holy Thursday' he writes of 'the children walking two and two in red and blue and green', of 'thousands of little boys and girls' like 'multitudes of lambs'. A touching, quaint, even idyllic picture of London children is painted, both in words and in the engravings that accompanied the poems. Yet five years later, he wrote *Songs of Experience*, a complementary, biting, satirical companion volume, in which, in a poem with the same title, Blake describes 'babes reduced to misery, fed with cold and usurious hand'. Can this be a holy land? The pastoral innocence of the world in which we like to believe we live is contrasted sharply with the adult world in which, in W.B. Yeats' words, 'the ceremony of innocence is drowned'. Blake's provocation of social action is plain to see.

Blake's theological perspectives were distinctive: publications such as *All Religions are One* and *There is No Natural Religion*, both dating around 1788, suggest a certain unorthodoxy, and some works around 1795 are openly critical of Christianity. In 1804, however, he wrote a long poem entitled *Milton: A Poem in two Books, To justify the ways of God to Men*, in which he sets out to improve upon Milton's vision expressed in *Paradise Lost*. In a section where Milton is seen to return to earth to change his mind, the words we now sing appear: 'And did those feet...' The words are subtitled with a quotation from the book of Numbers: 'But Moses said to him, "Are you jealous for my sake? Would that all the Lord's people were prophets, and that the Lord would put his spirit on them!"' (Numbers 11:29).

Blake perhaps saw himself as some kind of prophet, and in the verses of the hymn there is indeed a hint of prophecy which appealed not only to Parry but to the women seeking their emancipation in the early part of the 20th century. Blake hints at a desire to build the heavenly city, Jerusalem, the city of God, in England. As with 'innocence' and 'experience', there is a juxtaposition of the idyllic beauty of the 'pleasant pastures' over against the 'satanic' developments of industrialization. Good and evil dwell together—they may even be interdependent—but Blake has a vision to bring social reformation zeal to his native land.

The text is a mental call to arms, the new Jerusalem is a vision for the future, and although it draws upon the spurious myth that Jesus travelled with Joseph of Arimathea to England, it appeals to the thought that England might become what it once was, a land of milk and honey where peace and justice reign supreme, to the glory of God. We could hardly argue with that, except to acknowledge that no land has ever been that, and that there is plenty to do before anywhere can make that claim. This was Blake's point, and we can only admire his desire to see it happen.

Of Blake's influence there is no doubt. Poets and politicians read his work, and once Parry had written that soaring, elegant, rumbustious tune that opens and concludes so grandly, then the English took his words to heart, albeit perhaps without knowing their origin or their context. But to identify their visionary, inspirational nature is not difficult—not so difficult, certainly, as to identify the theological value of their meaning.

'Jerusalem' is something of an enigma, then, for ultimately we may be ambivalent about the words and wary of the tune, yet gain tremendous enjoyment from singing both. Ultimately we should be reminded of the vision of making the world a better place, and whenever and wherever we sing it, we must be sure to be singing of a better world brought about by and in Christ. The holy Lamb of God did not walk in bodily form on England's pleasant land, but the Spirit of God is abroad and the body of Christ present in every land, and we all await that day when Christ shall come again to redeem us and the very soil on which we walk. And until that day, we all work for and sing of a better world, here and hereafter.

O God, whose Son walked this world and reclaimed it for you, grant to this and every land, church and state, leaders of vision and integrity, through whom your kingdom may be brought near, that as your people struggle for justice and freedom, we may all be inspired to love our neighbours as ourselves, for the sake of the same, Jesus Christ our Lord, Amen.

ETERNAL FATHER, STRONG TO SAVE

✣

Eternal Father, strong to save,
Whose arm doth bind the restless wave,
Who bidd'st the mighty ocean deep
Its own appointed limits keep:
O hear us when we cry to thee
For those in peril on the sea.

O Saviour, whose almighty word
The winds and waves submissive heard
Who walkedst on the foaming deep,
And calm amid its rage didst sleep:
O hear us when we cry to thee
For those in peril on the sea.

O sacred Spirit, who didst brood
Upon the chaos dark and rude
Who bad'st its angry tumult cease
And gavest light and life and peace:
O hear us when we cry to thee
For those in peril on the sea.

O Trinity of love and power,
Our brethren shield in danger's hour
From rock and tempest, fire and foe

Protect them wheresoe'er they go;
And ever let there rise to thee
Glad hymns of praise from land and sea.

Words: William Whiting (1825–78)
Tune: Melita, John Bacchus Dykes (1823–76)

✤

This is the seafarers' hymn, sung without fail at every religious gathering of seafarers. In the second week of October of every year, the National Service for Seafarers takes place at St Paul's Cathedral, and the thought of this hymn not being sung would horrify many. At that service, young and old, Sea Cadets and retired Merchant Navy seamen, join together in worship, celebration of and prayer for the seafaring community.

Seafarers worldwide are ministered to by various Christian charities, among them the Anglican Missions to Seafarers (formerly the Missions to Seamen), the British Sailors Society (Free Churches), the Apostleship of the Sea (Roman Catholic), the Mission to Deep Sea Fishermen, and the Naval Chaplaincies, all of whom work together. Anyone who has had any association with any of these organizations will testify to the importance of their work. Even today, most of what we need, consume and enjoy is brought to us on a ship. There are ships plying the seas all the time, and it used to be said that one went down every day. As the hymn describes, the angry tumult of the sea can be very dangerous, and the power of creation unleashed in a storm at sea can be terrifying. Modern ships are stronger and bigger than they used to be, but they are still vulnerable. Large oil tankers can take several miles to turn around, and in a storm things can go badly wrong.

Many people will remember the terrible sinking of the Russian submarine *Kursk* on 12 August 2000 with the loss of all the crew. Such spectacular disasters at sea raise public awareness of the dangers of seafaring, as do stories of modern piracy, which is now one of the greatest dangers at sea. Ships are robbed and their crews threatened, attacked or even murdered daily.

I once worked as a lay chaplain at Seaham Harbour in County Durham. The coal-mining community has been very dependent upon the sea, and knows of the great traditions and the great tragedy that the sea can bring. On 17 November 1962 a local fishing boat, the *Economy*, got into trouble, and eight men and an eight-year-old boy died when the lifeboat was launched to rescue them. Only one man survived. What had begun as a simple day's fishing turned tragic when the weather behaved unpredictably, the fishermen got into trouble and summoned the lifeboat. On their way back into harbour, in the dark and in increasingly heavy seas, nine lives were lost in a few minutes as both boats were lost. Such incidents strike at the heart of seafaring communities, and are long remembered. They also serve to illustrate how little control we have over the great forces of sea and wind, and how quickly things can go wrong.

The Bible has plenty to tell us about the sea, from the beginnings of creation to the shipwrecks that St Paul endured. Jonah has a bad experience when he is thrown overboard by sailors who think he has caused a storm, and the prophet Isaiah writes of 'God, who stirs up the sea so that its waves roar' (Isaiah 51:15).

Psalm 107 describes those who go 'down to the sea in ships', who 'saw the deeds of the Lord, his wondrous works in the deep. For he commanded and raised the stormy wind, which lifted up the waves of the sea. They mounted up to heaven, they went down to the depths; their courage melted away in their calamity; they reeled and staggered like drunkards, and were at their wits' end' (Psalm 107:23–27).

St Paul also experiences danger at sea:

But soon a violent wind, called the northeaster, rushed down from Crete. Since the ship was caught and could not be turned head-on into the wind, we gave way to it and were driven... we were scarcely able to get the ship's boat under control... We were being pounded by the storm so violently that on the next day they began to throw the cargo overboard, and on the third day with their own hands they threw the ship's tackle overboard. When neither sun nor stars appeared for many days, and no small tempest raged, all hope of our being saved was at last abandoned.

Acts 27:14–20

St Paul is saved, as are the sailors in the Psalm, but there is no doubt who their saviour is: 'Then they cried to the Lord in their trouble, and he brought them out from their distress; he made the storm be still, and the waves of the sea were hushed' (Psalm 107:28–29).

Jesus has some watery experiences too. We find him walking on the water immediately after having performed the miracle with the loaves and fishes (Matthew 14:22–33), and earlier there is the calming of the storm during which 'a windstorm arose on the sea, so great that the boat was being swamped by the waves' (Matthew 8:24). Afraid of the storm, the disciples wake the sleeping Jesus. Jesus' reproach to them, that they are of 'little faith', seems a little harsh, as they had every reason to be afraid of the sea—Peter and James and John were fishermen who knew and lived from the sea. To underline their faithlessness, and to emphasize that 'even the winds and the sea obey him' (Matthew 8:27), Jesus calms the storm. It is these 'almighty words' of our saviour to which the hymn refers in the second verse.

The hymn is Trinitarian in structure. In the first verse we address the Father, the Creator, who appointed the limits of sea and land. Then in verse two we address Jesus, performer of those two nautical miracles, and in the third verse we address the Spirit, who 'moved upon the waters' at creation (Genesis 1:2). In the final verse we address all three together as powerful protector of all who are at sea, physically or spiritually!

William Whiting had surprisingly few maritime connections, and it is said that he wrote the hymn in 1860 for a boy at Winchester College whom he knew, and who was to sail to America. The words were revised more than once, thereby accounting for discrepancies and even disagreements over some lines, but it is Whiting's 1869 version that appears here.

There are adaptations that appear on both sides of the Atlantic, including one by Robert Nelson Spencer containing the splendidly appalling lines, 'O Christ the Lord of hill and plain / O'er which our traffic runs amain', and, 'Save all who dare the eagle's flight / and keep them by thy watchful care / from every peril in the air'. The final line of this arrangement reveals an all-encompassing agenda—'glad praise from space, air, land, and sea'. It is a nice idea, but no seafarer will applaud such a wholesale hijacking of this, the sailor's hymn.

The tune MELITA, by J.B. Dykes, is named after the haven that St Paul reached after being shipwrecked, for Malta was once known as Melita (see Acts 28:1). The tune is also used for a hymn about St George, which begins, 'Lord God of hosts, within whose hand / Dominion rests on sea and land'. The sentiments are similar, but 'Eternal father' surely holds its premier loyalty. MELITA is a 'storming' tune, brought to its best in brass band arrangements. It will always be associated by many with sailors, and so will keep them in the prayers of those who can so easily forget 'those in peril on the sea'.

Eternal father, we hold before you all who sail the seas. Be with them and guard them in danger, temptation and loneliness, and uphold them when sick, sad or afraid. Bless those who care for them, and guide us all to your heavenly haven, through Jesus Christ our Lord, Amen.

GUIDE ME, O THOU GREAT REDEEMER

✢

Guide me, O thou great Redeemer,
Pilgrim through this barren land;
I am weak, but thou art mighty,
Hold me with thy powerful hand:
Bread of heaven,
Feed me till I want no more.

Open now the crystal fountain
Whence the healing streams doth flow;
Let the fire and cloudy pillar
Lead me all my journey through:
Strong deliverer,
Be thou still my strength and shield.

When I tread the verge of Jordan,
Bid my anxious fears subside;
Death of death, and hell's destruction
Land me safe on Canaan's side:
Songs of praises
I will ever give to thee.

WORDS: WILLIAM WILLIAMS (1717–91), TRANS. PETER WILLIAMS (1727–96) AND OTHERS
TUNE: CWM RHONDDA, JOHN HUGHES (1873–1932)

✢

The City of London is thought of by many people as the place to go to make money. And most people who make money in the City do so by getting involved with stocks and shares, or banking. But the City of London is also the domain of the sandwich. In and around those famous streets of the City, with their wonderfully holy names, like Creed Lane, Sermon Lane, Paternoster Row and Amen Corner, there is a wealth of sandwich shops, all serving the thousands who work in the City. Even the supermarkets devote a considerable amount of shelf space to sandwiches of all shapes and sizes, a positively postmodern plethora of variety and choice that confounds the untutored tongue.

And not only can you have the humble British beef sarnie, invented by John Montagu, the 4th Earl of Sandwich (1718–92), who ate nothing else while gambling in 1762. There are also baps, bagels, baguettes, wraps and ciabatta to choose from. And if you are still wary of British beef, you can have almost any filling—avocado, prawns, pastrami, or any one of a number of Swiss cheeses. The choice is immense, and you can have something different every day of the week —which, of course, is what the numerous sandwich shops want you to do, and that's how they make lots of money in the City.

But the sandwich, despite its dubious beginnings in an 18th-century casino, has seen service in the humblest and direst of situations. For, dress it up with whatever fancy fillings you may, it basically consists of our staple food, bread. In adversity, it is bread alone, perhaps with fat or butter. In prosperity, the bread flanks or is even dwarfed by a full meal tucked inside. But bread it is, and it would not be a sandwich if it were not made with bread.

In the trenches of the First World War, both sides ate bread, and perhaps little else. Welsh Guards sang of bread in the latest hymn composed by an official of the Great Western Railway named John Hughes. In that barren land of dirt and blood, they sang of the 'bread of heaven', of God their defender and shield, begging his protection and strength. They sang, 'Guide me, O thou great Jehovah' as it was originally entitled, and they sang so melodiously that it wasn't long before the German armies were singing it too.

The same bread—the same God, the same faith—was called upon and drawn upon amid the darkness of war and fear. And today, the same bread—the same God and the same faith—is drawn upon among the bright lights and computer terminals of the City of London and countless other cities and towns. For whatever we do to the bread of life, it remains itself. Even though it can be obscured by flavourings, garnishes and various breeds of lettuce, no triviality can prevent it being the bread of life.

But of course, we do surround our faith with triviality and with all kinds of dressings and paraphernalia that can affect the taste of the bread. Sometimes we have to look quite hard to find the faith buried underneath. And there are times when we may have to admit that we don't like the taste of bread very much, that we want to spice it up, because bread alone is quite boring. The basic bread and butter of our faith can be quite uninspiring sometimes, even tedious.

We may even want to say that bread alone is for those in adversity: raw faith is for those in extreme need, and most of us in the 21st-century Western world are not in that position. Instead we turn bread into a luxury item, sometimes disguising its true character, or even hiding it completely. Indeed many people today think of a religious or faithful life as being a luxury in itself.

But bread, as Jesus knew, has always been the staple of diet. Without it, you are dead. The Israelites in the wilderness had none, but God sent manna from heaven and thereby saved them. The words of the hymn make specific reference to this episode in Jewish history—the time when, during the Exodus, there was not enough food (Exodus 16). The 'bread of heaven' refers not only to Jesus as the 'bread of life' (John 6:48), but it is also the heavenly manna, and thus the connection is made in quite a subtle way. Inasmuch as we work this out for ourselves, this hymn has a teaching, explanatory purpose. Similarly, the 'healing stream' is the water from the rock (Exodus 17), but it is also the blood flowing from the crucified Christ, who is our strong deliverer, our redeemer. The 'fire and cloudy pillar' signify the presence of God guiding both Israelite and contemporary pilgrim as they, or we, approach the 'verge of Jordan'. And, as we approach the 'promised land', we realize that it is all made possible because Christ has gained victory over death:

> *Death of death, and hell's Destruction*
> *Land me safe on Canaan's side.*

Christ it is, then, who opens the way across the river and who brings us home. And 'home' is not just an eternal home, it is here also the realization of salvation brought about in Christ. This hymn has an evangelistic purpose, which it fulfils so well, not by stating the obvious but by subtle allusion, making us make the connections and thereby inspiring thought, reflection and conversion.

The staple food in our diet of faith, says the hymn, is our Lord Jesus Christ. Dress your bread of faith up as you will, but don't lose sight of the bread itself. The dressing and filling out of faith is not so important, but there must be living bread holding it all together.

For just as a sandwich without bread is not a sandwich, we can hardly speak of faith without reference and deference to Christ. The filling may be the tastiest part in the middle of a sandwich, but it is the bread that holds it all together. So it is with faith and life: whatever we fill our lives with, we need God, who creates, sustains and saves all things, to hold it all together in Jesus Christ our Lord.

O God our Father, who sent bread from heaven to feed and sustain your people, continue to nourish us in our faith, that we may continually feed on Christ the bread of life, ever mindful of your saving love shown in the same Jesus Christ our Lord, Amen.

CHRIST IS MADE THE SURE FOUNDATION

✤

Christ is made the sure foundation,
And the precious corner stone,
Who, the two walls underlying,
Bound in each, binds both in one,
Holy Zion's help for ever,
And her confidence alone.

All that dedicated city,
Dearly loved by God on high,
In exultant jubilation
Pours perpetual melody:
God the One in Threefold glory,
Singing everlastingly.

To this temple, where we call thee,
Come, O Lord of hosts, today;
With thy wonted loving-kindness,
Hear thy people as they pray;
And thy fullest benediction
She within its walls for ay.

Here vouchsafe to all thy servants
Gifts of grace by prayer to gain;
Here to have and hold for ever
Those good things their prayers obtain,
And hereafter in thy glory
With thy blessed ones to reign.

Laud and honour to the Father;
Laud and honour to the Son;
Laud and honour to the Spirit;
Ever Three and ever One:
One in love, and One in splendour,
While unending ages run. Amen.

WORDS: LATIN, CIRCA 7TH CENTURY, TRANS. JOHN MASON NEALE (1818–66)
MUSIC: WESTMINSTER ABBEY, HENRY PURCELL (1659–95)

✣

Henry Purcell was one of England's finest composers, and he devoted almost all of his relatively short life in the service of church music. He began his career as a chorister at the Chapel Royal, which was the official heart of regal music in London. His father was a lay clerk, or 'Gentleman of the Chapel Royal', and Purcell adopted his father's trade. The life of a chorister was not like it is at one of our major cathedrals today. Just up the road at St Paul's, choristers were accustomed to drinking large quantities of beer each day (London water was undrinkable), and often sang in taverns and playhouses as well as in church. Thus the young Henry would have had an interesting and varied education.

At 14 his voice probably broke and he became a tuner of organs and wind instruments at Westminster Abbey and other places. Eventually, in 1679, he became organist of Westminster Abbey, and then in 1682 he also became organist of the Chapel Royal. He took part in the coronations of James II and of William and Mary, at which both choirs sang. Like many musicians of his day (and thereafter) he occasionally fell out with the Dean and Chapter who administered the Abbey, but by the time of his untimely death his ecclesiastical superiors were keen to give him a free, stately funeral and a grave in Westminster Abbey, where he still lies buried.

Strangely, though, WESTMINSTER ABBEY is his only hymn tune, and it was not really written for that purpose. The tune to which we usually sing 'Christ is made the sure foundation' was so named because of Purcell's associations with the place, but it is actually taken from the final 'Alleluya' section of an anthem setting of the first verses of Psalm 62: 'O God, thou art my God, early will I seek thee'. The rhythm of the anthem music has been smoothed out a little, but basically it is the same music.

And a fine tune it is, flowing like a stately dance, and it is ideally suited to an entrance procession, particularly at state or civic celebrations. It is not a quick tune, and it lends itself to large-scale accompaniment and hearty singing, yet it never loses its dignity under these circumstances.

The words are also ideally suited to such occasions. They draw their initial inspiration from St Paul, who writes:

You are citizens with the saints and also members of the household of God, built upon the foundation of the apostles and prophets, with Christ Jesus himself as the cornerstone. In him the whole structure is joined together and grows into a holy temple in the Lord; in whom you also are built together spiritually into a dwelling place for God.
Ephesians 2:19–22

This idea of Christ as the cornerstone of a building is also found in 1 Peter 2:6: 'See, I am laying in Zion a stone, a cornerstone chosen and precious.' This combination of allusions makes the words excellent for a civic occasion or a festival commemorating a church building. The original Latin version of the hymn, '*Urbs Beata Hierusalem*', was officially designated for occasions such as the dedication of a building. When we think of our church buildings, it is good to think of Christ as a kind of metaphorical foundation-stone, or as the basis of our faith, on which all else rests. And if we build our faith on firm foundations, then it will not topple in a storm, as in the illustration that Jesus himself gave about the man who built his house on sand (Matthew 7:24–27). Wise faith is built on rock, with Christ himself as the cornerstone.

The words of the hymn are very ancient, and they point us towards the city of Jerusalem, which in medieval devotion was seen as the heavenly Salem, or Zion, the city of God. The Latin words date back possibly as far as the seventh century, yet they still resonate today, as they did in 1851 when John Neale made his translation. The text had already been translated by the Reverend John Chandler (1806–76) in 1837, and this version is still with us as 'Christ is the cornerstone'.

The words are, in fact, the second part of a longer hymn, the first part of which was also translated by Neale, and is still extant as 'Blessed city, heavenly Salem', which can also be sung to Westminster Abbey. Unlike the verses we have here, the opening verses are often still sung to the original plainsong melody which accompanied the original nine-verse Latin text, *Urbs Beata*. The main four verses we have here were sung at the service of Lauds, which was the first service of the day in the monastic tradition, whereas the opening four verses were reserved for Vespers (the evening service). Neale preserved the metre of all the verses, so it would be theoretically possible to sing all nine verses consecutively, to either the plainsong or Purcell's tune, but this would not only be very long, it would also break with the long Latin tradition of singing the hymn in two separate parts.

The first verse of this, part two of the hymn, conjures up images of old, strong buildings bound together in Christ, who himself is heaven's help and the only source of confidence for Christians. Verse two takes us to that 'dedicated', heavenly city, in which all the inhabitants sing in everlasting praise. Verse three brings us back to earth, and more specifically to the place where we sing, 'this temple', to which the singers invite God and on whom his blessing is sought. 'Come from heaven to our temple here in this city, and hear our prayers,' the verse seems to say. The fourth verse continues in that vein, with words that are reminiscent of the Marriage Service: 'Here to have and hold for ever'. We are very much 'here' in this verse, and then, as a poetic twist in Neale's translation, we find ourselves in the 'hereafter', in God's glory, reigning with the saints of God.

The final verse is a doxology, and doesn't appear in some American hymn books, although it was added by Neale to both parts of the hymn in the assumption that they would not be sung consecutively. The doxology is very appropriate as an ending to such a majestic hymn. Typically, it extols and offers praise to God, Father, Son and Holy Spirit, three and one, for ever, Amen. The 'Amen' is important as a proper ending to a doxology: the 'let it be so' adds a final closure to the hymn of praise.

O God our Father, who hears us as we pray and gives to us all good things, bind us together in the love of Jesus Christ, the cornerstone of our life and the foundation of our faith. Pour on us the perpetual melody of your grace that we may hope for that heavenly city, where you reign, Father, Son and Holy Spirit, now and for ever, Amen.

FOR ALL THE SAINTS

✣

*For all the Saints who from their labours rest,
Who thee by faith before the world confest,
Thy name, O Jesu, be for ever blest,
Alleluya! Alleluya!*

*Thou wast their Rock, their Fortress, and their Might,
Thou Lord, their Captain in the well-fought fight;
Thou in the darkness drear their one true Light.
Alleluya! Alleluya!*

*O may thy soldiers, faithful, true, and bold,
Fight as the Saints who nobly fought of old,
And win, with them, the victor's crown of gold.
Alleluya! Alleluya!*

*O blest communion! Fellowship divine!
We feebly struggle, they in glory shine;
Yet all are one in thee, for all are thine.
Alleluya! Alleluya!*

*And when the strife is fierce, the warfare long,
Steals on the ear the distant triumph-song,
And hearts are brave again, and arms are strong.
Alleluya! Alleluya!*

The golden evening brightens in the west;
Soon, soon to faithful warriors cometh rest:
Sweet is the calm of Paradise the blest.
Alleluya! Alleluya!

But lo! there breaks a yet more glorious day;
The Saints triumphant rise in bright array:
The King of glory passes on his way.
Alleluya! Alleluya!

From earth's wide bounds, from ocean's farthest coast,
Through gates of pearl streams in the countless host,
Singing to Father, Son and Holy Ghost.
Alleluya! Alleluya!

WORDS: WILLIAM WALSHAM HOW (1823–97)

TUNE: *SINE NOMINE*, RALPH VAUGHAN WILLIAMS (1872–1958)

ENGELBERG, CHARLES VILLIERS STANFORD (1852–1924)

✣

The Christian thinker, writer and Cistercian monk Thomas Merton (1915–68) once said that his greatest ambition was to be a saint. But he was not seeking special honour or hierarchical favour in the eyes of God. Sainthood, for Merton, was not about who we are and what we've done for God—it's about what we are and what God has done for us. All we have to do to be a saint is to be a believer along with countless others who share the faith among different denominations, languages and cultures all over the world, and throughout the span of time. The community of believers, the faithful, extends throughout space and time, and it is that—it is we—who are the saints. Wanting to be one of them is neither ambitious nor even very difficult.

And yet, that is not, and hasn't been for hundreds of years, the kind of meaning we generally attribute to the word 'saint', for historical and secular convention has determined that saints are special people, with special gifts from God—nearly perfect people for whom the victor's crown of gold is specially reserved.

But if that is so, none of us is a saint. None of us has made it—we have all messed up parts of our lives, we all have regions in our hearts that we do not care to revisit, areas perhaps of forgiveness but not of forgottenness. We have hurt and damaged others, and been on the receiving end too. We may have loved, but we have used others or failed them or ourselves at times. None of us is fit to be awarded the title 'saint' in the sense that the world has come to use it. In personal, private and public life we are no more than human, and there is something definitive about being human that makes life imperfect. To be human is to live in the midst of cloudy and imponderable issues. The faithful are all saints, in this mixed-up wonder of a world. But for exactly the same reason, none of us is one.

Yet we do want to say that some people, in the way they live their lives, are very special to us and to God, and they are so because they are blessed with spiritual gifts of faith, love and hope. They are people who are able to respond to Christ's call of service, humility, generosity, kindness and love; people who, in all they do, point to God, reflecting his glory through themselves like stained-glass windows. Those lives become like windows in that it is the life of Christ that the world sees and not their own natural living as such.

Some people, to human minds at least, have something to offer— some quality or appearance of the holy that they wear both lightly and authentically. And we honour them accordingly, both paying them respect and holding them up to ourselves and others as mirrors, hinting to us what is possible in the realm of humanity. Such saints are for our benefit, not God's, for in their service to God they serve us. And God has raised up saints in every generation, many of whom have witnessed to the faith by their lives and their deaths.

It is these people to whom William Walsham How refers in his hymn so wondrously set by the English composer and hymnologist Ralph Vaughan Williams. It is a long hymn, especially with the 'Alleluya's at the end of each of the eight verses, and it is seldom sung entire. When the organ plays over the tune before we sing, we know we are in for a long haul, and we need the springboard that the first, unsung beat of each verse provides, as we launch into another verse. As we sing of the glorious battle, we may be tempted to hope that we might fight our way through this triumph-song for all the saints. Yes indeed, for all of them!

But of course the sentiments expressed are right and proper: we hear of the earthly strife which gives way, in the end, to that more glorious day when God the Trinity reigns, surrounded by countless hosts of the redeemed, all of whom have survived the spiritual onslaught that is portrayed so vividly in the words.

But these saints are human beings, just like you and me, and we cannot, indeed should not, expect them to be much different from us. That they have made mistakes, even led riotous lives, does not detract from their sainthood, because they are not meant to be perfect, nor have ever claimed to be. St Francis of Assisi (1181–1226), St Augustine (354–430), and St Paul all led lives that were far from exemplary at times. There are no good people. There are only those whose natural beings have been transformed. A saint is a human being who is transformed and redeemed by God, and through whom, in their human being, the loving light of God shines.

God can and does shine through all of us. We are all called to the 'riches of his glorious inheritance among the saints', as St Paul puts it (Ephesians 1.18). In our churches, stories are always being told of ordinary people who approach sainthood in virtue of actions and attitudes that shine with God's glory—stories of goodness and mercy, of generosity and selflessness, in times of war, famine, peace and prosperity. The church calendar is peppered with saints throughout the year, to remind and encourage us that although these people are special, they are no different from us. It reminds us, perhaps, that we too can be saints, and that it is fine to want to be one, as Thomas Merton did. It is fine to want to be a saint, because we are saints, albeit unworthily so.

We can hold together the idea that all are saints, that none are saints, and that some are saints. This is not three different uses of the word, nor three kinds of saint, but an acknowledgment that we are imperfect human creatures, made and redeemed by God who reveals and gives us access to perfection in our Lord Jesus Christ.

O God, who calls all your saints to witness to your love even unto persecution and death, give us grace to lead lives worthy of our calling, that we may rejoice with the saints who have gone before us to dwell with you in your heavenly kingdom, where you reign, Father, Son and Holy Spirit, now and for ever, Amen.

I VOW TO THEE, MY COUNTRY

✧

I vow to thee, my country, all earthly things above,
Entire and whole and perfect, the service of my love:
The love that asks no question, the love that stands the test,
That lays upon the altar the dearest and the best;
The love that never falters, the love that pays the price,
The love that makes undaunted the final sacrifice.

And there's another country, I've heard of long ago,
Most dear to them that love her, most great to them that know;
We may not count her armies, we may not see her King;
Her fortress is a faithful heart, her pride is suffering;
And soul by soul and silently her shining bounds increase,
And her ways are ways of gentleness and all her paths are peace.

WORDS: CECIL SPRING-RICE (1859–1918)
TUNE: THAXTED, GUSTAV HOLST (1874–1934)

✧

Rather like JERUSALEM, which is much-loved and much-criticized, especially in Britain, this hymn is a contentious one. This is rather a shame, because THAXTED, whatever anyone says, is a good tune. It was not originally composed for this poem, which Cecil Spring-Rice wrote in Stockholm around 1908, but Gustav Holst did make the arrangement of his own tune from the 'Jupiter' movement of his *The Planets* suite. The two have been inseparable ever since, and it is sometimes difficult to hear the orchestral movement without thinking of the words that have become wedded to it. In this way the popularity of the orchestral suite has undoubtedly been boosted by the presence of the THAXTED tune as the middle section of 'Jupiter'.

Holst, who composed music as soon as he could write, earned his living first as a trombonist and then as a music teacher, most famously at St Paul's Girls' School in West London. During the First World War he went to encourage the troops in music-making, teaching them harmony and singing, and displaying an innate gift for teaching and communicating music. *The Planets*, which is a seven-movement suite for orchestra, was composed during the First World War, and owes the titles of its movements to the then-known planets in the solar system. Pluto was not first discovered until the American astronomer Clyde Tombaugh (1906–1997) spotted it in 1930.

Holst's interests in the planets was largely astrological and, combined with his interest in Hinduism and gnosticism, made for quite a mixture! In his *Hymn of Jesus* he used a text from the apocryphal Acts of St John which describes a story of Christ dancing with the disciples. Another work, *Savitri*, uses a Sanskrit text. Holst himself, although born in Cheltenham, had a Swedish great-grandfather, and it is via Sweden that we can connect him to Cecil Spring-Rice, who wrote the words in the Swedish capital.

Spring-Rice was in the diplomatic service, and worked in the Middle East and Russia before going to Stockholm in 1908. In 1912 he was sent to be British ambassador in Washington, and was there while the First World War raged in Europe. The USA remained neutral while he was there (he left in 1917), and we might think of him working there having already written the second verse of the hymn. Spring-Rice had dreamed of a place far away, where 'all her paths are peace'; and yet he was serving in America, trying to persuade her to help save Europe, while far away in France millions died in the trenches. The first verse had been written too, but the effect of the war caused him to rewrite it, making it less aggressively patriotic than it had been. Those who feel that 'I vow to thee, my country' is too nationalistic may want to remember that its author felt so too, and toned it down! For Spring-Rice, a diplomat, the greatest hope was peace, and he worked for it at the highest levels. The hymn is not about war at all, it is about peace, albeit gained at great cost.

To be fair to the author, the hymn presents a vision of a land of peace, a land that is to be compared and contrasted with heaven. After revising the poem in America, he returned home, and very soon died. His vision of heaven is as a place of peace, that 'other country' where faithful souls are at rest. His vision of earth is of a place where sacrifice and love go together, the kind of love that Jesus spoke of: 'No one has greater love than this, to lay down one's life for one's friends' (John 15:13). To be fair again to Spring-Rice, we must remember that he was working, and therefore writing, at the cutting edge of world politics, world war and world peace. As a negotiator between Britain and the United States he was involved in discussions the results of which had a direct impact on the lives of those fighting on the front. Of all people, Spring-Rice himself would have known about the costs of certain policies and actions, and just as those who have dealt with problems in the Balkans or the Middle East in later generations know, there are inevitably consequences to almost any course of action in these situations. Spring-Rice's is a personal poem, and it speaks from and about a situation in which few find themselves. Many men fight and die, but there are few who actually send them to do so.

The words of what became the hymn are complex, even if they appear at face value to be extolling mindless sacrifice and unquestioning loyalty, both of which are no longer fashionable. We live in a different, though no more peaceful age. Yet many still want to sing these words and find them very moving, and get very upset if they are prevented from doing so.

Ultimately, they are words of faith encountering dilemma, and faith convinced of a certain course of action. There are many people in history who have advocated war in order to obtain peace. In the past, tremendous sacrifices have been made to obtain lasting and righteous peace, and while later generations may not remember those sacrifices so readily, they should not be forgotten. To some extent we still see, and will continue to see, cases where military force, or the possibility of it, is deemed to be the only way to save innocent lives.

Whatever we think of 'I vow to thee, my country', it is important to know the context of its authorship and to understand the role in world history that its author played. Those who like the tune but not the words might be inclined to try 'O God beyond all praising' by Michael Perry (b. 1942), which was written to fit the unusual metre of Holst's tune. These words are fine enough, although for many they do not carry the poignancy of Spring-Rice's poem, but now at least it is possible to please those who feel that the original words of the hymn are jingoistic.

Whether it is jingoistic or not, its second verse is a vision of heaven and a prayer for world peace. In speaking of heaven as a 'country', the poem conveys it as a real place, and as *the* real place, whose fortresses of love are our true home, calling to us and inspiring in us true loyalty. These are sentiments that can hardly be challenged. May our vision be always one of peace, in heaven and on earth.

Father in heaven, hear the prayers of your dear children who pray for peace. Give relief to all who are damaged by war or violence, and give to all who suffer, wholeness, and to all who work for peace, a faithful heart, so that your kingdom on earth may increase, for the sake of Jesus Christ, the Prince of Peace, Amen.

KING OF GLORY,
KING OF PEACE

✣

King of glory, King of peace,
I will love thee;
And that love may never cease,
I will move thee.
Thou hast granted my request,
Thou hast heard me;
Thou didst note my working breast,
Thou hast spared me.

Therefore with my utmost art
I will sing thee,
And the cream of all my heart
I will bring thee.
Though my sins against me cried,
Thou didst clear me;
And alone, when they replied,
Thou didst hear me.

Seven whole days, not one in seven,
I will praise thee;
In my heart, though not in heaven,
I can raise thee.

Small it is, in this poor sort
To enrol thee:
E'en eternity's too short
To extol thee.

Words: George Herbert (1593–1633)

Tune: Gwalchmai, Joseph David Jones (1827–70)

✣

George Herbert is now revered as something close to a saint by the Anglican Church. He is remembered especially on 27 February, when he is commemorated as a pastor. The anniversary of his death is actually 1 March, which is, of course, St David's Day, the feast day for Wales.

Herbert was born in Wales, in Montgomery Castle, and was related to the family of the Earl of Pembroke. His father died when he was three, so he grew up very close to his mother, Magdalen, who was a very good friend of John Donne (1571–1631), the famous poet and later Dean of St Paul's. At 10, Herbert gained a scholarship to Westminster School, where he came under the influence of the Dean of Westminster, Launcelot Andrewes (1555–1626), one of the great thinkers and preachers of his day, whose piety and wisdom formed the basis of the church that was to dominate English spirituality thereafter.

In 1609, Herbert went to Trinity College, Cambridge, where he was to spend the next 20 years as student, College Fellow and University Orator. He was hoping for a diplomatic or political career. As University Orator, it was his task to compose speeches in Latin for any appropriate official occasion. In 1623 he was elected as Member of Parliament for Montgomery, his home town. Herbert's glittering career seemed to be going nicely, but the state of Parliament and the Crown was not, for civil war was only a few years away. For him and for his friend Nicholas Ferrar (1592–1637), the dilemma of how to serve both the nation and God began to prove difficult, and Herbert left London life for a while, possibly suffering from a depressive illness.

Sometime between 1624 and 1626, Herbert was ordained deacon, and soon became a Prebendary of Lincoln Cathedral, a title which gave him an income and the daily task of reciting Psalms 31 and 32. With the title came the dilapidated church of Leighton Bromswold, which Herbert set about restoring.

In 1629 Herbert got married, and the following year moved to the parish of Fugglestone-with-Bemerton in Wiltshire. This move was to change his life and mark the beginning of a new and important ministry conducted almost entirely in Bemerton, but which took on international and long-lasting significance. Herbert only lived another three years, but in that time he gained a reputation as something of a saint within those villages, and he wrote much poetry and a book on rural ministry entitled *A Priest to the Temple, or The Country Parson, his character and Rule of Life*. That book is still highly respected today, not only as a description of early 17th-century ecclesiastical life but as a manual of pastoral care.

Herbert's poetry became even more famous, even though it was not published until after his death. In *The Temple* we find these words, which were turned into a hymn in about 1889, and published in the *Yattendon Hymnal*. Thereafter they found their way into the *English Hymnal*, remaining in use ever since.

The tune that is invariably used for this hymn was written by another Welshman from Montgomeryshire. Joseph David Jones was born in Brynerygog, and spent his life teaching. He published a book of psalm tunes, but this is the only one still in use today. GWALCHMAI was written in 1868. It is a delicate tune in a very unusual metre, alternating long and short lines, and until Michael Saward (b. 1932) wrote 'Welcome to another day' the tune had been confined to this text. By the same token, no other tune has married itself to Herbert's fine words. The first two and the fourth lines of the tune are very similar, while the third line takes us up to the top of the scale on the words 'Thou hast heard me' before returning to an exact repetition of the first line. Rather like the tune for 'Teach me my God and King' (SANDYS), GWALCHMAI does not invade the piety of the words. We might expect a grand tune for these words, but they are far too subtle for that, and with GWALCHMAI we can spend some of our mental energy reflecting on the meaning of the phrases rather than on belting out a big tune!

The words themselves have been altered to make a hymn, omitting one of Herbert's seven four-line verses. To make the hymn, verses were joined to make three eight-line verses, and this meant that Herbert's sixth verse was left out. The missing verse is:

> *Thou grew'st soft and moist with tears,*
> *Thou relentedst:*
> *And when Justice call'd for fears*
> *Thou dissentedst.*

The first line of the hymn derives from Psalm 24: 'Lift up your heads, O gates! and be lifted up, O ancient doors! that the King of glory may come in. Who is the King of glory? The Lord, strong and mighty, the Lord, mighty in battle' (Psalm 24:7–8).

While this is the king of glory, Herbert's is not the king of battle, but the king of peace, mentioned in the letter to the Hebrews: 'His name, in the first place, means "king of righteousness"; next he is also king of Salem, that is, "king of peace"' (Hebrews 7:2).

The text is a prayer, and in each verse there is a balance of 'I' and 'thou'. In verse 1, the singer promises to love and 'move' God, all because thou, God, hast heard and spared me. In the second verse, 'I' will sing, and bring, because God clears and hears me. The final verse, which has been chopped about, should involve the singer praising God and raising the heart, in return for which God in Christ relents and dissents. Thus the final stanza, which stands alone as the seventh, speaks of 'extolling' and 'enrolling'. The fact that there were originally seven verses is significant, because it reflects the 'seven whole days' of praise that Herbert mentions. In all these verses we find the rhythms of faith, forgiveness and praise. Herbert loves because he is forgiven; he sings and brings praise because he is cleared.

Some individual words need a little attention: the idea of 'moving' God is archaic, and perhaps confusing. Herbert's prayer is that in order to ensure God's continuing love for him he will 'move' or petition him—move God to love him. The 'enrol' of the final verse means to 'celebrate'. It is an insignificant thing, Herbert says, in this way of worshipping, to celebrate with God, but then even eternity isn't long enough for God to be properly praised.

This is above all a humble hymn of praise, not a glorification of God, as the first line might initially suggest. In humility Herbert offers the 'cream' (the best) of his heart, because God has noticed the emotion of his heart (his 'working breast'), which beats with the ever-present awareness of human unworthiness to approach God. Herbert expresses similar sentiments in other poetry, where he characterizes God as a host who welcomes us at his feast, even though we do not deserve his love

('Love', see p. 126). Much of Herbert's poetry resonates with the Prayer of Humble Access, first introduced into the English Communion Service in 1548, which contains the words, 'We are not worthy so much as to gather up the crumbs under thy table. But thou art the same Lord, whose property is always to have mercy.'

It is true, we are not worthy; but it is also true that God in Christ has spared us and raised us up, so that we may be freed to live lives of service and joy, and to praise God. That we may do so with words and music of such subtle beauty is simply another reason for praise and thanksgiving.

King of Glory, and Prince of Peace, hear us as we turn to you and accept our prayers and praises, unworthy though they be. Forgive us our sins, and heal our infirmities, so that we may be made ready to serve you daily with the cream of our lives and the love of our hearts, and by your Spirit grant us humility and patience until that day when we shall be enrolled in the court of heaven, ever dwelling with you, Father, Son and Holy Spirit, Amen.

TEACH ME, MY GOD AND KING

✣

Teach me, my God and King,
In all things thee to see;
And what I do in anything
To do it as for thee!

A man that looks on glass,
On it may stay his eye;
Or if he pleaseth, through it pass,
And then the heaven espy.

All may of thee partake;
Nothing can be so mean,
Which with this tincture, 'for thy sake',
Will not grow bright and clean.

A servant with this clause
Makes drudgery divine;
Who sweeps a room, as for thy laws,
Makes that and the action fine.

This is the famous stone
That turneth all to gold;
For that which God doth touch and own
Cannot for less be told.

WORDS: GEORGE HERBERT (1593–1633)

TUNE: SANDYS, FROM W. SANDY'S 'CHRISTMAS CAROLS' (1833)

These simple but telling words originate from the pen of George Herbert, who was one of England's greatest poets, and whose piety and pastoral ministry have served as an example to countless clergy and laity for the past three centuries. His most famous set of poems, entitled *The Temple*, contains the text of the hymn 'Teach me, my God and King'. The collection of 160 poems was published after Herbert's death, by his friend Nicholas Ferrar (1592–1637). Herbert sent them to Ferrar from his deathbed, with the words, 'He shall find in it a picture of the many spiritual conflicts that have passed betwixt God and my soul, before I could subject mine to the will of Jesus my master; in whose service I have now found perfect freedom', and he suggested that if the poems be thought of no value, then Ferrar should burn them.

It is rather ironic that Nicholas Ferrar, himself the founder of a religious community at Little Gidding near Huntingdon, should have been Herbert's posthumous agent. Ferrar was also a writer, but nine years after he too died, in the midst of the English Civil War, his own works were burned by the Puritans, who feared that his influence might inspire the reintroduction of religious practices that they had abolished. Suspecting that Little Gidding was some kind of monastery, the Puritans broke it up in 1646. It was actually a community of Christians who ordered their lives around the *Book of Common Prayer*, seeking to serve God in daily work, charity and prayer, rather in the same spirit expressed by the words of this hymn. The poet T.S. Eliot (1888–1965) entitled one of his *Four Quartets* 'Little Gidding', after he became inspired by Ferrar's life and ministry and the example of the Little Gidding experiment, which was revived in the 20th century.

Ferrar did not burn Herbert's inspiring poetry, but wisely published it. The volume was an instant success, selling some 70,000 copies and being reprinted ten times by 1670. The poem from which the hymn is taken is called 'The Elixir' and there are at least two hymn versions of it. The most well-known in England is the one found originally in the 1906 edition of the *New English Hymnal*, reproduced above. Another version, edited by John Wesley (1703–91) in 1738, runs as follows:

Teach me, my God and King,
In all things Thee to see,
And what I do in anything
To do it as for Thee.

To scorn the senses' sway,
While still to Thee I tend:
In all I do be Thou the Way,
In all be Thou the End.

All may of Thee partake;
Nothing so small can be
But draws, when acted for Thy sake,
Greatness and worth from Thee.

If done to obey Thy laws,
E'en servile labours shine;
Hallowed is toil, if this the cause,
The meanest work divine.

This version is more common in the United States, and is sung to the tune EMMAUS, written by Joseph Barnby (1838–96). In England the tune SANDYS is generally used, being derived from a Christmas carol tune. Ralph Vaughan Williams (1872–1958), one of the editors of the *New English Hymnal*, chose SANDYS, and it has stuck ever since. It is a simple, memorable tune, with few harmonic complications, and its simplicity mirrors the gentle piety of the words.

The first verse is self-explanatory, consisting of a request to God our king to help us see his handiwork in all things and to do all things for him. A simple prayer, perhaps, but not an easy task! It is not easy to see Christ in people who disturb us, nor among criminals, enemies or troublemakers. Neither is it easy to see every task as befitting the service of God. Herbert knew this, so the first verse indicates the goal to which he aspires, and on which he then elaborates.

There are two ways of looking at the world, says the poet, just as when we look on glass we can treat it as a mirror or a window. One way sees no depth—the eye is 'stayed'—but one can also look beyond the surface realities and see deeper truths and meanings. Herbert's implication is that we should look deeper, and see the world as a window on heaven. He goes on to say that anyone can do this: all may partake. Herbert is alluding to the eucharist, which represents and remembers (but does not re-enact) the sacrifice made by Christ at Calvary, made 'for our sake'. Receiving Christ in the bread and wine cleanses us, making us shiny and whole.

Herbert goes on to suggest that if our lives are centred upon Christ's loving gift of himself to us, then whatever we are doing can be directed as a thank-offering to him. And there can be nothing more finely done than every task offered and completed for the glory of God. Then we reach the final verse, in which Herbert offers his conclusion that this daily working out of God's love for us, if recognized, is like the acid test of faith and life. In Herbert's day, it was a popular pastime to try to make gold out of base metal (alchemy). It was also believed that there was a 'philosopher's stone' that could turn base metal into gold, and of course everyone wanted to discover what it was or how to do it! (Readers of the first *Harry Potter* book will have heard about this!) As far as the hymn is concerned, Herbert uses this idea metaphorically, saying that God is like this magic stone, for everything that he touches becomes pure gold. The greatest thing that God can touch is the human soul, and the golden soul is one that is made bright and clean by grace and, through daily work, offered back to God.

George Herbert's vision of daily life offered to God, which was in some sense lived out in the community established at Little Gidding, remains an inspiration to us all. Many do not generally live in religious communities today, but there is a sense in which we can consider all the various communities in which we move as having a religious dimension. We are placed on this earth to serve one another and to serve God, and Jesus teaches us that whatever we do for others, we do for him (Matthew 25:31–46). In Christ we can be taught this, for he is our God, and our King.

O Christ our King, shine your light on our souls, that we may reflect your love. Deepen our vision, that we may see you more clearly. Refine us like gold, that we may become pure in your sight. Touch our hearts and lives, that we may always act for your sake, for you lived and died for us, but now reign in glory. Amen.

✧

ALPHABETICAL LIST OF HYMNS